Return to the Street

Pavement Books
London, UK
www.pavementbooks.com

First published 2015 © Sabina Andron, Dhanveer Singh Brar, Mihaela Brebenel,
Chris Collier, Sophie Fuggle, Tom Henri, Femke Kaulingfreks, Ashley Lavelle,
Jennifer Preston, Regner Ramos, Holly Eva Ryan, Rachel Segal Hamilton, Patri-
cia Anne Simpson, Linda Stupart, J.D. Taylor, Paulius Yamin

Cover Photograph by Emmanuelle Groult. Reproduced with permission from
the artist.

British Library Cataloguing in Publication Data.
A catalogue record for this book is available from the British Library.

ISBN: 978-0-9571470-5-8

Return to the Street

edited by
Sophie Fuggle & Tom Henri

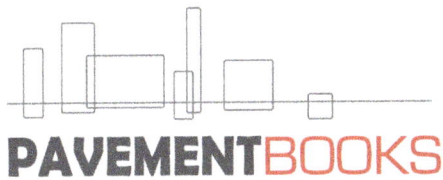

PAVEMENTBOOKS

STRANDS book series

A strand is a thread, a trajectory, a train of argument or thought. It is also a road, a promenade, the place where beach meets cityscape. It is a limit as well as a line. It is the site of encounter, conflict and confrontation. As borders are reinforced and sea levels rise, spaces of inclusion become those of exclusion. The strand gives way to the stranded, marooned, isolated, imprisoned and alienated. This series presents a range of perspectives and critical methodologies aimed at questions of space and our sociocultural engagement with it. As such it incorporates approaches from cultural studies, literature, film and media studies, anthropology, political science, architecture and geography.

Current and forthcoming titles

Return to the Street edited by Sophie Fuggle and Tom Henri

Taking Up Space edited by Jamal Aridi and Jessica Glendennan

La Ligne d'écume: Encountering the French Beach edited by Sophie Fuggle and Nicholas Gledhill

For Emile Blake-Hutnyk and his inspirational street stunts

CONTENTS

Acknowledgments — ix

Notes on Contributors — xi

Introduction — 1
- SOPHIE FUGGLE & TOM HENRI

I. MARKED TERRITORIES — 11

1. The Stairway as Street: Urban Form and Political Space — 13
   - JENNIFER PRESTON

2. Barcodes and Barricades: Parisian Street Art and Global Capitalism — 33
   - RACHEL SEGAL HAMILTON

3. The City and the Virtual: The Use of Digital Technology in 3D Street Art — 47
   - SABINA ANDRON & REGNER RAMOS

4. Escaping Psychogeographical Cul-de-Sacs — 63
   - MIHAELA BREBENEL & CHRISTOPHER COLLIER

II. FERAL YOUTH — 79

5. The Rebel without a Cause as Protagonist of Unruly Politics — 81
   - FEMKE KAULINGFREKS

6. 'We Hate Humans': Some Problems in Reading the 2011   97
   English Riots within a Recent History of Working-Class
   Violence
   - J. D. TAYLOR

7. Black Outbreak   113
   - DHANVEER SINGH BRAR

III. PUBLIC SERVICE ANNOUNCEMENTS   129

8. Politics (and Mime Artists) on the Street   131
   - PAULIUS YAMIN

9. Enlightened Streets: Public Art and International   143
   Anti-Violence Campaigns
   - PATRICIA ANNE SIMPSON

10. Moving Forwards, Looking Backwards: Street Art   169
    Against Authoritarianism in Brazil
    - HOLLY EVA RYAN

IV. UNEASY PRESENCE   187

11. Whose Streets? Our Streets! The Place of the Streets in   189
    the Occupy Movement
    - ASHLEY LAVELLE

12. Walking in the Street: SlutWalk and the Street   205
    - LINDA STUPART

13. Imbibing Neoliberalism   219
    - TOM HENRI

Index   231

ACKNOWLEDGMENTS

Some of the chapters of this book originated from papers given at the Return to the Street Conference hosted by the Centre for Cultural Studies at Goldsmiths, University of London in June 2012. The editors would like to thank all at Goldsmiths who were involved in and supported the event. Special thanks also go to John Hutnyk and Sophie Wood.

NOTES ON CONTRIBUTORS

Sabina Andron is a PhD candidate at the Bartlett School of Architecture, University College London, with a project on street art, graffiti, and their relation to the built environment. She has a background in literature and visual culture, and is a keen photographer of urban inscriptions and surfaces. Sabina is also an artistic advisor and facilitator, and she runs the arts education group I Know What I Like, where she organizes critical gallery visits and art walks, and curates exhibitions with work by artist members. http://sabinaandron.com/; @sabinaandron.

Dhanveer Singh Brar is a scholar of black studies, with a specialization in the intersections of black diasporic thought, culture and aesthetics. He is currently Andrew W. Mellon Postdoctoral Fellow in the Humanities at Penn Humanities Forum, University of Pennsylvania.

Mihaela Brebenel is a visual studies researcher and writer. She is a doctoral student and associate lecturer at Goldsmiths, University of London. Her research project is on the politics and aesthetics of moving image. Her research interests take shape around the relations enacted by screen-based media and the processes of production-reception of moving images.

Christopher Collier is a PhD candidate in the School of Philosophy and Art History, University of Essex. His research examines the re-emergence of psychogeography in the 1990s. He is particularly concerned with how it relates to an autonomous and activist production of material culture, along with its changing potential for criticality in a transforming context. He has several published several articles on the subject and on other related topics.

Ernest is a multiple-use name referring to a shifting collective of people collaborating over shared interests in urbanism, art and cultural experimentation. Whilst Ernest does not self-define as an artist, she has certainly used the structures and resources available in this guise in order to support her experiments.

Sophie Fuggle is lecturer in French at Nottingham Trent University. She is author of *Foucault/Paul: Subjects of Power* (Palgrave, 2013) and co-editor of *Word on the Street* (IGRS Books, 2011). She is currently working on a collection focusing on the beach in the French cultural imagination. Her recent research looks at the framing of criminality within and beyond the French carceral space.

Tom Henri studied sociology, social policy and social work at the University of Southampton. He then worked as a social worker and a social work educator before taking up a lectureship at Goldsmiths, University of London. His academic and research interests include the construction of youth as a problem, racisms, substance misuse, and how discourses of social class and nationality both inform and are reproduced by and through social work and social policy.

Femke Kaulingfreks received her Masters degree in Philosophy at the University of Amsterdam and completed her PhD at the University for Humanistic Studies in Utrecht. Her dissertation consisted of an interdisciplinary research into the political meaning of public disturbances and urban violence caused by adolescents with an immigrant background from deprived neighborhoods in France and the Netherlands. She currently works as a researcher in the research group 'Diversity and Citizenship' of the The Hague University in Applied Sciences. Besides her teaching and research work Femke regularly organizes youth exchange projects and is engaged in activism related to housing, migration and social justice issues.

Ashley Lavelle researches in the area of radical politics and social movements. His most recent book, *The Politics of Betrayal: Renegades and Ex-radicals from Mussolini to Christopher Hitchens* was published by Manchester University Press in 2013.

Jennifer Preston is an honorary research fellow of the University of Queensland and a registered architect with a practice in Sydney. She was awarded a doctorate of philosophy in the field of architecture in 2014 with a dissertation titled 'Social Climbing: The Architectural, Cultural and Heritage Significance of Sydney's Public Stairways'. Jennifer has taught in architectural history and theory at the University of Technology Sydney, and been a guest lecturer on accessible design at the Queensland University of Technology. She has written several conference papers and journal articles exploring various aspects of stairways principally concerned with their use value.

Regner Ramos obtained his undergraduate and Masters degrees at the University of Puerto Rico's School of Architecture and is currently a PhD candidate at The Bartlett School of Architecture, UCL. His research focuses on how GPS mobile apps are changing the use, understanding, and perception of urban spaces, whilst simultaneously creating new forms of identities and embodiments. Regner is also an Associate Lecturer at Central Saint Martins, the Editor-in-Chief of *LOBBY* - The Bartlett School of Architecture's new magazine - and a contributing writer for *Glass Magazine*.

Holly Eva Ryan's research centres on international politics and aesthetics, with a focus on uses of cultural power and forms of resistance in Latin America and the Caribbean. Holly currently holds teaching posts at King's College London and City University London, where she recently established an interdisciplinary research group on social movements and civil society.

Rachel Segal Hamilton is a London-based arts writer and editor, specialising in visual culture. She has contributed to *The Telegraph*, *VICE*, *British Journal of Photography*, *Photomonitor* and the *Royal Photographic Society Journal* and is Commissioning Editor at *IdeasTap*. She holds an MA in Cultural Studies from Goldsmiths, University of London, and a BA in Modern Languages from the University of Cambridge. @rachsh // www.rachelsegalhamilton.com

Patricia Anne Simpson is Professor of German Studies at Montana State University. She is author of *The Erotics of War in German Romanticism* (Bucknell University Press, 2006), *Cultures of Violence in the New German Street* (Fairleigh Dickinson University Press, 2011) and *Reimaging the European Family: Cultures of Immigration* (Palgrave, 2013).

Linda Stupart is an artist, writer and educator from Cape Town, South Africa. She is currently a PhD candidate at Goldsmiths, University of London, with a project engaged in new considerations of objectification as well as an Associate Lecture in Critical and Theoretical Studies at London College of Communication.

J.D. Taylor is a writer and PhD researcher at the University of Roehampton, working broadly within cultural studies and contemporary political theory. He is the author of *Negative Capitalism: Cynicism in the Neoliberal Era* (Zero, 2013), and is currently working on a state-of-the-nation travelogue about a four-month journey across Britain. He blogs at www.drownedandsaved.com.

Paulius Yamin is an anthropologist from the Universidad de los Andes (Bogotá, Colombia) with an MA in Cultural Studies from Goldsmiths, University of London. He works as a public policy consultant for the Mayor's Offices of Bogotá and Quibdó (Colombia) and as a lecturer in anthropology.

INTRODUCTION:
TOWARDS A NEW POLITICS OF THE STREET

Sophie Fuggle & Tom Henri

This book is an attempt to think through two sets of questions. The first set concerns what might be termed a 'return' to the street. This is not a bright, new dawn. It is not the first steps out into the light following an environmental or technological apocalypse. Rather, this return concerns a renewed and heightened awareness of the vast social inequalities, violence and exclusion which continue to be perpetuated across the world. To challenge such inequality requires confrontation with the individuals, agents, institutions and authorities who actively promote and enact such violence and exclusion. It requires the occupation of sites and spaces which make visible such acts of exclusion. The street constitutes one such site of confrontation and visibility.

Identifying the street's continued importance as a highly visible space of confrontation requires consideration of the different motivations, stakes and tensions arising from this 'return' in the form of riots, protests and occupations of recent years. How might we situate this 'return' in relation to earlier political and social movements focused on and around the street?

The second set of questions is linked to the first and concerns more precisely the shifting role of public space and the everyday processes of inclusion and exclusion enacted here. How far does the street as myth, metonym and discourse of public space correspond to the private walkways, corporate-sponsored playgrounds and heavily policed pavements of today's urban centres? To return to the street is therefore also to acknowledge and challenge the ways in which public spaces have become private. This might be considered as part of a wider privatization of the public realm which includes the outsourcing of state provision including healthcare, education and law and order turning these into neo-liberal 'quasi-markets'. Perceived as such, public services are eroded and welfare undermined in the name of 'competitiveness'.

The street, the square, the park have all become sites where spontaneous public exchange has been transformed into carefully regulated public performance and economic exchange, where one's access depends upon one's perceived (or performed) economic value. To accept this transformation is, at the same time, to affirm one's complicity in the processes which exclude individuals and groups via terms like 'renewal' and 'regeneration'.

Real Bodies in Real Spaces

At the end of Jonathan Mostow's 2009 film, *Surrogates*, a group of neighbours step one by one out into their street, dressed for the most part in dressing-gowns and pyjamas, cautious, unsteady and blinking in the daylight. In this particular rerendering of Plato's Cave narrative, the world in 2054 is a world where it has ceased to be dangerous to go out quite simply because no one needs to go out anymore at all. Instead humans have been relegated to a life lived vicariously through their surrogates - robot replicas operated via headsets. This all changes when, for the first time in a number of years, a murder is committed. To destroy a surrogate is nothing more than criminal damage to private property. The murder enquiry led by a bored, jaded detective, Greer (Bruce Willis) forces society to call into question the vicarious mode of living they have come to take for granted.

Once liberated from their headsets, individuals are invited to embrace both a new dawn and a return to a former time of unmediated social and physical interaction with one another. The film's overriding and condescendingly predictable message seems to be that we should take heed of anything and everything that, whilst claiming to 'enhance' real experience and enjoyment, ends up circumventing such experience. At the same time, the film also suggests something else about our understanding of public and private space and the role of these spaces in identity formation.

Where the surrogates operated by the main character, Greer, and his wife, Maggie (Rosamund Pike), take the form of slightly younger, better groomed versions of themselves, narcissism is off-set against the 'inauthenticity' or even 'betrayal' of those who opt for surrogates of different appearance, race or gender. This sense of deliberate deceit is articulated at one point by Greer who echoes common persistent attitudes towards those who create online avatars especially when such personas assume a role beyond the limits of the Internet. However, in the world of surrogates, the risks of online grooming have faded since everyone is now embodied by their surrogate at all times. Homicide and violence have been replaced by theft and vandalism.

Throughout the film it is clear that surrogates are chosen by individuals according to established norms as to how a person should appear in order to command respect, acceptance and also desire in a given role. Beyond the pure superficiality of Greer and Maggie, explained away by the film as a mismanagement of grief, there lies an awareness that those who do not conform to standard representations of the male and female body, those who are overweight, infirm, old or simply unattractive are excluded or limited from public space and social agency. If 'real' physical bodies are what matter, some bodies matter more than others (cf. Butler, 1993).

In *The Inhuman*, Jean-François Lyotard asks whether we can think without our bodies before suggesting that the very question itself is moot (Lyotard, 1991). As films like *Surrogates* amply demonstrate, hypothetical exercises in 'thinking' beyond and without our bodies end up reproducing fairly standard conceptions of the human body as stand-ins. Where this is perhaps necessary for the characters in *Surrogates* who are still required to operate their robot replacements via a prosthetic device, it should perhaps strike us as odd in *The Matrix Trilogy* that all those coma-induced bodies providing energy to the machines should need the construction of an imagined life-world based on a form of embodiment and body-image completely unknown to them. Bodies continue to matter and consist of matter. In the absence of telekinesis, technological prostheses continue to be mapped onto physical bodies, functioning as extensions to these bodies.

Wider debates about the body and space are key in explaining the importance of the street as both actual, physical space and ideological concept within late capitalist society. The street functions as a limit between public and private space, between here and elsewhere. It is both territory and trajectory. The street is where we encounter the other firsthand whether as friend, neighbour, stranger or enemy. In an age defined by our connection to the 'virtual', the physical street continues to function as the site where real bodies operate in real spaces even while such notions undergo radical contestation and reconfiguration. The street is therefore indispensable to discussions of political action, activism, responsibility and resistance.

*

The essays included in this book approach the street via a range of different critical lenses, methodologies and objects of enquiry. Multiple sites and spaces are covered including the streets of London, Paris, New York, Sydney, São Paulo, Rio de Janeiro, Bogotá, Port Louis, Nuremberg and Hillsborough. While various chapters are focused on site-specific analysis, notably, Yamin's examination of street theatre as pedagogy in Bogotá, Chapter 8, and Brar's discussion of the London Grime scene in Chapter 7, elsewhere a more comparative approach is taken to teasing out what is at stake in this space we refer to as 'street.' In Chapter 3, Andron and Ramos demonstrate the ways in which technology pushes the boundaries of the material street using the example of 3D street art and advertising. Also looking at street art in Chapter 2, Segal Hamilton explores the way in which Parisian street artists enact both a countermapping and re-colonisation of public space in and beyond their own 'territories'. In her chapter on 'Enlightened Streets', Simpson juxtaposes public education campaigns in Germany, Brazil and Mauritius in order to challenge existing notions of 'enlightenment' within a postcolonial context. Highlighting the various tensions at work in the 'SlutWalk' events taking place around the world, in Chapter 12, Stupart considers what it means for women to be seen 'walking the streets' in various global cities.

While recent events constitute the starting point for thinking about a 're-turn to the street' as amply demonstrated in Kaulingfreks' analysis of 'unruly politics' in Chapter 5, the idea of 'return' is frequently explored via historical contextualization. Lavelle's analysis of the 2011 Occupy Wall Street movement in Chapter 11 situates this within a history of political activism, questioning the validity and long-term impact of such interventions. In Chapter 10, Ryan calls into question contemporary celebrations of street art in Brazil and elsewhere via extensive reflection on the Grupo Tupinãodá's art-based activism during the dictatorship. Taylor's reading of British skinhead subculture in Chapter 6 pro-vides a wider contextualization for thinking about class warfare and the 2011 London riots.

Read together these interventions demonstrate the primacy of the street as an object of ongoing analysis, critique and debate for a range of disciplines including architecture, urban geography, gender and race studies, sociology, political science, history, cultural and media studies as well as the need for a multidisciplinary approach to exploring the uses and abuses of public space. In this respect, the book avoids offering a prescribed route in favour of a series of loosely linked explorations. Thus, Collier and Brebenel's attempt to escape 'Psy-chogeographical Cul-de-sacs' in Chapter 4 lends a self-reflexivity to the volume through a critical assessment of the legacy and continued validity of the Situa-tionist and Letterist movements.

Like all signposts, the chapter groupings are there primarily to be ignored unless you are cornered and desperate. It is perhaps telling, however, that the collection is bounded by two chapters focusing on the materiality of the street and its 'furniture'. In the chapter 1, Preston looks at the stairway and the exclu-sion and encounters it engenders as a common element of the cityscape, identi-fying its role in progressive town planning ideology and gentrification processes which privatize public space for consumer activity. In the chapter at the end of our journey, Henri looks the Deptford Anchor, the relocation of which repre-sents a gentrification process aimed at removing lower class drinkers from the streets. Like the street itself, the book is contained by both its physical and ide-ological limits. There is an awareness in each chapter that the street as a site of resistance and radical political potential risks recuperation at every moment by the very same forces that are being contested.

Reading and Writing the Street

There is, of course, a danger in overreading the street which is worth noting here. Not least given the rabid recuperation at work on all aspects of street life, culture, art, food and music. One of the main objectives of this book is to insist the street constitute an object of ongoing, rigorous and multidisciplinary analysis and critique due to the rapid erosion of public freedom and civil liberties occurring in postindustrial cities. This implies that crossing the street always involves looking both ways and taking some risks. It is not about keeping your head down and hoping no one bumps into you as you go on minding your own business. Rather, our street, the one found in the pages of this book, requires drawing attention, speaking out and acting up.

Consequently, when reading and writing the street, we should be particularly attentive to the problems involved in reducing space to 'literary analogy' as identified by Henri Lefebvre in *Toward an Architecture of Enjoyment*:

> The application to architectural space of a semiological concept, the zero degree, does not imply that we could use other concepts, such as "reading-writing." It's true that a monument and an architectural space can be read. But that they can be defined as texts is something else entirely. Neither the concept of reading nor that of writing are appropriate for space, nor is the concept of a code, mainly because practice (social and spatial) is not part of those concepts (Lefebvre: 2014, 124-5).

While the symbolic omissions, exclusions and violence perpetuated via linguistic categories are frequently acted out with real material and physical force in public space, to define everything that occurs on the street in terms of 'text' is to oversimplify and homogenize very different sets of acts, events and experiences within such spaces. The common result takes the form of a compromising romanticism which redefines those alienated or excluded by the street, its architecture, practices and agents, as 'readers' free to tell their own story. Thus, where Michel de Certeau's notions of reading the city in *The Practice of Everyday Life* were intended as tactics which enabled the city-dweller to 'resist' the overarching strategies of the urban planner and architect, Lefebvre reverses the notion of 'reading' to suggest that we are the ones being read here. 'Space decodes people's impulses...it is not people who decode space' (125).

Yet, the street with its multiplicity of surfaces and sign systems together with the unpredictability of the encounters it engenders, cannot but lend itself to an overeager academic enquiry which has thus far relied heavily on semiology. Such enquiry finds objects of analysis everywhere but fails to tell us anything new or useful about the world let alone provide the political impetus to change it.

James Agee pinpoints the difficulty of accurately 'writing' the street in *Let Us Now Praise Famous Men*:

> Trying, let us say, to represent, to reproduce, a certain city street, under the conviction that nothing is as important, as sublime, as truly poetic about that street in its flotation upon time and space as the street itself. Your medium, unfortunately, is not a still or moving camera, but is words. You abjure all metaphor, symbol, selection and above all, of course, the temptation to invent, as obstructive, false, artistic. As nearly as possible in words (which, even by grace of genius, would not be very near) you try to give the street in its own terms: that is to say, either in the terms in which you (or an imagined character) see it, or in a reduction and depersonalization into terms which will as nearly as possible be the 'private' singular terms of that asphalt, those neon letters, those and all other items combined, into that alternation, that simultaneity, of flat blank tremendously constructed chords and of immensely elaborate counterpoint which is the street itself. You hold then strictly to materials, forms, colors, bulks, textures, space relations, shapes of light and shade, peculiarities, specializations, of architecture and of lettering, noises of motors and brakes and shoes, odors of exhausts: all this gathers time and weightiness which the street does not of itself have: it sags with this length and weight: and what have you in the end but a somewhat overblown passage from a naturalistic novel: which in important ways is at the opposite pole from your intentions, from what you have seen, from the fact itself (Agee and Evans: 2006, 207-8).

More recently, Astra Taylor's 2008 film *Examined Life: Philosophy in the Streets* inadvertently demonstrated just how ill at ease academics can be when asked to engage with public space in anything other than abstract terms. In one chapter, Judith Butler takes a walk with Sunaura Taylor who is confined to an electric wheelchair. Setting off around San Francisco, Butler and Taylor identify the city as being one of the most accessible in the world despite its intensely hilly terrain and public transport system with far from comprehensive disabled access. Notions of walking, access and mobility are framed according to a U.S. worldview which continues to place the abled-bodied motorist at the centre of such notions. Yet, the most disturbing part of the exchange between Butler and Taylor is the moment they exhaust the potential of the street itself as topic of discussion and enter a vintage store. What is being implied here, albeit unintentionally, is that one's presence on the street is predicated less on one's physical mobility as a 'body' and more on one's ability to act as a consumer. Here, to analyse the street is to consume the street.

Written in the immediate aftermath of the Occupy Movement, David Harvey's *Rebel Cities* goes some way to declaring a return to the streets as essential to the anti-capitalist struggle. Harvey's point is basically the same as ours: real bodies in real spaces are what count, 'the collective power of bodies in public space is still the most effective instrument of opposition when all other means of access are blocked' (Harvey, 2012:161-2). But for Harvey such a struggle continues to be predicated on the figure of the abled-bodied, male worker. More focus is required as to how a crowd or collective risks reproducing existing forms of exclusion in claiming to speak for the masses as a homogeneous whole. Those whose access to the street is already restricted due to race, gender or disability must frequently concede their voices to those for whom the street is taken for granted as usable, occupiable and negotiable space. At the same time, a more critical stance is needed towards both the romanticisation and demonization of the crowd in public space. It is, for example, naive to think that issues such as the systemic street harassment of women in Cairo disappeared completely during the occupation of Tahrir Square in 2011, yet this was the rhetoric widely presented. Conversely, how might the pervasive politics of fear which posits the crowd as unruly mob or herd, keeping people off the streets, through the imposition of curfews and devices like the sonic 'mosquito' be redressed?

A new politics of the street would not simply take into account other figures and bodies – those who do not or cannot produce, consume and exchange – but accord such bodies primacy. Public space should be designed and organised according to the needs of the weakest and most vulnerable members of society. Disabled access should not be an afterthought or the token gesture that it continues to be in the most 'progressive' of cities became clear after the 2012 Paralympics in London. Where disabled access to the games had been facilitated to promote an image of London as disabled-friendly, in the years since the games, reforms to the UK welfare system has seen increasingly cruel and punitive measures targeted at disabled claimants.[1] Yet we are also witnessing new forms of disability activism taking place in the street. In January 2012, DPAC (Disabled People Against Cuts) chained their wheelchairs together across a street in central London bringing traffic to a halt on Regent Street.

Violent Spectacle

Implicit in the call to 'return' to the street, is the recognition that the body still remains the focus of a whole series of different power relations, subject to and subject of a range of techniques aimed at producing the docile body and normalising the deviant body (Foucault, 1977). In 1978, Michel Foucault declared that disciplinary power was all but over. In 1990, Gilles Deleuze announced the shift from a disciplinary society to one of control. Both, it seems, were too hasty in their prognosis.

If the growing prison populations in the U.S. and most of Europe demonstrate anything it is the continued prevalence of disciplinary power within late capitalist society. The taking to the streets – as a response to widespread changes in material, social conditions – demonstrates a belief, which a few years ago was considered to be outdated, a belief that this is where political, social change occurs. Although Facebook and Twitter along with other social media provide

---

[1] The number of suicides and deaths linked to cuts in benefits rose sharply between 2011 and 2014, according to the *Disability News Service* (RT.com, 2014).

a space in which to construct accompanying commentary or narrative to such events, there is also the recognition of the limitations of such virtual spaces – the unreliability of the twitter feed, the issues of self-policing and surveillance engendered by social media - even as they remain tools of organisation along with the ability of different governments to regulate and control access to such media in the first place.

Yet, the open displays of police brutality we are witnessing in towns like Ferguson, on university campuses across the U.S. and in cities like London, Cairo and Hong Kong together with the fact that victims of such brutality frequently face charges for violent disorder also seem to imply something other than a disciplinary mode of power.[2] The direct use of blunt force publicly and unapologetically employed by those in power seems to embody a doctrine of might is right. The return to the street coincides with a return to the spectacle of the scaffold.

Public displays of force involving small town police chiefs posing by armoured vehicles or the Mayor of London ordering water cannons appear to supplement the open admission of torture by Western governments along with the photos of the Whitehouse 'Situation Room' purportedly taken during the shooting of Osama Bin Laden by U.S. Navy Seals. But perhaps this is not a 'return' to a sovereign mode of power or even, as Giorgio Agamben (1998) might suggest, a *thanatopolitics*, defined in terms of the persistence of the sovereign deeply embedded within the structures of the biopolitical. The relatively small incidences of violent disorder which erupted across cities in the UK in the summer of 2011 and which largely involved a series of arsons and lootings did not signify a reactivation of the unruly mob of medieval society. Instead, they seemed to signal the exhaustion of the biopolitical – what Agamben might call its moment of *inoperativity* – the point where it is both fulfilled and suspended. It is the very question of the biopolitical or, more precisely, the question that underpins the biopolitical, which is at stake here. What does it mean to be alive today? Who is really alive today? Slavoj Žižek asks these same questions in *Welcome to the Desert of the Real* (2002) where he, somewhat reductively, juxtaposes the Middle Eastern suicide bomber with the New York jogger. His point being that the radical calling into question of what it means to be alive can only ever involve risking everything that this is taken to mean. In this respect the 'Situation Room' is the image *par excellence* of this moment of exhaustion. Is this image of top government officials of a Western superpower watching a 'snuff' film (Hutnyk,

---

[2] During the UK student protests in late 2010, Alfie Meadows suffered severe brain injuries requiring intensive surgery following a blow to the head by riot police. Meadows was subsequently charged with violent disorder before being acquitted by a jury in 2013. Mathieu Rigouste, an French political activist and author of *La Domination Policiére* (2012) about the rise of the police state in France was arrested and charged with violent disorder in June 2013. At the time of his arrest Rigouste had spent 3 days in hospital after being beaten up by police officers in Arnaud Bernard, a run down district of Toulouse earmarked for gentrification.

2012) the final taboo – the only remaining transgression (besides paedophilia) – or is it the apotheosis of the Western biopolitical imagination? Here we are witness to the taking of life or the experience of death as mediated by the limit of the TV or computer screen. Again, what this possibly signals is the primacy of the physical body in real physical space. We are presented with a deferred image in which members of the Obama administration do the looking for us, themselves already at a distance from the events being relayed back. Where individual subjectivity is not formed wholly within the space of the Internet, it is precisely the mediatory space of the screen which enables and encourages us to actively deny all responsibility, agency and culpability.

Obama left the situation room seemingly blinking in the light of his own new dawn, facing the cameras and reaching out to the man and woman on the streets of America virtually inviting them to partake in the disgusting scenes of gross patriotic jubilation which ensued on streets across the country. Yet, the curious thing here is the double staging that went on, the press conference photograph was staged along with the one taken in the situation room – Obama gave the press conference, then re-enacted his arrival at the press conference for the cameras. The double deferral of presence here can be mapped onto the endless deferral of both power and responsibility. The *mise en scène* turned *mise en abîme* of these images reminds us that what we are witnessing is not a return of the sovereign but something far more sinister. And consequently, a return to the streets and other public spaces should be read as the refusal, no matter how limited, to deny or give up individual and collective responsibility.

References

Agamben, G. 1998. *Homo Sacer: Sovereign Power and Bare Life*. Stanford, CA: Stanford University Press.

Agee, J and Evans, W. 2006. *Let Us Now Praise Famous Men*. London: Penguin.

Butler, J. 1993. *Bodies that Matter: On the Discursive Limits of 'Sex'*. London and New York, NY: Routledge.

De Certeau, M. 2011. *The Practice of Everyday Life*. Berkeley and Los Angeles, CA: University of California Press.

Deleuze, G. 1990. 'Post-Scriptum sur les societes de contrôle.' *L'autre Journal* 1. May.

Foucault, M. 1978. *Discipline and Punish: The Birth of the Prison*. New York, NY: Pantheon.

Foucault, M. 1978. 'La Société disciplinaire en crise.' *Asahi Jaanaru* 20:19. 12 May. Reproduced in Foucault, M. 2001. *Dits et écrits II, 1976-1988*. Paris: Gallimard.

Harvey, D. 2012. *Rebel Cities: From the Right to the City to the Urban Revolution*. London and New York, NY: Verso.

Hutnyk, J. 2012. 'Beyond Television Studies'. *South Asian History and Culture* 3:4. 583-590.

Lefebvre, H. 2014. *Toward an Architecture of Enjoyment*. Minneapolis, MN: Minnesota University Press.

Lyotard, J.-F. 1991. *The Inhuman: Reflections on Time*. Cambridge: Polity Press.

Rigouste, M. 2012. *La Domination policiére: Une violence industrielle*. Paris: La Fabrique.

RT.com. 2014. '"Damning Revelation": Cuts to Disability Benefit "Killed 60" in 3 Years – report'. 14 November. Available: http://rt.com/uk/206247-benefit-cuts-related-deaths/. Last accessed 30/11/2014.

Žižek, S. 2002. *Welcome to the Desert of the Real*. London and New York, NY: Verso.

Filmography

Examined Life: Philosophy in the Streets. 2008. Directed by A. Taylor. USA: Sphinx Productions. 87 mins.

Matrix, The. 1999. Directed by The Wachowski Brothers. USA: Warner Bros. 136 min.

Surrogates. 2009. Directed by J. Mostow. USA: Touchstone Pictures. 89 mins.

I. Marked Territories

1

THE STAIRWAY AS STREET: URBAN FORM AND POLITICAL SPACE

Jennifer Preston

When the physical form of the urban street is considered, it is usually imagined as a public road with pavements on either side, lined with buildings, but there are other urban typologies; canals, bridges and stairways that perform the functions of a street. Like the more typical street typology, these are places that permit the movement of traffic, places where people live, where business is transacted and where a social life is conducted. These are also largely public places whose very publicness determines their political nature. Each of these alternate street typologies has a physical form which shapes the way it is used and the possibilities open to those who use it. The public urban stairway, with its ranks of tiered levels, often contained on either side by balustrades, handrails or the walls of buildings, provides a distinct architectural form within the urban environment. This urban form affords the possibility of political action in a variety of ways but it also restricts or even prevents other actions.

Using a variety of examples, primarily from Sydney, Australia, this essay will explore the political nature of the public urban stairway as a location not only of overt political protest but also as a place of subtler meanings; the privileging of some users over others, the shifts from public spaces of transition to private spaces of commerce and as places where the public nature of the space allows, and sometimes conflicts with acts and desires of the private individual. An examination of the public urban stairway can illuminate the complex relationships operating within a given society, particularly those relationships concerned with the establishment, maintenance and contestation of authority and power.

A public urban stairway is a social space, a space where people gather and interact, and being a social space it is a social product (Lefebvre, 1991: 26). The social character of a stairway space is produced by the actions of the individuals and groups of people that created it, the people that have used it in the past, currently use it and those that observe its use. The design of a public stairway and the social space that results, is also influenced by those that may use it in the future. Henri Lefebvre argued that social space was not only the outcome of past actions but also 'what permits fresh actions to occur, whilst suggesting others and prohibiting yet others' (Lefebvre, 1991: 73). This essay argues that the manifestations of both social and political actions that take place on a public stairway have similarities to those that occur on other forms of public street but that the physical form of the stairway conditions the actions that take place here in different ways. The physical form of the stairway also facilitates practises that are not accommodated as effectively by the usual street typology. The public urban stairway, by forming an exclusively pedestrian street fosters its own 'street life', one that is removed from vehicular traffic and one that embodies political aspects in a variety of ways; as a notice board for dissent or commemoration, as an exclusionary space, as comodified space and as a stage for shifts and changes in authority and control. It is important that we examine differing typologies within the urban landscape so as to take account of the complexities of the material form and use of public space. Failure to do so can lead to a homogenized view that assumes simple dichotomies such as public-private, motorist-pedestrian, or worker-consumer.

The stairway as a notice board of dissent

The physical and spatial materiality of the stairway form gives it distinct advantages for the purpose of displaying a message. It is a space where dissent and critique can be brought to the public eye. From a distance the risers of the stairway appear to form a single vertical plane providing a potential canvas for an image or lines of text. As the pedestrian moves closer the image or text stratifies into individual bands, breaking up the image. To use the stairway, the pedestrian is forced not only to face the image but to pass over it.

When climbing a stairway the pedestrian's eyes focus a few steps in front, so that the riser of the stairway is an optimal location for advertising and political slogans (Miyasike-da Silva and McIlroy, 2010). Those walking up the stairway cannot avoid seeing the message. Graffiti practitioners clearly understand this, using the risers of the stairway as a notice board or gallery space where the personal expression of private individuals is displayed. Two stairways that regularly display new graffiti on their risers are within the 'Graffiti Tunnel' at Sydney University. This space contains two stairways within the tunnel and a third just outside that play host to almost daily changes from graffiti artists, students and those with a message. It hosts political statements, declarations of love, of being 'out and proud' and endless campaigning at student election time. No part of this stairway or tunnel is left untouched, although attempts by the university have been made to prevent the painting of doorknobs and stair treads by use of signage and security patrols.[1] The risers of the stairway are sometimes used to construct images that can only be seen as a whole when approaching the stair

---

[1] See http://www.legal-walls.net/walls/21.

and fragment as one reaches it. Such was the case with a representation of the Aboriginal flag painted in 2007.

The stairway risers are routinely used as a place to campaign by students running for student council elections. They present their candidates and political agendas in brief catch phrases and slogans which may only last a few hours before another candidate covers these over with a new set of messages.

Figure 1: Sydney University Graffiti Tunnel, 2007. Photograph by the author.

Figure 2: Sydney University Graffiti Tunnel, 2013. Photograph by the author.

The stairways of the graffiti tunnel change daily, the university permits any form of graffiti provided it is 'not offensive'. It is used as a place of campaigning, protest and memorial. The vibrancy of the tunnel and the rapidly changing images, illustrate a freedom of personal expression that is rarely permitted within public space.

A more dramatic example of the public stairway as a canvas for protest and indeed memorial occurred during the Gezi protests in Turkey in 2013. A group protesting against the proposed destruction of Gezi Park in central Istanbul were moved out by police. The denial of the protesters' rights to peaceful assembly and the violence used by police in moving them sparked anti-government protests across Turkey (Amnesty International, 2013). Etham Sarisuluk was one of the protesters. He was shot in the head and killed by a member of the riot police. Initially a government spokesperson claimed that Sarisuluk was killed by rocks thrown to him by other protestors but after a video of the apparent shooting was released on the internet, Sarisuluk became a symbol for the resistance to police brutality and the violent suppression of opposition by the government (Koplawitz, 2013).

The memorialisation of Sarisuluk was solidified in the form of his image which was applied to the risers of a stairway to a pedestrian bridge in Kizilay, central Ankara. In the image a monumental Sarisuluk is shown towering over riot police, tear gas and armoured vehicles (Kayabali, 2013). Pictures of the Sarisuluk image on the stairway have in turn been used in the media to further express outrage at the behaviour of the police and government (Özesen, 2013). The physical form of the stairway and the vertical canvas created by the risers enable the image to be seen from some distance, yet it also has an intimate relationship with those wishing to use the pedestrian bridge, who come into physical contact with it.

The physical form of the stairway with its tiered ranks of treads, provided the necessary form of terrain to enable a protest on the Spanish Steps in Rome in 2008. The Italian activist and artist Graziano Cecchini, purportedly in an attempt to raise awareness of the plight of the Karen people in Burma, released five hundred thousand brightly coloured balls at the top of the stairway. These bounced down the steps in a colourful casade many ending up in the Barcaccia Fountain in Piazza di Spagna at the foot of the stairway. This colourful protest action used the form of the stairway to maximise the movement of the balls. It also used the fame of the Spanish Steps themselves to maximise tourist and media exposure. Although many saw it as a stunt by the artist to gain attention for himself, the cascading effect also caused delight with passers-by and tourists collecting the balls as souvenirs (Nizzi, 2008).

Cecchini's activities used the stairway playfully, reminding the city's users of the stairways physical form and presence in the everyday life of the city. This opened up the possibility for people to rethink their relationship with the physical space and recognise potentials of the city in which they live and move. This type of prompt, which breaks us out of our daily habits and assumptions and causes us to reassess our urban environment often only comes to the everyday user of the street at times of violence; accidents, falls, confrontations or exclusions.

These overt forms of political protest that appropriate the physical properties of stairways within the public realm are highly visible and often dramatic but there are more subtle political forces embodied in the public stairway and indeed central to the stairways very meaning; the politics of equitable access.

The Politics of Equitable Access

On a purely pragmatic level stairways provide a traffic route for pedestrians, overcoming what otherwise can be unnegotiable terrain. They provide a clear route of pedestrian travel that is invariably a more direct route than is otherwise available. People experience the stairway in different ways because in reality the public is not one homogenous mass. Rather, as Hannah Arendt argued in her 1958 work *The Human Condition* the earth is populated by individuals (Arendt, 1958). This seems obvious, yet many authors speak of 'the public' and 'the pedestrian' as if these masses were comprised of identical human beings with identical likes and dislikes, abilities and disabilities, interests and annoyances. An effective investigation of the stairway as street requires a recognition of the diversity of people that make up the category of both 'public' and 'pedestrian'.

In many contemporary societies in developed countries such as Australia, Britain, Japan, Sweden, and the United States there is a widespread view that all people regardless of their level of physical ability have the right of equal access to public buildings, public transport and public space. This ideal however has proved difficult to achieve in reality, largely due to the financial costs involved in implementing accessible systems. It has required political will to enact legislation to force the issue of equitable access.

The public stairway is an exclusionary space, clearly a problem for the aim of equitable access. Some of the individuals who make up the diverse 'public' have a physical disability or impairment or they may be old and frail. Stairways therefore privilege certain types of users, the able bodied, and exclude or limit the participation of others. The nature of this exclusion is both physical and political, a fact very clearly illustrated by protests in Washington in 1990 where people with disabilities left their wheelchairs and crawled up the steps of the United States Capitol building in support of the Americans with Disabilities Act (Winter, 2008).

Much has been written on the privileging of the car over the pedestrian within the city (Durning, 1996; Purcell, 2000; Sheller and Urry, 2000; Brown, Morris and Taylor, 2009). Much less has been written on the privileging of some members of the public over others in pedestrian space. Even when the stairway is a public space whose creation and maintenance is paid for from the public purse, the stairway still excludes selected members of the public. An examination of the public stairway makes it apparent that in the street some pedestrians are privileged over others, those who are fit and able bodied. Recent attempts to counter this privileging have resulted in improvements to stairway design and the addition of lifts or funiculars. It is possible to design stairways to increase the level of accessibility to a larger section of the population. Those with vision impairment for example, are significantly benefited by the addition of tactile ground surface indicators, contrasting nosings on the stair treads and carefully detailed handrails. Ancillary design measures such as lifts, ramps or funiculars have the potential to open up access to a much wider public. These alternative mechanical methods are however expensive and the political will for their installation would appear to require a higher demand than from only the percentage of the public who are not physically able to climb. Here the pressure of tourism and commerce is having an appreciable influence where the requirements of tourists and everyday users of the city coincide. It also presents conflicts in instances where the demands of tourists and the money they bring in are prioritised over the needs of the everyday user of the city and conflicts with the commitment a government has to residents.

For those concerned with the design and use of public space, achieving equity and universal access presents many challenges. The reality of a city's topography would seem challenge enough but the often historic nature of many stairways presents an additional political conflict, that of heritage versus access. The desire to preserve the heritage of a city can conflict with a desire to provide equitable access for all.

Equity of access is clearly problematic for public stairways; exclusionary by their very nature, but it is not an unresolvable issue. Since the Santa Justa lift was built in Lisbon in 1874, public lifts have been augmenting stairways to enable easier and more universal access. With the rise of lobbying and awareness of disability discrimination the occurrence of public lifts is increasing. Commercial interests are not absent in this change as is illustrated by the 2003 lift project in the Spanish City of Teruel. The British Architect David Chipperfield in association with b720 Architectura tackled the problem of equitable access conflicting with heritage fabric in Teruel where a lower square was connected to the upper part of the city by an imperial stairway built in 1921 with decorative elements in the Mudejar tradition. The lower square was the proposed location for the arrival point of a high-speed rail link and this prompted its development which included the restoration of the stairway and the insertion of new lifts within the wall of the city. This solution provided 'a respectful juxtaposition' between the historic stairway and the new lifts (Bordas, 2003). Equitable access resulted but it was the economic power of the proposed high-speed rail link that galvanized political will and brought about the change.

The Stairway as Comodified Space

The politics of control and access on the stairway is not limited to issues of disability. Increasingly stairways that at one time were public spaces of transition are becomming spaces of commerce. In Victorian era Sydney, when the vast majority of the population walked, urban stairways were created by the city council, not only as elements of pedestrian infrastructure but as expressions of aesthetic and moral ideals and manifestations of civic pride. In the current city of Sydney some of these spaces are becoming commodified spaces, providing seating or advertising space for commercial enterprises such as cafes, bars and restaurants.

Agar Steps leads to Observatory Hill, the highest natural landform in the city of Sydney and provides the sole access to five Victorian Italianate terrace houses that line the south side of the stairway. Calson Terrace and shop, dating from 1882, ends the run of terraces at the lower level onto Kent Street and accommodates a cafe. The cafe uses the landings of the stairway to provide additional space for outdoor furniture (Figure 3). This creates a shady location for customers with a view through the trees to the water. The steps at their widest point measure five metres and this allows the owner of the cafe, to set out tables and chairs onto the landings without obstructing the passage of the residents who live on the stairs and the tourists making their way to and from The Observatory, The National Trust Gallery and parklands on the Hill. The use of the landings in this way allows the cafe owner additional space to carry out a commercial enterprise, it provides funds to the council as rental for the space that the table and chairs occupy, it promotes social interaction between the neighbours, cafe patrons and users of the stairway and it provides a pleasant outdoor environment, with dappled shade and views which despite its use as a commercial space is, at least theoretically, open to all.

Other stairway spaces in the city of Sydney do not necessarily embody the same open access and variety of uses. In recent years the creation of a stairway into the privately owned World Square shopping complex, designed by Crone Nation Architects and completed in 2008, has created a stairway that provides access through the site to retail outlets. The entry from George Street comprises two sets of steps on either side of a ramp. The ramp provides access for those with shopping trolleys, prams or in wheelchairs making it widely physically accessible (Figure 4). The entry arrangement provides views and access from the landings into the shops that line the stairways. The entry from the street has been designed with commerce as a central motivation. The stairway/ramp configuration maximises the number of people that can use it. The landings connect to the entrances of shops and the display windows of these shops line the facades adjoining the stairway and ramp. In addition places to sit and rest along the stairway and ramp direct the individual's eyes to the goods on display in the shop windows. Although this stairway/ramp configuration presents as being in the public realm, it is in fact part of a private development, and as such owners of the development can set the rules as to who enters or remains within the space.

Figure 3: The public stairway as commodified space. Agar steps Sydney, 2005. Photograph by the author.

The World Square development obliterated a small street, Swan Street which had at one time been a public street lined with residences.[2] From the turn of the twentieth century there were several attempts to buy the street as the area was developed by the large department store Anthony Horden's[3] and it was finally closed and sold by the council in 1950.[4] This relieved council and the rate payers of the financial burden of the streets maintenance but it also removed one of the small city spaces from public ownership. The World Square development restored public access although not public ownership to the site with a series of cross block links. One of these links is entered by the stairway and ramp configuration described above.

As the architecture scholar Esther Charlesworth observes, the concept of the private realm is no longer that of the family but rather 'the corporate forces that increasingly control our urban planning processes and the resultant spatial

[2] City of Sydney Archives items 26/78/251, 26/78/252, 26/276/1622.

[3] Ibid., 1906/0914, 1089/1/112.

[4] Ibid., 011/37 and 12/025.

outcomes' (Charlesworth, 2005: 5). Being a privately owned piece of public infrastructure, the stairway has a different set of constraints and regulation than those that are publicly owned. There are on-site security personnel who query those taking photos of the shopfronts and move on people resting on the stairway who appear to be homeless or possibly offensive to potential shoppers. The complexities of the overlapped private and public domains allow entry and use by some members of the public but not others. Those who are likely to spend money and not cause any inconvenience are admitted but skateboarders, buskers and the homeless are not allowed and are moved on by security. This is a space for commerce not a place for free social interaction. This creates an unusual paradox because the usual nature of a public stairway as a social space is not occupied by institutions, security staff or generally even surveillance cameras. The typical public stairway in Sydney is therefore a largely uncontrolled space. By creating a private commercial space of the publicly accessible stairway, a ridgidly controlled and surveilled space is created where freedom of behaviour is limited to that acceptable to the property owners. This not only limits those that can access this space but also the social interactions that are able to take place here. The objective here is to encourage consumerism rather than to promote any type of social interaction and yet, as I will discuss further in the next section, social interaction is a key ingredient in public space.

Figure 4: World Square Sydney, privately owned public space. Photograph by the author.

The social and anti-social space of the stairway

Public urban stairways, like other street typologies, can be viewed as both social and anti-social spaces. The urban designer, Allan Jacobs expressed the view in his book *Great Streets*, that a good street is one that helps make community and encourages participation. He explains, 'Participation in the life of a street involves the ability of people who occupy the buildings…to add something to the street, individually or collectively' (Jacobs, 1993: 3). Appropriation of the public stairway space by individuals and groups is one way that social interactions flourish. Appropriation of public space 'can use the fact and occasion of the city as the site of interventions and new socio-spatial creations' (Borden et al., 1996: 12).

Figure 5: Agar Steps residents with potted plants on the landing around their doorway. Photograph with permission by Ross Thornton, 2012.

It can be as quotidian as the chaining of a bicycle to the stairway handrail, as ordinary as the potted plants of residents on the steps and landings, or as rarefied as an artwork of light for the limited period of a festival. During the 2011 'Vivid' festival in Sydney, Moore's stairs were used for an interactive lighting artwork called 'Hopscotch' which involved pedestrians using the stairway in creating light rainbows generated by their movement. Unlike many appropriations of the public space of the stairway, this was sanctioned and formalised. Its temporary and entertaining nature not only created an interaction between the pedestrian and their physical environment but also between strangers as they commented on the work and teamed up to create different lighting effects.

There are subtly reactionary forms of behaviour that occur on public stairways. In one light these can be seen as forms of play and social expression but from a different perspective these practises are viewed as aberrant behaviours. Many forms of unstructured play occur on public stairways, frequently enacted by adults. There are conventional forms of play such as jogging and fitness training but there are also more daring, more physically dangerous forms of play, observed particularly amongst younger male adults, such as sliding down the handrail, trying to trip up one's companions, walking down the balustrade rather than the stair itself, skateboarding, rollerblading, parkour, and even cycling.

The public stairway can have an air of danger, mystery and surprise with the potential for discovery. The pre-existing conditions of protection from traffic, openness to observation and an unusual physical form that can be put to testing skill and stamina lend a stairway to play activities. Lefebvre notes when observing activity in public space that,

> all 'subjects' are situated in a space in which they must either recognize themselves or lose themselves, a space which they may both enjoy and modify. In order to accede to this space, individuals (children, adolescents) who are, paradoxically, already within it, must pass tests. This has the effect of setting up reserved spaces, such as places of initiation, within social space (Lefebvre, 1991: 35).

This appropriation of the stairway and the understanding of the possibilities that it provides results in activity where, as Lefebvre notes, 'the ages and sexes tak[e] from the available space the part that "belongs" to them, which then attracts one group and repels others' (Lefebvre, 2003: 131). Skateboarders are a clear example of this, with groups of predominantly young males taking over the steps in Martin Place, Sydney on weekends to hone and display their skills. Other skateboarders of a similar age and the same gender are attracted to join in but passers-by, although perhaps stopping to watch, do not walk through the space of the skateboarders. It is temporarily their space.

Skateboarding, particularly in public space, is often viewed as a subversive or anti-social activity as evidenced by signs prohibiting it and the fines attached to breaching regulation. This view is problematic because it demonises and potentially alienates legitimate users of urban space. It also deprives non-skaters of a form of entertaining street life. Efforts to exclude this group from the public life of the street frequently result in aggressive forms of street control that have a negative impact on a far wider range of citizens than was intended. Metal fins set in between the stone blocks of low walls and parkland edging in an attempt to prevent skating the edge mean skaters may move elsewhere but the everyday user of the city can no longer lie on the park wall in the sun or even sit comfortably with others as the physical space between them is now determined by anti-skate fins. Prohibition signs add to the visual clutter of urban parks and other public spaces.

The most often cited cause for attempting to ban skateboarders from public space is economic, the cost of the alleged damage that they do to public property in the form of chipped edges, scratched handrails and unsightly wheel marks. There is evidence that some skateboarding activities can cause damage to public space but instead of presenting skaters as a threat and spending money on devices to move them elsewhere or corral them in separated skate parks, perhaps a more inclusive approach would be beneficial to a wide section of the public. Celebrating skateboarders creative use of space and focusing money previously spent on providing deterrent devices towards designing into the urban environment skateable edges and handrails more resistant to damage would benefit a much wider section of the population than simply the skaters. Freedom to experience the urban environment in ways outside the norm, benefit a wider section of the public than just those who participate. Certainly, the freedom to explore the urban terrain in unexpected ways, raises the issue of contestation within public space. Doreen Massey observes, echoing earlier ideas of Hannah Arendt, that the 'public' is not one homogenous mass. Exercising the freedom of the individual in public space 'can encroach on the freedom of others. "The public" for whom this place was dreamt and built turns out to be multiple and differentiated' (Massey, 1996: 76). Whilst various demands on space may raise contestations the persistence of the image of 'the public' as only consisting of middle class office workers and affluent consumers, subtly forces people to comply with certain behaviours and uses in order to feel accepted within public space. This potentially leads to a limited group of people belonging to the space rather than the space belonging to all the people.

The stairway like other forms of street can also be an anti-social space. In a society that is increasing its surveillance and control over private individuals with speed cameras, security cameras, private security guards and terrorist legislation, public stairways in Sydney provide a venue where people can often still be private in public. Perhaps surprisingly, even in 2011 Sydney's stairways including those within the red light district of the Kings Cross area police command, did not have surveillance cameras, although the police have requested that the council provide them.

The City of Sydney in 2014 had 98 council-funded cameras in the city area for a population of 177,000 (City of Sydney, 2014). In 2009, The City of London [borough] had 619 cameras to cover a population of 9000 (*BBC News*, 2009). In addition, both cities have many privately funded cameras that view public space at the entries to businesses or residences. The selection of council funded camera locations in Sydney is determined by the council working in conjunction with 'crime mapping experts within NSW Police' (ibid.) using data provided by the NSW Bureau of Crime Statistics that showed public spaces in central Sydney which 'experienced a significantly higher rate of crimes against the person than other areas' (ibid). Given that the selection of the location for cameras was based on the intensity of crime events and no surveillance cameras were located on public stairways, the implication is that public stairways are in reality, comparatively safe.

There is also an issue here of who, if anyone, surveillance cameras protect. Many studies have shown that cameras alone do not prevent crime, at best they assist in identifying the perpetrator after the event has occurred and the quality of equipment can make even this an uncertainty. Indeed the presence of CCTV cameras may increase the incidents of some offences (Isnard, 2001: 3). In addition rather than reducing the fear of crime as is often claimed, the presence of surveillance cameras has been attributed to a rise in anxiety about crime in some instances (Isnard, 2001: 3).

There is big money in the business of 'security' and 'crime prevention'. In Australia in 2014 Telstra reportedly spent up to 60 Million Australian Dollars to buy slightly more than half of SNP Security, a back-to-base alarm and security camera business (Commins, 2014). An anxiety about crime translates into dollars spent on 'security'; putting cameras on streets, building protective fences, installing anti skate devices and in some cities, anti-homeless spikes. But the aesthetics of 'security' feeds the anxiety about crime. A public space with surveillance cameras, extreme levels of lighting and imposing fences, spikes and anti-skate fins does not look or feel 'safe'.

Whilst the rhetoric that surrounds closed circuit television businesses is one of crime prevention and security much of the surveillance is directed not towards criminal behaviour but to behaviours that the owners of the systems label anti-social. The term is frequently misused, often perhaps intentionally. Antisocial behaviour is behaviour that is inconsiderate of other people and thus may cause damage to society, yet the term is increasingly being used to describe behaviours simply outside the norm, behaviours that are not inconsiderate or cause damage but are simply unusual. This is problematic because it moves anti-social behaviour into a subjective realm where it seems to be often confused with anti-capital generating behaviour. People who are homeless, begging or loitering, for example, are moved on not because there activities damage society but because in reflecting unpleasant aspects of the reality of society they provide visible evidence that the notion of a singular 'public' is false. Their presence, which confronts middle class values and expectations and challenges us with the reality of others lives, is bad for business. It questions the dominant discourse as to who the street belongs to and how one should behave in public space. It forces us to face questions about what we spend and what we consume, what we have and how we got it.

Removing people from public space because they do not fit preconceived ideas of how public space should be used is dangerous. It opens the door to removing from the public domain any person or activity who those in power simply do not like. The removal of the skateboarders and the homeless sets a precedent for the removal of buskers, charity collectors, and fund raising cake stalls. In attempting to sanitise society by removing sections of the public from public space, we cause damage to that society for it is no longer complete, representative and open but becomes an artificial stage set that does not reflect reality and the problems and challenges that exist within it.

Inconsiderate or anti-social behaviour happens on a wide variety of street types including stairways and it is not a recent phenomenon. Historical complaints can be found in the archives of the City of Sydney. One example is a complaint about Merriman, Caraher and Playfair stairs which was written by the honorary secretaries of the Citizens Vigilance Committee in July 1900 (Citizens Vigilance Committee, 1900). The citizen's vigilance committee was formed at the beginning of the outbreak of bubonic plague in Sydney in 1900, to work with the NSW government in an effort to control the plague epidemic. They held meetings, whose proceedings were published in the newspapers; they produced pamphlets on how to trap rats; (ibid) and were active in establishing rat collecting depots and forwarding citizens' complaints regarding unsanitary conditions to the relevant government authorities. The Citizens Vigilance Committee continued after the plaque epidemic had passed to lobby governments for sanitary reform (Golder, 1995).

In a letter from the Citizens Vigilance Committee to the Town Clerk dated 10 July 1900 it was reported that:

> It appears that these stairs are the resort of people who continually lounge about them and cover the steps with expectoration, tobacco juice etc. It is also stated that frequently there are rotten eggs thrown on the stairs in addition to the dust and dirt caused by continual traffic. Under these circumstances we are directed to ask that they be swept at least once a day and that they be hosed with water twice a week. In their present state they are almost impassable to ladies who wish to keep their dresses clean (Letter to the Town Clerk from the Citizens Vigilance Committee, 10 July, 1900).

The complaint was referred to the 'Inspector of Nuisances' for action.

This letter evidences the way in which the stairway was used during a particular historic period. It was heavily used, not only providing access for the 'continual traffic', which included 'ladies', but it was a place where people 'lounged about', chewing tobacco and spitting out the juice. This contrast of 'ladies who wish to keep their dresses clean' and the people who lounged about chewing tobacco and spitting, points to a mix of people of different genders and social classes using the stairway in a variety of ways.

The committee was not alone in their appeals to improve the detrimental conditions of stairways caused by the anti-social practises of users around the turn of the twentieth century. In March 1901 R.W. Richards the City Surveyor, wrote to the Mayor recommending that a lamp be erected on a stairway in the Rocks as he believed ' …the erection of a lamp on these steps would probably prevent indecencies that are now committed there' (Letter from R W Richards to the Mayor dated 26 March, 1901).

Figure 6: Light fixture and signage Chard Stairs, Sydney, 2012.

Increased lighting alone was not necessarily a guaranteed way to improve people's behaviour in public. In 1925 complaints were received by the Council from William Chard, that 'people at night commit nuisance… (in solid and liquid form)' on Chard Stairs in Darlinghurst.[5] This stair had been designed with integrated wrought iron lamps, yet it also provided a convenient platform from which 'boys and thieves' were able to enter the premises of Larkc, Hoskins & Co. Ltd., importers of motor cars, at the first floor level (ibid). Whilst windows overlooked this stairway, they were from commercial premises and not usually occupied at night. These situations reinforce Jane Jacobs' notion for the need to have 'eyes upon the street' but lighting and 'eyes upon the street' are not sufficient in themselves (Jacobs, 1965: 45). The individuals behind the eyes that observe the activities must be prepared to act if lighting and observation is to have an impact on criminal and anti-social behaviour. The space of the street and the stairway needs to be affirmed as community space, not just as a means for accessing property. Where the lighting of the twentieth century has failed to control public behaviour sufficiently, today this attempted control is supplemented by signage, Acts of parliament and financial penalties. On Chard stairs a sign by the City of Sydney council prohibits a variety of activities including consuming alcohol, 'feeding pigeons' and the 'sale of goods and services' with the stated objectives of preventing damage to the area and 'inconvenience or injury to others' (City of Sydney site plaque). Lighting, signage and surveillance cameras, euphemistically called 'safety cameras' on occasion, are all methods by which public and private institutions attempt to regulate and control real bodies in real spaces. These attempts at control can lead to a process of exclusion.

There are a variety of conditions that lend a stairway to acts of anti-social behaviour. There is often a lower likelihood of being clearly seen and a high likelihood of being able to escape if necessary. Stairways are inaccessible to police cars, police horses or bicycles, and the necessary slow and visible nature of pursuit from one end, results in the likelihood of an escape from the other end. Minimal surveillance, often low lighting and a place that may present few interruptions, create near to ideal conditions for a variety of what society generally considers anti-social behaviour from littering to public drunkenness, urinating and defecating, drug taking, soliciting, and more serious criminal behaviour such as mugging, rape and murder.

One branch of literature on public and private urban space focuses on crime and security promoting notions of 'designing out crime' (Geason and Wilson, 1989). In Britain the architectural response to crime and anti-social behaviour has generally been a hostile and defensive one with the establishment of gated communities, (Kelbie, 2003; Glancey, 2010) heavy use of CCTV cameras and recently spikes in the streets (Carter, 2014). But there is a counter discourse that argues the heightened electronic surveillance and personal data collection is in itself anti-social and a threat to both our private and public lives and our public space (Cida de Aragon, 2007). We need to consider carefully our definitions of

---

[5] City of Sydney Archives, CRS 2432/24.

anti-social behaviour and how we respond to it. The promotion of fear through the proliferation of electronic surveillance and movement control that creates provocative rather than calming spaces is not the only option as developments such as Sluseholmen in Copenhagen have demonstrated (Laville, 2014).

Public stairways have a specific architectural form that contributes characteristics to the public realm that are both similar and different to the usual form of public street. Their risers can present space for messages of dissent, their form restricts their use to only ambulant users of the city, they are public spaces that can become commodified by private businesses and they are spaces that facilitate both social interaction and anti-social behaviours. Whilst it is only on rare occasions that stairways are seen as exceptional urban places, all urban stairways have a value beyond their physical form and the pedestrian route of travel that they provide. They are places where things happen and where the complex relationships of people and groups particularly those relationships concerning power and authority are played out. In cities that are becoming increasingly controlled by interventions such as CCTV cameras, fences, anti-skate fins and anti-homeless spikes can the public stairway remain an open and free public space in the future of the city? The stairway is not only a transitory space to pass through it is a politically charged space that provides a lens through which questions of who the street belongs to, how it is used and occupied and who is excluded from it, can be examined.

References

Amnesty International. 2013. 'Turkey: Gezi Park Protests: Brutal Denial of the Right to Peaceful Assembly in Turkey'. 2 October. Available: http:// http:// www.amnesty.org/en/library/info/EUR44/022/2013/en. Last accessed 04/08/2014.

Arendt, H. 1958. *The Human Condition*. 2nd ed. Chicago, IL: The University of Chicago Press.

Australian Heritage Database. 1978. 'Agar Steps Houses'. Available: http://www. environment.gov.au/cgi-bin/ahdb/search.pl?mode=place_detail;place_ id=2157. Last accessed 04/08/2014.

BBC News. 2009. 'The Statistics of CCTV'. 20 July. Available: http:// http://news. bbc.co.uk/1/hi/uk/8159141.stm. Last accessed 04/08/2014.

Bordas, D.B. 2003. 'Remodelación del Paseo del Óvalo, la Escalinata y su entorno Terue (Spain)'. *Public Space*. Available: http://www.publicspace.org/en/ works/c041-remodelacion-del-paseo-del-valo-la-escalinata-y-su-entorno/ prize:2004. Last accessed 04/08/2004.

Borden, I. 2001. *Skateboarding, Space and the City: Architecture and the Body*. Oxford: Berg.

Borden, I., Kerr, J., Pivaro, A., and Rendell, J. (eds). 1996. *Strangely Familiar: Narritives of Architecture in the City*. London and New York, NY: Routledge.

Brown, J., Morris, E. and Taylor, B. 2009. 'Planning for Cars in Cities'. *Journal of the American Planning Association* 75:2 (Spring), 161-177.

Carey, P. 2001. *30 Days in Sydney A Wildly distorted Account*. London: Bloomsbury Publishing.

Carter, C. 2014. 'Tesco removes spikes over claims they are "anti-homeless"'. *The Telegraph*. 12 June.

Cecilia, F. M. and Levene R. (eds) 2004. *Dense Minimalism: David Chipperfield 1998 – 2004*. Madrid: El Croquis Editorial.

Chard, W. 1925. 'Letter to the Town Clerk'. *City of Sydney Archives*. Item CRS2432/24.

Charlesworth, E. 2005. *City Edge: Contemporary Discourses on Urbanism*. Oxford: Architectural Press.

Citizens Vigilance Committee. 1900a. *Rats and the Plague: How to Catch and Trap Rats*. Sydney: Government Printer.

_____ . 1900b. 'Letter to the Town Clerk'. 10 July. *City of Sydney Archives*. Item 1900/2571.

City of Sydney. 2014. 'Street Safety Cameras'. 28 July. Available: http://www.cityofsydney.nsw.gov.au/community/safety/street-safety/street-safety-cameras. Last accessed 04/08/2014.

Commins, P. 2014. 'Markets Live': Iron-Wrought Rally'. *Sydney Morning Herald*. 23 June. Available: http://www.smh.com.au/business/markets-live/markets-live-ironwrought-rally-20140623-3amzq.html. Last accessed 04/08/2014.

Corsini, J.M.O. 2007. *Urban Design: Accessible and Sustainable Architecture*. Barcelona: Instituto Monsa de Ediciones.

De Aragon, C. 2007. *...On Public Space*. Sydney: Infinite Press.

Dick, T. 2005. 'Fixing the Hole'. *Sydney Morning Herald*. 8 January.

Durning, A. T. 1996. *The Car and The City*. Washington: Northwest Environmental Watch.

Emmett, P. 2000. *Sydney Metropolis Suburb Harbour*. Sydney: Historic Houses Trust of New South Wales.

Finance Committee [Minutes of the]. 1950. 'Proposed Sale of Swan Street'. 1 February, 1949 – 21 November, 1950. *City of Sydney Archives*. Item 012/025.

Geason, S. and Wilson, P.R. 1989. *Designing Out Crime: Crime Prevention Through Environmental Design*. Canberra: Australian Institute of Criminology.

Gehl, J. 2010. *Cities for People*. Washington, DC: Island Press.

Glancey, J. 2010. 'Gated Communities are a Social Ill'. *The Guardian*. 8 July.

Golder, H. 1995. *A Short Electoral History of the Sydney City Council 1842-1992*. Sydney: City of Sydney.

Isnard, A. 2001. 'Can Surveillance cameras be Successful in Preventing Crime and Controlling Anti-social Behaviours?' *Australian Institute of Criminology*.

Jacobs, A. B. 1993. *Great Streets*. Cambridge, MA: MIT Press.

Jacobs, Jane. 1972 [1961]. *The Death and Life of Great American Cities: The Failure of Town Planning*. 3rd edn. Harmondsworth: Pelican Books.

Kayabali, Y. 2013. '#occupygezi: Protests Progress'. *Victoria and Albert Museum*. Available: http://www.vam.ac.uk/b/blog/posters-stories-va-collection/occupygezi-progress. Last accessed 04/08/2014.

Kelbie, P. 2003. 'Rise in gated communities could pose a threat to public services'. *The Independent*. 27 September.

Koplawitz, H. 2013. 'Ahmet Sahbaz, Officer who Shot and Killed Protester Etham Sarisuluk in Turkey Protests, Released from Jail.' *International Business Times*. 24 June. Available: http://www.ibtimes.com/ahmet-sah-baz-officer-who-shot-killed-protester-ethem-sarisuluk-turkey-protests-re-leased-jail-video. Last accessed 04/08/2014.

Laville, S. 2014. 'Designing out Crime in Scandinavia: "Cities cannot be completely Safe and Completely exciting at the same time"'. *The Guardian*. 24 June. Available: http://www.theguardian.com/cities/2014/jun/24/designing-out-crime-scandinavia-copenhagen-cities-safe-exciting. Last accessed 19/01/2015.

Lefebvre, H. 1991. *The Production of Space*. Translated by Donald Nicholson-Smith. Malden, MA: Blackwell publishing.

_____ . 2003. *Henri Lefebvre Key Writings*. Translated and edited by S. Elden, E. Lebas and E. Kofman. New York, NY: Continuum.

Legal Walls. 2008. 'Sydney University Graffiti Tunnel'. Available: http:// http://www.legal-walls.net/walls/21. Last accessed 04/08/2014.

Lonely Planet. 2014. 'McElhone Stairs.' Available: http:// http://www.lonelyplanet.com/australia/sydney/sights/landmarks-monuments/mcelhone-stairs. Last accessed 04/08/2014.

Miyasike-da Silva, V. and McIlriy, W. 2012. 'Does it Matter Where You Look when Walking on Stairs? Insights from a dual-task Study.' *Plos One* 7:9 (September).

Nizza, M. 2008. 'A Ball Bonanza at the Spanish Steps'. *The New York Times*. 16 January. Available: http://thelede.blogs.nytimes.com/2008/01/16/a-ball-bo-nanza-at-the-spanish-steps/?_r=0. Last accessed 23/07/2013.

Özesen, E. 2013. 'Etham Sarisuluk on Ankara Streets'. *Bianet*. 13 June. Available: http://www.bianet.org/english/people/147552-ethem-sarisuluk -on-ankara-streets. Last accessed 04/08/2014.

Purcell, D. 2000. 'The Car and the City'. *Bulletin of Science, Technology and Society* 20:5 (October), 348-359.

Richards, R. W. 1901. 'Letter to the Mayor.' 26 March. *City of Sydney Archives*. Item 1901/998.

Sheller, M. and Urry, J. 2000. 'The City and the Car'. *International Journal of Urban and Regional Research* 24:4 (December), 737-757.

Simmel, G. 1997 [1903] 'The Metropolis and mental life'. In Leach, N. (ed.) *Rethinking Architecture: a Reader in Cultural Theory*. London: Routledge.

Winter, M. 2008. 'I was there…Washington DC 1990.' *ADAPT History Project*. Available: http://www.adapt.org/freeourpeople/adapt25/narratives/15adapt.htm. Last accessed 04/08/2014.

Works Committee [Minutes of the]. 1950. 'Closing and Sale of Swan Street'. 2 February 1949 – 22 November 1950. *City of Sydney Archives*. Item 011/37.

Zjawinski, S. 2008. 'Guerilla Artists Bombs Spanish Steps with Plastic Balls'. *Wired*. 18 January. Available: http://www.wired.com/2008/01/guerilla-artist/. Last accessed 04/08/2014.

2

BARCODES AND BARRICADES:
PARISIAN STREET ART AND GLOBAL CAPITALISM

Rachel Segal Hamilton

Like graffiti before it, street art has in recent years undergone a process of commodification, acquiring mainstream acceptance and, according to its detractors,
losing its edge. Cultural institutions have embraced it - in 2008 Tate Modern
held the first major UK exhibition dedicated to the form, inviting artists to paint
on the walls of the building.[1] Art dealers have exploited its economic potential,
with a string of six-figure sales of work, most notably by Banksy, street art's en-
fant terrible turned national treasure.[2] Brands have adopted its visual language
and deployed its techniques and aesthetic for commercial ends, commissioning
guerrilla marketing campaigns and employing street artists to work with them.[3]
Property developers have become wise to street art as a visual precursor to gentrification in areas such as Hackney Wick in London, Kreuzberg in Berlin and
Belleville in Paris.[4]

   Whatever its status today, street art originated as a bottom-up reaction to the
material urban environment and its dwellers. The first proponents of what we
recognise as contemporary street art were the French artists Ernest Pignon-Ernest and Gerard Zlotykamien, who started illegally painting and fly-posting pic-
torial work on the streets of Paris in the 1970s. Pignon-Ernest and Zlotykamien's
early efforts were followed in 1981 by Blek le Rat (real name Xavier Prou) who,
inspired by the New York subway graffiti movement, set out to paint his own
graffiti piece on a wall in Paris.[5] But he found it impossible because the environ-

---

[1] Also MOCA's *Art in the Streets* in 2011 and Fondation Cartier's *Né dans la Rue* in
2009.

[2] The most expensive Banksy artwork sold to date is *Keep it Spotless*, a defaced Damien
Hirst canvas, which went for $1,870,000 at Sotheby's, New York in 2008.

[3] Louis Vuitton has a range of street art silk scarves with designs by artists such as
EINE and Os Gemeos. See http://uk.louisvuitton.com/eng-gb/articles/street-art-on-
silk. Last accessed 16/09/2014.

[4] In 2006 property developer Caroline Cummings funded a street art exhibition on
the walls of 11 Spring Street, a popular destination for street artists, before she had it
converted into apartments. See Kennedy (2006).

[5] In graffiti terminology, a 'piece' (short for masterpiece) refers to a large and complex
work, often involving multiple colours, arrows, shading and 3D effects. See Cooper and

ment of Paris, the architecture, was 'nothing like America' (Reiss, 2007). Instead, he developed a distinctive stencil technique, which has influenced subsequent generations of street artists, especially Banksy. The particularity of the Parisian architectural aesthetic warranted its own response. More recently, in the 1990s and 2000s, Paris has produced a multitude of well known street artists, such as Zevs, JR, Invader, Andre, C215, l'Atlas, and many others.

A vernacular art form, street art has always resisted capitalism. However, such resistance is by necessity tactical rather than strategic. Michel de Certeau defines the two in *The Practice of Everyday Life*. Those in power - town planners, the police - attempt to organise and control city life from above, strategically, but, in opposition to this, the users of a city - skateboarders, cab drivers, dog walkers - engage with it tactically, in unpredictable, creative and constantly-changing ways, to suit their everyday needs. Street artists, working as individuals and as collectives, carve their own routes through the city and don't adhere to any one, unified politics or code of ethics, although explicitly political street art can be found in many contexts - on the streets of Cairo during the Egyptian revolution, for example.

Looking at three Parisian street artists – JR, Zevs and Invader – I will explore the way that street art is indicative of a wider tension between privatisation and activism in contemporary urban space. Rather than seeing street art as having 'sold out', I wish to argue that any notion that street art was 'free' is itself a myth. Street art, like many urban practices is engaged in a continual struggle with capitalism, a process of feedback and blockage. It attests to the continuing significance of the street as a site for creativity and resistance, while at the same time making visible both capitalism's instability and its ingenuity - its gift for continually co-opting and commercialising any flows of resistance which seek to undermine it.

Paris has been decisive in shaping our understanding of the modern city, and the tensions inherent within this space. That coherent architectural aesthetic to which Proust refers is the result of the urban renewal project led by Baron Georges-Eugène Haussmann between 1853 and 1870. Haussmann sought to rationalise the city, demolishing its labyrinthine medieval streets and replacing them with wide, long, straight *grands boulevards*. In his *Arcades Project*, Walter Benjamin argues that the aim of this was 'to secure the city against civil war.' He goes on to note that:

> Widening the streets is designed to make the erection of barricades impossible, and new streets are to furnish the shortest route between the barracks and the workers' districts. Contemporaries christened this 'strategic embellishment' (Benjamin, 2002: 12).

Chalfant (2009:6).

While Paris is an enduring symbol of global empire – a point from which, since the first *Exposition Universelle* in 1855, culture has been exported outwards, it also is a city with its own strong history of resistance, from the barricaded revolutionary street of 1830 and 1848 to the street of the student revolts of May 1968, and, more recently, the *banlieue* riots of 2005, during which the then interior minister Nicolas Sarkozy described rioters as 'scum' [*racaille*], which he promised to wipe from the streets.[6] Anxieties about the changing use and meaning of the Parisian street preoccupy media commentators who lament what they perceive to be the city's transformation into a *ville musée* [museum town], a theme park, devoid of 'real people', good only for visual consumption by crowds of gawping tourists (Scemama, 2006).

Within this socio-historical context of resistance and struggle, street art might be defined as a form of barricade. A barricade constitutes a bottom-up recycling of the material substance of the city for use in social-political struggle. The term comes from *barrique*, the French word for barrel. However, a barricade can consist of virtually anything since they are improvised from whatever materials are to hand. Thus, no two barricades are the same, but a loose definition would be: a temporary improvised structure, erected by civilians, to obstruct or control the street as a means intervening in and reclaiming urban space from the authorities. They have been used in street battles all over the world, from the Warsaw Ghetto uprising of 1944 to the incidents in the Pembury Estate in Hackney during the 2011 London riots,[7] and, more recently, in Maidan Square, Kiev, in the 2014 Ukranian protests, but they have a particular resonance in Parisian cultural memory, where the widening of the streets under Haussmann failed to prevent barricades being used once more in May '68. If Haussmanisation was a 'strategic embellishment', Parisian street art is a 'tactical counter-embellishment', descended from the barricades of street battles past. Like barricades, street art reshapes social interaction from top-down city planning and wider market forces.

Logos on the street

Already in 1999, Naomi Klein had noted the way in which brands have overtaken products. In No Logo she analyses the way that what is being sold by Nike, say, is no longer simply a pair of trainers but a lifestyle philosophy for which consumption is a mode of expression. Here, advertising works at the level of subjectivity; it no longer exhorts us to do something – to buy a product – but to

---

[6] Sarkozy vowed to do this using Kärcher, a high-power pressure hose used to clean graffiti from walls. See Sciolino (2007).

[7] Although much has been made of the looting which took place during the 2011 London riots, rioters on the Penbury Estate built barricades and launched an attack against the police (Lewis and Khalili, 2011).

be a particular kind of person. Central to this is the logo. Klein writes: 'Logos have grown so dominant that they have essentially transformed the clothing on which they appear into empty carriers for the brands they represent' (Klein, 2010 [1999]: 28).

More than its precursor, graffiti, street art has grown up immersed in post-modern branding culture. Like graffiti, it is illegal and ephemeral: the risk of being removed by the authorities, weathered by the elements or scrawled over by other artists is an intrinsic part of the process. But whereas graffiti privileges elaborate typography, street art tends to be more iconographic, experimental and aesthetically accessible (Manco, 2004). Graffiti is a cipher, a complex sub-cultural code, often illegible and unappealing, to all but those in the know. Street art, by contrast, vandalises through decoration, working with rather than against the city and seeking out the approval of a lay audience. If we broadly define the practice of street art as unsanctioned, impermanent intervention in the physical presence of the street, this can encompass anything from stencils, defaced billboard adverts to painting, flyposting and mosaics.

What these divergent modes of creative action share is the way in which they operate – like logos. Individual works may vary but will retain a strong overall consistency of aesthetic, technique or tactic. This is evident in the different approaches of these three artists. Invader uses square, coloured bathroom tiles to create mosaics of pixelated Space Invader characters from the classic computer arcade game. Self-proclaimed 'photograffeur' JR flyposts portraits, shot in black and white, using a wide-angle lens and generally on a large scale. Zevs, meanwhile, visually attacks and 'liquidates' logos by pouring paint on them so it looks as if they are melting (Figure 1). Street artworks tend to be instantly recognisable as the work of a given practitioner, who builds their reputation through repetition, deploying marketing-style methods of dissemination. Mimicking global brands, many street artists now have an international reach; they travel abroad, exporting their logos to streets across the world. Consciously or not, this carries with it an element of neo-colonialist aspiration. Making a street artwork on a foreign wall, like planting a flag, is a way of marking territory, making visible your claim on space.

JR, Invader and Zevs all use pseudonyms. The letters 'JR' are apparently his real initials, 'Invader' refers to the space invader mosaics that are his calling card, while 'Zevs' (pronounced 'Zeus') named himself after a metro train that almost ran him over while he was out painting in the streets. All use different methods to disguise their faces when appearing in photographs or in public. JR wears sunglasses and a hat, Invader fittingly opts for a pixelated effect over his face and, until fairly recently, Zevs was always shown wearing a translucent leopard print scarf tied around his face, like some masked anti-superhero (Figure 2). These disguises aren't simply a pragmatic way to avoid arrest. In reality the authorities could identify the artists if necessary – as they have done in the case of Zevs.[8] They are a performance that perpetuates novelty and construct a rebel identity. But, as in the case of large 'faceless' corporations, the anonymity of the street artist also allows them to eschew individual responsibility. Some companies try to counter this using frontmen such as Steve Jobs or Mark Zuckerberg, who claim an intimacy with their consumers or users by being named and shown. These street artists, meanwhile, present themselves as outlaw Robin Hood-type figures. Both are attempts at creating emotional individuation against a background of too much information. At the same time, we are seeing the rise of new leaderless political movements, such as Occupy or Anonymous, both of which use anonymity and replicability as a form of branding.

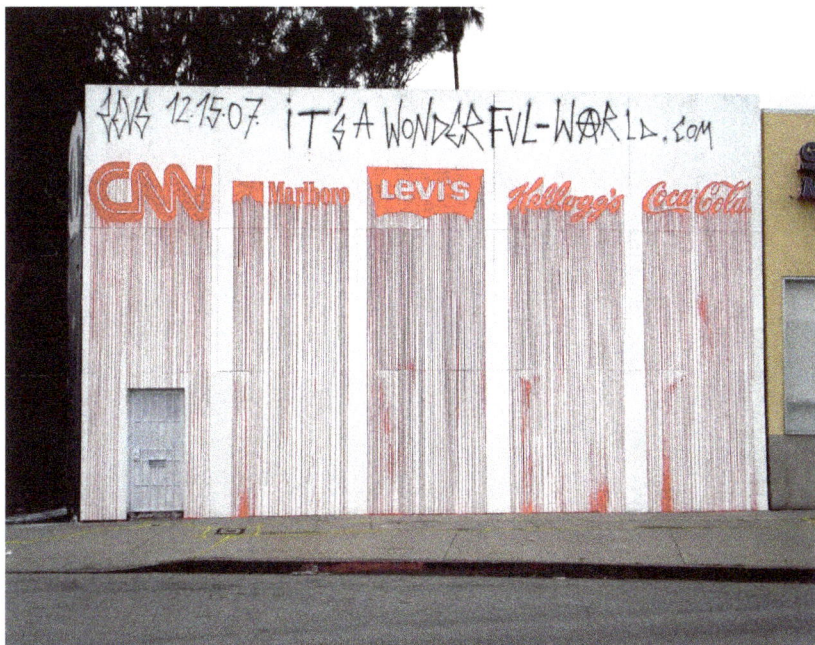

Figure 1. 'Liquidated Logos'. Photograph by Lord Jim. Creative Commons License. Logos by Zevs (2007).

Zevs: The street art culture industry

Rather than adding objects to the surfaces of the city, Zevs adapts what is already there. He is known for 'liquidating' logos – throwing buckets of paint onto Nike swooshes and Mcdonald's golden arches and leaving them dripping. He writes:

> I want to take their logos and reverse the effect – reverse the flow of energy. It isn't about anti-advertising, though; it's more to show that the power of the logo can be reversed against the company. If a company asked me to liquidate one of their logos, I wouldn't do it. I make sure to keep a clear distance between me and

---

[8] Zevs was arrested in Hong Kong in 2009 for painting a liquidated Chanel logo on an Armani store (Wooster Collective, 2009).

the companies whose logos I operate on. But if they wish to buy one of my paint-
ings – then, sure, this isn't a problem (qtd in Nguyen and Mackenzie, 2010: 34).

This statement highlights an ambiguity in the relationship between street art and
consumerism. Zevs claims to 'keep a clear distance' but this is impossible. In the
sense that it manipulates the informational content of logos, his work is indicative of an age in which the machinations of consumer culture have become pro-
foundly communicational. We no longer simply buy products from companies,
we converse with them on Facebook and Twitter. They send us emails asking
how we feel about them. Tell us jokes. Apologise when they get things wrong.
Brands strive to achieve intimacy with their consumers. Coca-Cola's declared
mission is 'to refresh the world' - but also to 'inspire moments of optimism and
happiness.'[9] For the recent *Share a Coke* campaign, they released limited-edition bottles featuring common first names, inviting consumers to share selfies
of themselves, posing with their personalised bottles at 'Share a Coke' parties.[10]

Figure 2. Screenshot of Zevs from *Visual Kidnapping* (2002).

Unlike corporate branding, which is more explicitly motivated by financial gain,
street art does not appear to be asking anything of its viewer beyond recognition. Yet, like many contemporary street artists, Zevs, JR and Invader all sell
artworks through galleries. Consequently, any work they put in the street functions to some extent as advertising, generating of flows of profit, through print
sales, tickets to art shows and merchandise. This relationship of negotiation
with, rather than outright rejection of, the art world is evident in the relative
ease with which street art has been integrated into the mainstream compared to

---

[9] See http://www.coca-colacompany.com/our-company/mission-vision-values.

[10] https://www.cokezone.com/uk/en/coca-cola/share-a-coke.

graffiti in the 1980s. The overlap between street art and the art world is bolstered by the fact many street artists, in contrast to graffiti crews before them, belong to a privileged demographic of media and business-savvy, art-school educated, professional artists who develop their practice in studios before displaying work in the streets. As Luke Dickens has shown in his ethnographic research on the street art screen print company *Pictures on Walls*, street art is a creative industry predicated on a post-Fordist model of flexibility (Dickens, 2010: 64).

Figure 3. 'ZEVS bombs the Giorgio Armani building in HK' (2009). Photograph by Edwin Lee. Creative Commons License.

On 2 April 2002, Zevs cut out and removed an image of a model from a billboard advertising Lavazza coffee in Alexanderplatz, Berlin. He chose this particular image because, as a young, attractive woman, the model was 'the perfect victim'.[11] He threatened to 'kill' their image if the company didn't pay a ransom of €500,000. His proposed execution method was a 'big poster crusher in Vitry-sur-Seine outside Paris' (Zevs, 2002). Initially Lavazza ignored him but, following a sophisticated media campaign, including website, billboard posters, and press events at contemporary art galleries, they negotiated. The deal they agreed upon saw Zevs returning the image in return for an 'act of sponsorship' in the form of a €500,000 donation to the Palais de Tokyo in Paris. Instead of subverting the visual power of the Lavazza brand, Zevs basks in it. The staged confron-

---

[11] Nihls Christie's notion of the 'ideal victim' is 'a person or category of individuals who – when hit by crime – most readily are given the complete and legitimate status of being a victim.' He argues that female, child or elderly victims of crime gain disproportionate news media coverage because they are perceived to be more vulnerable and deserving of sympathy (Christie, 1986: 18).

tation with Lavazza becomes a form of mutual exploitation. Zevs achieves notoriety and exposure, while Lavazza gains cultural capital from associating their name with an 'edgy' street artist and a contemporary art gallery. Although on one level Zevs claimed to have held a major corporation to ransom, he is simply acting out the traditional relationship of art patronage.

JR: Street art space

Since Haussmannisation, power and wealth have been overwhelmingly concentrated in the centre of Paris, while industry and production have been pushed outwards, creating a suburban working class that is at once spatially and politically marginalised. This contrasts with London, for example, which has traditionally had social housing in even the wealthiest, most central boroughs of the city. Both, like most cities, grew up out of ancient walled configurations, but London is surrounded by a green belt whereas Paris is surrounded by housing estates. Unlike in London during the 2011 riots, middle class Parisians were unlikely to have experienced the *banlieue* riots of 2005 directly. Their visual interactions with rioters would have been restricted to mainstream media representations and the politics of fear inherent in such representations.

JR's street art project, *Portrait of a Generation*, which began in 2004, took on a defining urgency following the 2005 riots, presenting an alternative vision of young people from the suburbs.[12] JR started out documenting the street-level world he knew, taking photographs of his friends tagging or break-dancing or simply of the rooftops and backstreets where they spent their time, and wheat-pasting them up on walls around Paris. With coloured spray paint, he would create a frame around the images 'so you would not confuse it with advertising' and add the words 'Expo2rue' [street gallery] alongside.[13] The play on words between 'deux' [two] and 'de' [of] in Expo2rue reflects the way that this aestheticisation of street life occurs through a process of doubling. The photographic images in Expo2rue work both as documents and as artworks in themselves. For *Portrait of a Generation* JR photographed residents of the Les Bosquets housing estate in the eastern Paris suburb of Montfermeil, printed them out on a large scale, 6m x 8m – 'pictures so big that people couldn't ignore them' – and pasted them on walls, initially in the surrounding area, but later in the gentrified inner boroughs of Paris (qtd in Lichfeld, 2006). In *The Civil Contract*

---

[12] During October and November 2005, triggered by the deaths of two teenagers while hiding from the police in an electricity substation in the Eastern suburb of Clichy-sous-Bois, young people across the Paris suburbs rioted, looted and set fire to more than 9000 cars and scores of public buildings and businesses (Christafis, 2006).

[13] JR describes this at length in his 2011 TED Prize acceptance speech. The TED prize is an annual award of $100,000 given to an 'exceptional individual' to carry out their 'one wish to change the world' (JR, 2011).

of Photography, Ariella Azoulay talks about 'the citizenry of photography', which she describes as a collective to which anyone with any relation to photography belongs (Azoulay, 2008: 131). Photography, Azoulay argues, allows citizens to bypass the state and connect with one another directly, making visible the ways in which they are dominated. Shot in black and white, and showing mainly young men making faux-aggressive gestures or pulling faces, JR's portraits have a cartoonish quality. Instead of replacing the media stereotypes with alternatives more palatable to a bourgeois audience, the images draw attention to these stereotypes by parodying them.

Even though JR makes a point of refusing to work with corporate sponsors (JR, 2006), the scale and style of his works, which are glossy and often billboard-sized, echo the glamorised aesthetic of urban youth favoured by sportswear brands. Even as they seek to subvert such an aesthetic, the photographs participate in and unwittingly enhance this image world. Nonetheless, by interrupting the viewer's physical trajectory with a visual reminder of the *banlieusards*, the images draw the edges of Paris inwards to the centre in a gesture of tactical re-mapping. This has provided JR with a model for subsequent projects. In 2012 he posted an archive image from the 1968 Memphis sanitation workers' strike on the street corner where riots broke out following Martin Luther King's assassination. In another project, *the Wrinkles of the City*, JR flyposted portraits he had shot of elderly residents in Berlin, Shanghai and elsewhere on buildings around these places. Here street art acts as a form of collective archive, erecting new, temporary monuments to people and stories otherwise invisible or excluded by the dominant spatial narrative of a city.

Invader: Street art tourism

Invader's work, too, uses counter-cartography. Produced in 1999, *Invasion of Paris (IoP)* is a map that shows the locations of Invader's work around the French capital. Like Guy Debord's *Guide psychogéographique de Paris* before it, Invader's *IoP* rejects 'the categories and rhythms of capitalist urban life and its demands for discipline and utility as determined by the structures of work' (Pinder, 2005: 150). Invader installed his first mosaic in Paris in the mid 1990s but it was in 1998 that 'the Invasion', as he refers to his artistic practice, began in earnest. From Paris, Invader set out to 'invade' the world and his work can now be seen across the globe, from Manchester to Mombasa. His method represents a highly overt version of the territory marking which, as suggested earlier, is a defining characteristic of all street art. The space invaders are stylistically consistent, forming a distinctive street art brand, which is exported globally to the cities that he visits. Typically Invader spends two to three weeks 'invading' a city, documents it as he goes, and subsequently produces a limited-edition map which is sold on his website and in the gift shops of contemporary art spaces.

While replicating the traditional, fold-out format of a tourist map, the *IoP*, like the *Guide*, operates according to a logic that runs counter to conventional cartography. A traditional map claims accuracy and is intended to help people get from one point to another. However, where names of certain well-known buildings are provided in Invader's map, these monuments are presented simply as points of reference rather than attractions in themselves. The IoP directs the user to look for space invaders or, in some cases, the former sites of space invaders that have been destroyed. Invader's installations tend towards greater longevity than many street art works due to the durability of the tiles he uses, and the ability of his work to blend in with its architectural surroundings.[14] Nonetheless, it is fair to say that the IoP was produced in the full knowledge that it would almost immediately be rendered redundant by the inevitable removal of mosaics, as well as the insertion of new ones.

Figure 4. 'Coucou'. Photograph by Groume (2010). Creative Commons License.

Indeed, since the first map was created in 1999, the number of space invaders in Paris has doubled from 500 to 1,000, warranting in 2011 the creation of an updated version of the *Invasion of Paris* map.[15] A reminder that maps are, after all, socially constructed, highly contrived abstractions which cannot possibly

---

[14] As fellow street artist Shephard Fairey puts it, 'Space Invader's mosaics are rarely removed, because they're visible to the right people yet under the radar of the "wrong" people'. By 'right' people Fairey is referring to those 'in the know': a global community of street artists and fans (Fairey, 2010: 1).

[15] To mark his 1,000th space invader in Paris, Invader had an exhibition at La Générale gallery entitled '1000' from June-July 2011. See lagenerale.fr.

capture a city as it is experienced: in a continual state of flux. In *The Power of Maps*, Dennis Wood argues that 'knowledge of the map is knowledge of the world from which it emerges' (Wood, 1992: 18). Behind the object of a map is the process of cartographic practice, which consists of making a set of conceptual choices. A map is a statement - a visual expression of its creator's values. By playfully re-imagining sightseeing through the lens of artworks that are freely visible in the streets rather than consigned to museums and subject to an entrance fee, the *IoP* enacts a radical dis-embedding and re-embedding of the tourist gaze from one of 'imaginative, pleasure seeking' consumption to one that emphasises everyday urban life (Urry, 1990: 13).

Figure 5. 'Boulevard de Belleville'. Photograph by Aurélien Michaud (2011). Creative Commons License.

With the increasing ubiquity of smartphones, street art fans can share these images instantly with others beyond their geographical location by MMS [multimedia messaging service] or by uploading them to the internet via social media platforms such as Twitter, Facebook or Flickr, emailing them to dedicated websites such as *Wooster Collective*, or posting them on personal blogs. Using these images, fans have created their own geo-tagged city maps showing precise locations which users can click to view images of Invader's work. Invader's choice of a computer game as the inspiration for this work is not purely stylistic. Invader's street art *is* a game, complete with rules and scores, detailed on both his website and the map. Depending on its location, each space invader is worth a certain number of points. Some locations may be obvious, for example right next to a road sign, whereas others may be more obscure, with the point scores reflecting this. Although this creates a slightly bizarre scenario whereby Invader awards himself points depending on how many space invaders he manages to put up in a given city, it also enables fans to play too.

Figure 6. 'Made in India.' Photograph by poida.smith (2008). Creative Commons License.

But who are the intended players? Invader says, 'The Invasions of Kathmandu in Nepal and Varanasi in India were a great experience for me because it was like a *terra incognita* to explore, without any street art before my coming' (qtd in Peiter, 2009: 34). The notion of 'invasion' may be playful but here Invader's language echoes that of colonisers talking about 'discovering' new lands. His words presume that these countries do not have street cultures and art of their own. This is surprising given that in Varanasi, Invader made an effort to adapt his space invaders to the setting - painting or drawing them on walls (Figure 6) which were better suited to this than mosaics, giving them bindis and including Hindi text. Nonetheless, his words underscore the way in which street art is sometimes exported with little thought given to local history or cultural sensitivities. For example, when Banksy painted his trademark rats in street art pieces in Bethlehem they were defaced by local residents, insulted at the implied comparison between Palestinians and animals, however ironic the artist's objective (Harrison, 2007). This raises questions about who the favoured audience for this work is: the people who will have to live with his work or the global media who will photograph and disseminate images of it?

Conclusion

Street art simultaneously works with and against capitalism - as the three examples analysed here demonstrate. In visually attacking corporate logos and images, Zevs's work critiques capitalism, in particular advertising and the commercialisation of public space. JR's portraits set in motion fleeting visual encounters with otherwise ignored faces of the city, preserving struggles past and pointing to forgotten stories. The city walls are an archive on which layers of history accumulate, thicken, coalesce and disappear. The work of all three, but most obviously Invader, act as counter cartographies, which remap the city, both materially and virtually.

And yet, as we have seen, each of these processes lends itself readily to commodification. Capitalism re-appropriates any critique within its own operation as Lavazza's eagerness to comply with Zevs' 'visual kidnapping' reminds us. Documentation can be turned into an object to be bought and sold - JR, and the other two artist, all sell versions of their outdoor pieces in galleries. Counter cartography becomes a new form of colonialism - an exercise in territory marking as global branding.

But in spite of this, street art remains, in Certeau's terms, 'a practice'. It is best understood as a way of travelling through space, adding to, mixing with, but never fully possessing that space. As such street art will continue to draw attention to and disrupt existing hierarchies of public and private urban space - in Paris and beyond. As Certeau puts it:

> Beneath the discourses that ideologise the city, the ruses and combinations of powers that have no readable identity proliferate; without points where one can take hold of them, without rational transparency, they are impossible to administer (Certeau, 1984: 160).

References

Azoulay, A. 2008. *The Civil Contract of Photography*. New York, NY: Zone Books.

Benjamin, W. 2002. *The Arcades Project*. Translated by Howard Eiland and Kevin McLaughlin. Cambridge, MA and London: The Belknap Press of Havard University Press.

de Certeau, M. 1984. *The Practice of Everyday Life*. Translated by Steve Rendall. Berkeley and Los Angeles, CA: University of California Press.

Christafis, A. 2006. 'French Police Criticised over Deaths of Youths that Led to Riots.' *The Guardian*. 8 December.

Christie, N. 1986. 'The Ideal Victim'. In Fattah, E.A. (ed.), *From Crime Policy to Victim Policy*. Basingstoke: Macmillan. 17-30.

Cooper, M. and Chalfant, H. 2009. *Subway Art*. London: Thames & Hudson.

Dickens, L. 2010. 'Pictures on walls? Producing, pricing and collecting the street art screen print'. *City* 14: 1. 63-81.

Harrison, R. 2007. 'Bethlehem Residents Vandalise Banksy Graffiti.' *The Guardian*. 21 December.

JR. 2011. 'JR's TED Prize Wish: Use Art to Turn the World Inside Out'. *TED*. Available: https://www.ted.com/talks/jr_s_ted_prize_wish_use_art_to_turn_the_world_inside_out?language=en. Last accessed 17/09/2014.

Kennedy, R. 2006. 'Last Hurrah for Street Art as Canvas Goes Condo.' *The New York Times*. 14 December. Available: http://www.nytimes.com/2006/12/14/arts/design/14graf.html?_r=4&. Last accessed 17/09/2014.

Lichfield, J. 2006. 'Ghetto Fabulous'. *The Independent*. 11 March. 30.

Peiter, S. (ed.) 2009. *Guerilla Art*. London: Laurence King.

Pinder, D. 2005. *Visions of the City. Utopianism, Power and Politics in Twentieth-Century Urbanism*. Edinburgh: Edinburgh University Press.

Reiss, J. 2007. 'Interview with Blek le Rat'. *Swindle Magazine* 11. Reproduced at: http://jonreiss.com/2007/05/interview-with-blek-in-swindle-magazine/. Last accessed 16/09/2014.

Scemama, C. 2006. 'Paris, Ville Musée'. *L'Express*. 5 January. Available: http://www.lexpress.fr/actualite/societe/paris-ville-musee_483410.html. Last accessed 16/09/2014.

Lewis, P. and Khalili, M. 2011. 'Hackney Rioters Directly Target Police'. *The Guardian*. 9 August.

Klein, N. 2010 [1999]. *No Logo*. New York, NY: Picador.

Manco, T. 2004. *Street Logos*. London: Thames & Hudson.

Nguyen, P. and Mackenzie, S. (eds) 2010. *Beyond the Street: The 100 Leading Figures in Urban Art*. Berlin: Gestalten.

Urry, J. 1990. *The Tourist Gaze. Leisure and Travel in Contemporary Societies*. London: Sage Publications.

Wood, D. 1992. *The Power of Maps*. New York, NY: The Guildford Press.

Wooster Collective. 2009. 'Zevs Arrest in Hong Kong - The Video'. 20 July. Available: http://www.woostercollective.com/post/zevs-arrest-in-hong-kong-the-video. Last accessed 17/09/2014.

Zevs. 2002. *Visual Kidnapping*. Sycomore Films. Available: http://www.gzzglz.com/video-visual-kidnapping.html. Last accessed 17/09/2014.

3

THE CITY AND THE VIRTUAL: THE USE OF DIGITAL TECHNOLOGY IN 3D STREET ART

Sabina Andron & Regner Ramos

Introduction

The pervasive incorporation of technology within increasing areas of people's everyday lives throughout the past two decades has altered the way that the built environment is perceived and experienced. Whether the symbiosis with technology is viewed as an atrophying element for more humane, sensory-based perceptions or as a crucial piece to living an 'augmented reality' in the twenty-first century, the ubiquitous use of personal digital devices presents social, cultural, and spatial changes that apply to a number of different situations.

At the same time, the phenomenon of public artistic expression known as street art is emerging from its subcultural status and becoming an integral part of urban identities, through artists' commissions and murals painted with permission which lead to the formation of cultural destinations around street art (such as, for example, Shoreditch in London) and even to the use of this practice as a branding strategy for attracting tourists. A practice once considered undesirable due to its independent and often political nature, is now embraced by local councils and the public as a rich and expressive art form which can change our perception and interaction with public space. This also leads to an incorporation of such creative outlets within clearly managed systems of approval and control, changing their spontaneous and ephemeral nature into strategic commissions and interventions.

One such mode of creativity is 3D street art, a type of pavement drawing which uses *trompe l'œil* perspective to create the illusion of depth, adding an apparent third dimension to the flatness of the pavement surface. One of street art's strategies as a genre is to experiment with different types of site specificity, adapting to its immediate surroundings and opening them up in clever and surprising ways (Klanten, R. and Hübner, M., 2010). 3D street art is in fact one of the most praised examples of site-specific creativity, with pictures flooding the internet representing people about to fall into the jaws of sharks or be swallowed by bursting volcanoes. All these make spectacular images when seen on a computer screen, but the on-site reality can be slightly less captivating.

This paper connects the role of digital technologies in contemporary spatial perception to 3D pavement street art as a public expressive practice. By tracing the crucial function of digital display in the experience of augmented reality, we will explore the particular case of 3D street art, revealing its spatial assumptions. How does 3D street art manifest itself in the built environment, and what conceptual and spatial implications does it involve? To what extent does the perception of this art form depend on digital technologies, and how does this impact on its site specificity? Looking at a 2011, 3D street art piece sponsored by Reebok Crossfit in the London Canary Wharf quayside, this paper seeks to analyse the importance of the camera in the perception of the three-dimensionality of the artwork and attempts to begin filling some of the theoretical gaps related to the topic.

'Look Through a Camera Phone for 3D!!'

Figure 1. Drawing of cliffs and waterfall branded with the *Reebok Crossfit* logo

In mid November 2011, artists Joe Hill and Max Lowry - who professionally go by the name '3D Joe and Max' - worked their way into the Guinness World Book of Records with what was branded as the largest 3D street drawing in the world. The drawing was placed in London's Canary Wharf business development district, a financially thriving counterpart to the City of London, and hardly a cultural hotspot or a popular area for foot traffic. Using the clear surface of the Canary Wharf quayside, the two artists covered a large area with a sanctioned piece of 3D street art, in a gesture which proved to be more commercial than it was creative or functional. The piece, which presented a waterfall and cliffs, was painted on lino and stamped with the Reebok logo in honour of their sponsor, which branded the drawing as an outdoor activity space (Figure 1).[1]

Figure 2. Perspective from the back of the drawing, where its figuration is no longer apparent and the fencing designates an off-limits area

---

[1] More details on this can be found at http://arrestedmotion.com/2011/11/joe-hill-x-reebok-worlds-largest-3d-street-artwork/.

The drawing was widely mediatised and visitors travelled to Canary Wharf for the sole purpose of seeing it, and, to an extent, one must acknowledge that Reebok activated an otherwise socially dormant space in the city. Through this scope, one might argue that the 3D artwork was a way of reclaiming public space and restoring a social, playful function to it. On the other hand, the fact that the artwork was an immense, horizontal billboard advertising the company does not go by unnoticed, somewhat ameliorating the social impact of the piece itself. In theory, bringing people to Canary Wharf to interact and play with a piece of 3D street art - while also giving those people who work in the area something that breaks the routine of going to their office buildings - has an undeniable appeal. However, the experience of actually being there proved to be more confusing than expected, because whichever way one looked at it, with the exception for one very precise and strategic angle - the work showed a massive blue, white, and brown display of seemingly random lines, instead of the shocking waterfall illusion which had been promoted through the media and internet. Moreover, these lines seemed to take over public space for no apparent reason, designating a fenced off area which one could no longer walk through or completely make sense of.

In many ways, the area looked like a neglected construction site, or a piece of leftover space which barely held any traces of function or activity. This was because the drawing was constructed using a specific technique, which meant that its illusory effect could only be observed from a single threshold of perception, through the aid of a digital camera.

In order for the piece to actively behave as it was supposed to, one had to occupy a spot which consisted of two footprints and a guidance note: 'Look through a camera phone for 3D!!'

The way this was signalled felt entirely makeshift and did not in any way encourage a seamless transition into the space of the 3D drawing. In fact, the two plaques looked like they were placed on the ground without any thought to their integration in the wider construct, making apparent the break between the physical and the virtual in a coarse, improvised manner. This highly conditioned construction not only limited people's behaviour, but it actually altered the physical properties of that space to the point of annulment. The drawing had made the horizontal surface occupied by the lino-canvas virtually disappear from the spatial continuity of the quayside, making it physically inaccessible and practically unintelligible. An effort to create an engaging piece of public art ended up in a confusing result, with minimal response to the physical and a maximum dependence on the virtual. This is not to say that the 3D street art completely disengaged the public from interacting with it, but rather to make evident that people's ability to go inside the piece was heavily controlled by the physical boundaries surrounding it.

Figure 3. Unique vantage point for the desired perception of the 3D effect

This is a process which seems to characterise all such creative pieces, as the optical technique itself requires a camera in order to work and produce the desired illusion. However, there is a general reluctance to disclose this from the artists' side, as this drawing style increases in popularity and has various online hubs dedicated to it.[2] Neither of these websites seems to specify the manner in which these pieces produce the 3D illusion, while the artists themselves provide only brief explanations of what they do, how they do it, and what they wish to accomplish.

Kurt Wenner, well-known 3D artist, explains, 'Any work of art employs some illusion. A framed picture is a conventional illusion. The viewer can choose to see the frame as a window, a starting point from which to visually enter the painted world, or as a border, separating the real world from the imaginary' (Krolls, 2010). Throughout this discourse on illusion, no direct reference is made to the necessary mediation, which is the digital camera and the integral part it plays in the perception of the work. The choice of the user to see a frame as a window or border is a much more active and creative one, whereas this particular type of drawing allows for no such engaging participation. Similarly, 3D artist Tracy Lee Stum speaks about the conceptual framing of her work by saying, 'I have a passion for manipulating 2D surfaces to reveal an unlikely alternative in 3D, typically designing and creating interactive images which invite the viewer to become part of my imagined world. As a result, communicating through this manner of direct participation has certainly become the keystone of my philosophy on being a visual artist' (Krolls, 2010).

While the drawing technique itself does indeed deserve separate consideration as an artistic practice, the discourse around participation and communication becomes problematic. The interesting part about inviting a viewer to 'become part' of an imagined world is the dual experiences that take place within and around the piece. On the one hand, for many 3D street art pieces, the artwork is meant to be viewed and photographed, without necessarily inviting interaction within the piece, and this visual interaction becomes the sole experience around the 'imagined world.' Ironically enough, the participatory feature that Stum praises as the central concept of her practice is in fact completely despatialised, as walking, touching or posing are not actually possible. These drawings prescribe their behaviour in very rigid terms, not leaving much possibility for actual interaction or participation. In the *Reebok Crossfit* piece, however, the drawing is meant to invite the audience to engage within the piece itself, as the world Max and Joe imagined lures the viewers to become active inside it. But the physical space is unrepresentative of what the piece shows, and while users are able to move inside the drawing itself, their physical and spatial experience is entirely mediated, dictated, perceivable, and documented through the digital camera. Viewers within the 3D street art are required to live the space by using their imagination, while the person taking the photograph directs the subject being photographed. In essence, what occurs is an effect similar to actors performing in front of a green screen, where later in the production process,

---

[2] See for example http://www.3d-street-art.com/.

images of new, imagined surroundings are added on to the scene to create the illusion that the actors were truly there, in that fantastic, fictional world, responding to the various stimuli surrounding them. What we are left with is an interaction with the digital device that captures the illusion, taking over any other participatory function and enclosing it within its screen.

The alternative offered to the flatness of two-dimensional surfaces is completely dependent on technological mediation, and this fact seems to be entirely overlooked in promotional and artistic statements. The moment of discovering this necessary mediation becomes similar to learning the trick behind a magician's performance. It is a revelation which leaves an air of disenchantment, and it most certainly raises some issues regarding the promotion of this art form. On the one hand, this attests to the ubiquity of handheld digital cameras, and on the other, it also strengthens the need for such devices, excluding those people who do not own or have a camera at hand. Similarly, along with the advertising in much of this art, this is perhaps another indication of how art often affirms rather than challenges existing social and economic structures. Behind all the online pictures and participation statements promoted both on art pages and on artists' websites, the spatial and conceptual reality of these pieces is yet to be properly addressed, and their claim to audience participation yet to be problematised.

On Space: In Front of the Screen

In his introduction to *Urban Interventions*, Alain Bieber refers to artists' actions in urban spaces as 'temporary autonomous zones' (Klanten and Hübner, 2010: 4), celebrating their break with the rhythms and discourses through which we usually interact with our cities. Using the existing material and cultural cityscape as inspiration, artists create interventions which break with conventions of appearance and behaviour, producing spaces which are autonomous in their visual and conceptual stances. In a comprehensive presentation of these different interventions, the volume defines different types of relation between art and space, placing them under categories such as 'Urban Canvas' (the creative handling and inspired transformation of existing structures and surfaces); 'Localised' (highly contextual pieces which make a comment on the spaces they are part of) or 'Attachments' (refreshing artistic extensions and adjunctions within the built environment). In all these cases, there are different types of connections which get established between the art works and their material and cultural contexts, connections which make them responsive to site and to community. However, the practice of 3D street art seems to have no such connection to its urban context, occupying space in a seemingly random, non-responsive manner.

Similarly, Miwon Kwon opens a discussion of site specificity as criticality, responsiveness, community orientation or the social integration of different groups (Kwon, 2004), which are all practices of existing in space rather than removed from it (physically or conceptually). The spatial relation established between 3D street art drawing practices and their supportive environments seems to fall outside these types of response to site, as the works themselves, their representation and the discourse around them fail to acknowledge the spatial configuration of these pieces. In a moment when the tendency is to open up public space through various kinds of interventions and site-challenging concepts, this kind of artistic practice presents a paradox in its very spatial composition. Completely abstracted from its spatial or cultural context, 3D pavement art is a circus-like spectacle with its own tent of temporary fascination. Not only does it not communicate with its surroundings in any way, but it requires a type of immersive participation which is completely oblivious to the characteristics of the environment or the background of the observer.

In order for the drawing to perform as expected, the actual three dimensional physical space which supports it must be flattened into the two dimensional space of a screen, where it can then create the illusory effect of 3D. This is a spatial paradox which might create an engaging addition to our perception of space, were it not for its powerful and clear constraints. This is due to the fact that the physical space has been rendered inaccessible except through a screen, blocking off its given dimensions and material features. The Canary Wharf piece was the largest in the world to date, as it spanned across 12,000 square feet of public surface in the London quayside area. In the process, it annulled this surface from its physical existence and converted it into 4 inches of smart phone screen, in order to obtain its intended level of performance. Unless the viewer stood in the designated observation point and used their gadgets as mandatory visual aids, the only thing left to be witnessed was the visual and functional closing of that large portion of public space. The entire spatial dynamics of the place was reduced to a static, two dimensional experience of a virtual 3D.

The fact that this art form's specific relation to space and its dependence on the digital display fail to be entirely promoted in a direct manner is problematic in itself. The discourse around 3D street art is in fact largely responsible for creating the hype around this practice, as representations of different pieces are given a life of their own through web sharing and circulation. The issue of how much the artists are willing to acknowledge their work as a form of rigidly constrained spatial practice also becomes doubtful, as they fail to specify the parameters under which their work can be experienced. Photos of people "falling" into the jaws of a shark still lead the discourse surrounding this practice, creating a misleading visual and experiential representation that not even the artists themselves have showed interest in correcting.

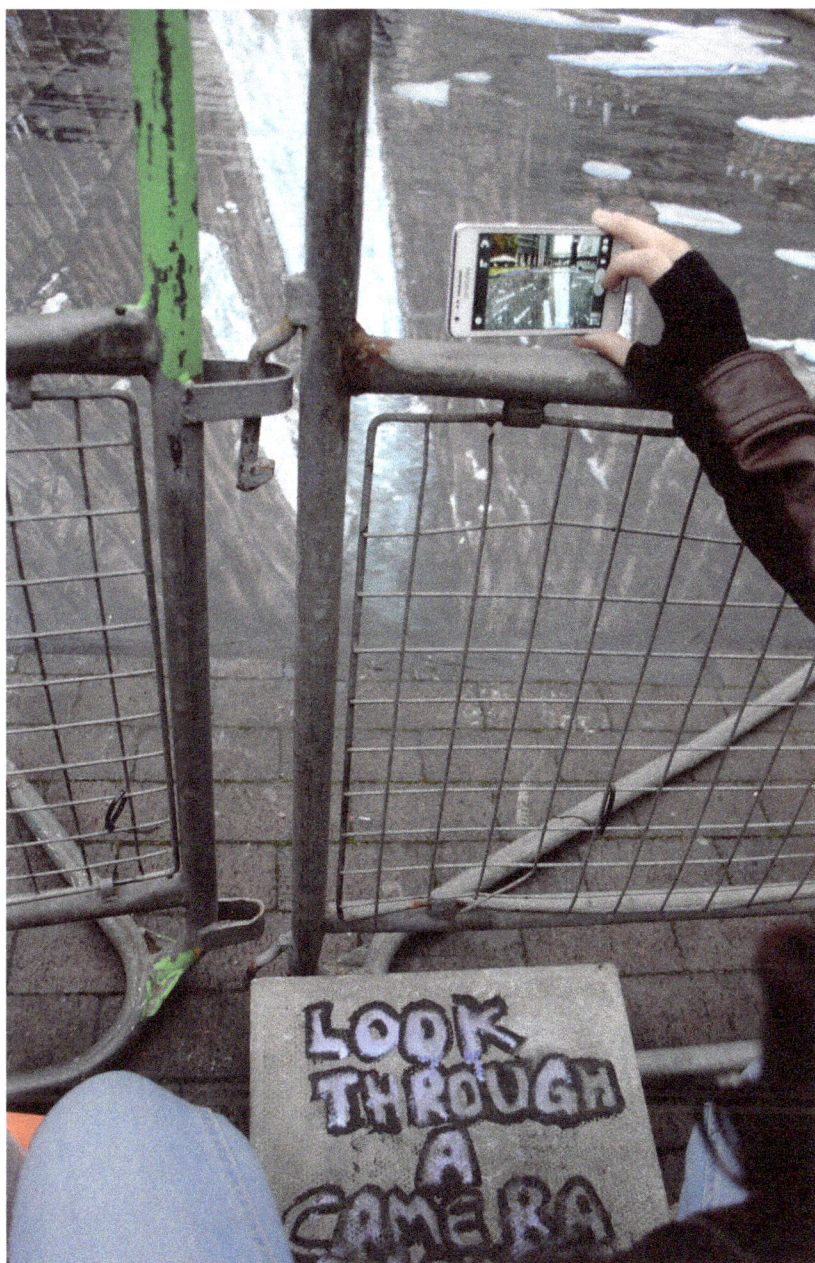

Figure 4. Double perspective: embodied and flattened space

The fact that this art form's specific relation to space and its dependence on the digital display fail to be entirely promoted in a direct manner is problematic in itself. The discourse around 3D street art is in fact largely responsible for creating the hype around this practice, as representations of different pieces are given a life of their own through web sharing and circulation. The issue of how much the artists are willing to acknowledge their work as a form of rigidly constrained spatial practice also becomes doubtful, as they fail to specify the parameters under which their work can be experienced. Photos of people 'falling' into the jaws of a shark still lead the discourse surrounding this practice, creating a misleading visual and experiential representation that not even the artists themselves have showed interest in correcting.

The spatial paradox of the Canary Wharf piece was made evident through the decision of sponsor *Reebok CrossFit* to brand the drawing as an 'outdoor workspace', a concept which does not fit with any of the characteristics of the space itself. The official photographs from the launch represented mock athletes posing in workout positions on top of the cliffs (sic!) – a situation whose physicality depended entirely on the lens capturing these positions. The actual passive perception that one is forced into by this art form is not being acknowledged through any kind of accompanying discourse, and the limitations it imposes on space are constantly being overlooked, thus seemingly adding another layer of privatisation to public space rather than opening up the space for different uses, as the sponsor seemed to suggest.

On Cyborgs: Behind the Screen

It is not just space that gets flattened in the performing mechanism of 3D street art, but the body loses its autonomy as well, becoming dependent on digital extensions that allow it to perceive reality in a certain way. Architect Antoine Picon is right when he states, 'It is at the urban level that issues such as the relation between physical and virtual reality take their full scope. In an age of digital social networks like Facebook, the future of public spaces will depend to a large extent on the successful interaction between the physical and the virtual' (Picon, 2010). In a space such as the one occupied by the *Reebok CrossFit* piece, urban space undergoes a series of reconfigurations produced by the function-technology-experience triad. Firstly an urban space is reconfigured to become a piece of art, with the intention of creating a virtual space that is layered onto the existing, physical space. This virtual space, composed of a painting with a 3D effect, serves a different function loaded with commercial value. The traditional, vertical billboard becomes horizontal, plastered over a walkable space, where citizens are invited to become participants of the virtual, supposedly 3D, space. However, this 3D virtual space is only visible through a digital display, and thus, an urban space is deprived of its function, to be lived through a camera-mediated experience. This phenomenon goes beyond merely being evaluated as a 'good' or 'bad' thing, as it becomes evidence of the twenty-first century citizen's prosthetic dependence on digital devices, particularly their phones.

Philosopher Marshall McLuhan addresses the pervasiveness of the digital within human life in his text *Understanding Media: The Extensions of Man*, by incorporating and relating the terms 'prosthetics' and 'autoamputation.' According to McLuhan, autoamputation consists of adding a technological element to a body so that it extends and enhances the body's performance, while in the process, amputating the nervous system of the organ whose function it magnifies. Autoamputation's relation to prosthetics is concretised in the *Reebok CrossFit* 3D street art piece precisely because it addresses the coupling between technology and citizens and its reverberations on the built environment. These reverberations thus move even further into the creation and perception of 3D street art, which indeed walks the fine line between real and virtual in our interaction with public space, as bodies need an extension through a technological component, losing their autonomy and equating the camera to the spectator's eyes.

In the mid 1980s Donna Haraway published *A Cyborg Manifesto*, in which she problematises technology, feminism, and theories of embodiment by turning to the figure of the cyborg. With technology becoming increasingly ubiquitous in society, Haraway advocated for a new type of embodiment, one who is free from past restrictions and looks forward to future changes. The traditional notion of the cyborg as 'a fictional or hypothetical person whose physical abilities are extended beyond normal human limitations by mechanical elements built into the body' is challenged by Haraway, as she grants the cyborg political agency, a consciousness, a purpose. She writes, 'The machine is not an it to be animated, worshipped, and dominated. The machine is us, our processes, an aspect of our embodiment. We can be responsible for machines; they do not dominate or threaten us. We are responsible for boundaries; we are they' (Haraway, 1985). Though her theories may appear to be extremist, bordering on techno-fetishistic, Haraway, like McLuhan, was able to shrewdly predict future relationships that would redefine the human-society-city triad. Technological advances are fascinatingly subtle, because they occur imperceptibly, in small doses allowing the body to adapt quickly to them. For example, if society had encountered a technological leap from the telegram to the iPhone, it would have been much harder to adapt to the technology, learn it, accept it, and engender its widespread use. However, with these technology leaking into society - drop by drop - we are suddenly immersed within them, coexisting with them, as they become extensions of our bodies. As Haraway predicted nearly thirty years ago, 'we are they.'

In his article 'Cyborg Urbanization: Complexity and Monstrosity in the Contemporary City', urbanist Matthew Gandy writes about the importance of rethinking the idea of the cyborg in relation to our current context. Gandy states, 'It may appear arcane - abstruse even - to utilise the idea of the cyborg as a means to explore the contemporary urban condition. Yet a cursory glance at the recent literature shows that the earlier incarnations of the cyborg as an isolated yet technologically enhanced body have proliferated into a vast assemblage of bodily and machinic entanglements which interconnect with the contemporary city in a multitude of different ways' (Gandy, 2005). Gandy thus becomes a catalyst in a debate that centres around urbanism and technology, not through the mere sense of technological infrastructure and transportation, but rather through the experience of the citizen. The use of the camera or photo-camera in the perception of 3D space in 3D street art is a testament to how the modern human, the 'cyborg,' needs a prosthesis to be able to perceive a particular virtual space; without it, there is no three dimensional space, there is only paint on a surface, and thus the relationship between people, city, space, and technology is redefined and experienced in new ways.

For the *Reebok CrossFit* piece, an interesting phenomenon occurs, pertaining to the reconfiguration of urban space. A virtual space, perceivable through a digital display, overlaps on a physical space, completely altering the traditional use of the Canary Wharf space. This dual layer that coexists in a given space is called 'augmented reality,' in which the physical world and the digital world interact. According to Picon, 'the digital realm can be considered as a culture because it is synonymous with various habits and rituals, because it influences our conducts as well as our representation of the world. Ubiquitous computing and augmented reality thus meet with the structures of everyday life' (Picon, 2010). However, in the case of this particular 3D street art, the structures of everyday life are interrupted, as the piece becomes a temporary installation, closed-off on all sides, except from the strategic, picture-taking point. Rather than merging and integrating with the urban condition of the Canary Wharf quayside it becomes an isolated entity, much like Canary Wharf itself. Therefore, as an urban space that involves user-performance, the *Reebok CrossFit* street art provides very rich grounds, as a result of this impoverishment, to explore the relation between space, behaviour, and technology.

Like Haraway and McLuhan, Picon makes a series of bold predictions of his own, claiming that, 'Beyond tactile screens and digital gloves, architectural space itself will become one day an integral part of the interface between the physical and the virtual. At an urban level, the public spaces of tomorrow will be places where two realities are intertwined, allowing an even greater array of interactions than today' (Picon, 2010). This is already happening in a variety of ways, and Adriana de Souza e Silva speaks of a particular type of merging between physical and virtual when she speaks of 'hybrid reality (location-based mobile games.' She claims these games:

> are multiuser games played with cell phones equipped with location awareness and Internet connection. HRG allow players to use the city space as the game board. Botfighters, produced in Sweden in 2001 by It's Alive was the first commercially released location-based mobile game (LBMG). It was designed as the traditional first-person shooter video game. However, in order to be played, users must be moving through urban spaces. Depending on the relative position of each player in the city, users can shoot other players with text messages, be targeted to receive a shot, and get into battles (De Souza e Silva, 2006).

Technologies like these, which merge physical and digital, provide new ways to understand, navigate, experience, and discover urban spaces. These are then reconfigured, as they make the user an active participant within urban space, contrasting with the *Reebok CrossFit* piece at Canary Wharf, where the sole experiential quality of the artwork is limited to taking a picture.

Although taking a picture can be a valid, urban experience for some, we must critically evaluate the role of the picture in this particular 3D street art space. It is far from uncommon to see users pose in front of urban or architectural landmarks while out in the city. A trip to Pisa would reveal scores upon scores of tourists posing creatively in front of the Leaning Tower, in an attempt to show to others, who might later see their pictures, that they were there. Where the photograph provides the physical manifestation of a *memory* of people's experience and presence in a space, the photographs taken at the *Reebok CrossFit* piece are taken to be able to *experience* the space itself. The visitor becomes a performer, and the camera becomes the brain, recording the experience as well as making the virtual space visible. But we must then ask, is this type of experience any less real and valid? Or can it be a new way to experience urban space? Picon argues,

> If the city provides a common locus to envisage these three threads, what holds them together is probably a new understanding of what the real means for designers. The real: the use of such a loaded word needs some explanation. By real, I want to designate here not reality as it can be experienced, be it physical, electronic or augmented reality. The real, in my sense, corresponds rather to a set of underlying principles that are supposed to organize reality, principles beyond immediately observable phenomenon (Picon, 2010).

This is precisely why being critical and analytical of urban installations, such as 3D street art, becomes pressing in the twenty-first century. With the increase in technological devices, society, spaces, embodiments, and behaviours are changing; understanding these advances, not merely admiring them for their unquestionable allure, becomes pressing, as they provide an opportunity for people to critically think about the spaces they actually inhabit, enabling them to see the overlaps between virtual spaces and physical ones. The issue with 3D street art is that, first, it fails to convincingly cast technology in the role of protagonist, and second, it provides intense opportunities for marketing and advertising, while shutting down other uses of the surfaces they are worked on. The exposure Reebok got from the piece in Canary Wharf is intensified by the very nature of the artistic piece. Needing to be used with the help of a camera phone means that the artwork is even more easily distributable via the Internet, and so the marketing proliferates, as the artwork has an effect on the people who are physically present in the space, to then travel throughout the internet, so thousands of others can see it. However, while 3D street art and its relation to public space finds itself on politically shaky grounds, it also opens the door for other forms of inhabiting public spaces, and it exploits citizens' dependence on prosthetic digital devices while out in the city. 3D street art makes the habitual act of using a mobile phone while out in the city evident, by giving the technology a purpose and making the user use the space politically, in the sense that they are aware of the reliance of a mobile phone, while also knowing that even though their performance in that place/piece of art takes place in a physical space, they are inhabiting a virtual one, through the documentation of this performance.

Conclusion

Where the nineteenth century industrial city inspired notions of being 'organicist' (Gandy, 2005), the twenty-first century displaces this conception and gravitates towards the 'neo-organicist city,' in which urban space is experienced through prosthetic extensions of the human body. Through the neo-organicist perception a symbiotic relationship exists between the individual and the city; but this relationship stems deeper than mere physical and palpable traits of technology in spaces. The merging of the virtual world with the physical world paves the way for countless forms of interaction and an unprecedented sense of augmented reality, and 3D street art is just one of the ways this phenomenon is manifested. As advanced and tech-savvy as contemporary life can be due to the closeness between the physical and the virtual, there are various drawbacks.

One of the main discrepancies seems to be that while virtual spaces are being successful by incorporating elements of real life and thus creating places, the built environment seems to be lagging behind and has yet to raise the bar and provide places that are fitting for contemporary citizens, while satisfying the cravings for the augmented-reality hunger of the spatially-extended cyborg. Certainly Michel de Certeau reinforces this idea by speaking out about the loss of stories and legends in the urban space, which has hindered the creation of relationships, appropriations, and attachments to spaces in the city. He writes,

> The same is true of the stories and legends that haunt urban space like superfluous or additional inhabitants. They are the object of a witch-hunt, by the very logic of the techno-structure. But their extermination (like the extermination of trees, forests, and hidden places in which such legends live) makes the city a 'suspended symbolic order.' The habitable city is thereby annulled. Thus, as a woman from Rouen put it, no, here 'there isn't any place special, except for my own home, that's all... There isn't anything.' Nothing 'special': nothing that is marked, opened up by a memory or a story, signed by something or someone else. Only the cave of the home remains believable (Certeau, 1988).

Seemingly, the modern day cyborg's cravings for an augmented reality brings cases of autoamputation within the urban experience. Studying instances of autoamputation in London's urban scale is indeed an attempt to tread unfamiliar waters using previous theoretical and philosophical bases that, with the seemingly unexpected pervasiveness of digital spaces in people's lives, have failed to shed light upon this recent phenomenon. Through 3D street art, the artists are challenging notions of bidimensional art by trying to satisfy these cravings of cyborgs, not only by attempting to create new spatial perceptions in an already three-dimensional and perceptible space but also by giving a story back to the urban fabric. The dimensions of spaces versus places and the reconstruction of spatio-temporal patterns have everything to do with the way that contemporary urban dwellers live their daily life. From something as seemingly jovial as is the spectacle of 3D street art, to the way that the modern cyborg-like flâneur experiences the city aided by his prosthetic extensions, people's continuous relationship with digital devices and their pervasive displays are moulding society, as well as the understanding and the spatial perception of the built environment.

References

De Certeau, M. 1988. *The Practice of Everyday Life*. Berkeley/Los Angeles, CA and London. University of California Press.

De Souza e Silva, A. 2006. 'From cyber to hybrid: Mobile technologies as interfaces of hybrid spaces.' *Space & Culture* 9:3, 261-278.

Gandy, M. 2005. 'Cyborg Urbanization: Complexity and Monstrosity in the Contemporary City'. *International Journal of Urban and Regional Research* 291, 26-49.

Hansen, M. 2006. *New Philosophies for New Media*. Cambridge, MA. The MIT Press.

Haraway, D. 1991. *Simians, Cyborgs and Women: The Reinvention of Nature*. New York, NY. Routledge.

Hayles, K. 2005. *My Mother Was a Computer: digital and literary texts*. Chicago, IL. University of Chicago Press.

Klanten, R. & Hübner, M., 2010. *Urban Interventions. Personal Projects in Public Spaces*. Berlin. Gestalten.

Krols, B. 2010. *3D Street Art*. Antwerp. Tectum Publishers.

Kwon, M. 2002. *One Place After Another. Site Specific Art and Locational Identity*. Cambridge, MA and London. The MIT Press.

McLuhan, M. 1964. *Understanding Media: The Extensions of Man*. New York, NY. McGraw Hill.

Mitchell, W. 1999. *E-topia: Urban Life, Jim - But not as we know it*. Cambridge, MA and London. The MIT Press.

Mubi Brighenti, A. (ed) 2009. *The Wall and the City*. Trento. Professional Dreamers Press.

Nandrea, L. 1999. '"Graffiti Taught Me Everything I Know About Space": Urban Fronts and Borders'. *Antipode* 31:1, January. 110-116.

Norberg-Schulz, C. 1984. *Genius Loci: Towards a Phenomenology of Architecture*. New York, NY. Rizzoli.

Picon, A. 2010. *Digital Culture in Architecture: An Introduction for the Design Professions*. Basel. Birkhäuser.

4

ESCAPING PSYCHOGEOGRAPHICAL CUL-DE-SACS

Mihaela Brebenel & Christopher Collier

In this chapter we aim to discuss some of the problems and pursuits that cluster under the battered umbrella of psychogeography, one that rather seems to attract as opposed to repel a certain, somewhat unsavoury deluge. The practice known as psychogeography is one particular, sometimes problematic way in which artists, writers and would-be militants have opted to engage with the street as a site of potential political and social antagonism. Yet more than 50 years after its definition, does psychogeography have anything left to offer beyond a handful of dead ends?

We speak here from a particular position - one fluctuating between that of researchers and simultaneously as part of a collective that operates under the name Ernest. Formed in 2011, Ernest has variously comprised students and practitioners in multiple spheres - including art, curatorial practice, architecture, cultural and media studies. Although here we will primarily speak about psychogeography in an UK context, Ernest's participants originate not only from the UK, but from Italy, Romania and Japan, with activities also taking place in a number of other localities, including Berlin, Paris and Thessaloniki. The reason we turn to psychogeography here, is because Ernest's activities have largely involved disparate encounters with the street as a site of research, artistic intervention and political engagement, often loosely framed through a dialogue with a tradition of psychogeographic practice. If Ernest did not initially set out to 'do psychogeography' as such, we often found ourselves returning, stumbling back across it unexpectedly. Therefore our first motivation in this paper was to explore and understand why the practice of psychogeography appears to haunt our thinking in this way.

Yet this is not merely a self-reflective exercise. It in turn raises another question, providing perhaps a broader, more significant motivation for looking again at psychogeography. It seems clear that from the student protests of 2010 to the widespread urban riots of 2011, along with various iterations of the global occupy movement, recent years have seen the street return as a site of political antagonism in the UK. This return can be seen as a continuity and repetition of previous struggles, albeit one differently augmented by evolving layers of mediatised experience. Perhaps this apparent 'return to the street' might account for our own strange fascination with psychogeography, as a practice of the street. This might therefore also provide an opportune moment to return and look again at psychogeographic practice more broadly, to explore any continuing relevance it may possess for such struggles.

In doing so however, one immediately comes up against a problem. One must first acknowledge that, like the street, psychogeography has never truly been left behind, yet if not left, perhaps its roads have led practitioners down a few blind alleys. Psychogeography has long been seen critically as little more than a literary cottage industry, or worse, a nonsense activity for the nostalgic. It has been dismissed as mere branding, even by some of those for whom it has proved most lucrative, such as London-based practitioner, writer and filmmaker Iain Sinclair (Sinclair, 2011). As such, the very notion of psychogeography is a problematic one. If we are to think through some sort of return to its well-trodden paths, if it is still to offer clues as to the street's subversive potential, we must first explore in more depth some of the problems that have haunted recent iterations of this loose tradition of urban practices.

To address this, we are turning to a street-inspired metaphor, asking: what are the potential 'cul-de-sacs' of a continuing psychogeographic practice? Whilst unable to cover all the problems entailed in these dead roads here, perhaps we can attempt to summarise a number of them in relation to both a wider historical context, but also to our own psychogeographic experiments.

First we will retrace our steps slightly, to explain what we mean by this word psychogeography, and to address whether the notion of a return implies that psychogeography's proposed problems might be dissolved by reverting to some primary, more satisfactory original from which later practices have deviated.

The word on the street

In 1955, Guy Debord, most prominent member of the (anti)artistic avant-garde organisation the Letterist International, predecessor of the more well-known 1957-72 Situationist International, first defined the word 'psychogeography' in print (Debord, 1955: 8). Both these groups were concerned with developing a critique that would lead to the complete overthrow of 'the entirety of existing conditions' - including alienated living, the commodity economy, hierarchical power structures and the pseudo-activities characterising both work and leisure in modern society.

Debord suggests the term '*psychogéographie*' to describe 'the study of the precise laws and specific effects of the geographical environment, whether consciously organized or not, on the emotions and behavior of individuals.' In selecting this term, he claims to be appropriating the second-language invention of 'an illiterate Kabyle,' a term whose attraction he suggests, lay in the fact it was 'charmingly vague' (Debord, 2006: 8). It was perhaps this 'vagueness,' that in 2008 induced Merlin Coverley to publish the only sustained attempt at a historicisation and consolidation of psychogeography. Debatably his study threw the term open, far more than it pinned it down.

Coverley's particular emphasis on psychogeography's literary genealogy accurately reflects the reorientation of the term in a post-situationist UK context, particularly in light of the increasingly mainstream popularity of figures such as Iain Sinclair. One might perhaps cast this as a retreat from political practice, proposing that this literary status, in the absence of an explicitly revolutionary, practical orientation, contains the dangers of its irrelevance. Yet, it is perhaps also psychogeography's literary reiterations that allow it to evade reification in a singular, static and positive definition, offering an ongoing radical potential.

To elaborate: even whilst acknowledging Debord's deferral to an anonymous, 'illiterate', oral progenitor, we heed Jacques Derrida's warnings, when he counsels against accepting the primacy and presence of speech. Psychogeography, as a neologism grafted onto an alien literary tradition, can be seen to have always been at once 'literary', excessive and irreducible. The tale of its invention serves to illustrate that it cannot be reduced to a self-contained concept, or the intent of an originating subjectivity. The evasive quality of psychogeography's terminology is testified by a felicitous coincidence of language; Derrida deploys the same word the letterists used to describe their primary psychogeographic methodology – *dérive*, or drift – to suggest citability, the ability to shift context, and to remake context anew (Derrida, 1967: 69). Psychogeography appears as praxis for the SI and yet its literary articulation can also be understood as the material condition of its citability, complicating any simple dichotomy between words and practice, original and copy.

Expanded traditions

Beyond its letterist manifestations, an expanded array of practices conforming to psychogeography's characteristics can not only be traced into a literary past, but also forward into the present. Conceived by Debord as simultaneously an artistic and emancipatory political strategy, one way of understanding the various cul-de-sacs into which practices utilising psychogeographic methodologies today might fall is to understand these practices, as hinted at above, as having *lost* a strategic, practical and 'radical' dimension ascribed to the situationists (Hanson, 2007: 11). As also briefly eluded however, we do not find a simple, hierarchical dichotomy between Debord's conception and more recent practices a particularly useful methodology. Instead we will now seek to examine both recent psychogeography, and its letterist/situationist iterations within a wider frame, in the hope of stumbling sideways over what is of continuing value in practice. Doing so however, does entail an understanding of the development and diffusion of psychogeography beyond Debord's codification.

We could understand this development as a shift towards a more characteristically 'postmodernist' perspective in psychogeography, along with an attendant 'demarxification.' This shift has certainly foregrounded some important questions regarding potential colonial and masculinist overtones buried in historical psychogeography, along with a re-examining of the problematically teleological and totalising inheritances of a particular version of Marxist thought. However, one observation to be made is that these various shifts have also resulted in an evacuation of the overarching revolutionary programme central to the SI, of which psychogeography was but one element.

Accepting this shift, a certain open dialectic becomes apparent between psychogeography as negative method, opposing psychogeography as positive, constructive concept. This is the tentative framework within which we propose to understand the main orientations found in recent approaches, something which can be crudely simplified into twin cul-de-sacs. On one side, an aimless drift into self-referential autocritique and political impossibility, an encounter with the ineffable, awaiting the unprogrammed event. On the other, clinging to a troubling ontological ground, a world of stable presences, determinist, universalising logic, and a potentially teleological metaphysics of history that tempers fatalism with 'chiliastic serenity'. Though tending towards the second route, the success of a situationist psychogeography, in our view, was that at its best, it held these two in unresolved tension. We will now turn to more recent practices, to assess if they perhaps fall foul of these twin cul-de-sacs.

Psychogeographical cul-de-sacs

Firstly, the tendency to veer strongly towards the first cul-de-sac – what we might call a 'negative' direction - in much recent psychogeography, has arguably led to the important emphasis upon both play and participation evident in a number of situationist texts being differently understood in some cases via a postmodern notion of the free play of signifiers. This has also perhaps led to the utilisation and indeed instrumentalisation of psychogeography in various guises as participatory art practice. Here, a simplistic critique of earlier ideological forms, whereby play and participation were seen as the negation of disciplinary procedures, is conducted.

In fact, deploying psychogeography in this way, perhaps enacts rather than evades the disciplining of contemporary capitalism, producing subjective reconfigurations in more flexible, fluid, networked and recombinant forms. Such art practices appear congruent with the deployment of play and participation

MIHAELA BREBENEL & CHRISTOPHER COLLIER

entailed in a broadly relational approach to art as criticised by, for example, Claire Bishop (2012a). Moreover, these practices frequently find themselves subject to co-option by state and corporate agendas, as Josephine Berry Slater and Anthony Iles (2010) have, amongst others, noted. The attendant interpretation of situationist theory in many such practices, as a simplistic opposition between 'activation' and 'spectatorship,' overlooks the co-option of play and participation within the biopolitical machinations of post-Fordist capitalism.

The idea that playing in the city somehow gives special access to escaping circuits of control is taken as given by much contemporary psychogeography. This is attested by the uptake of such mobile phone apps for the facilitation of psychogeography's playful spirit as *Dérive, Random GPS, Serendipitor* and *Drift* – interactive mobile platforms for s(t)imulating the experience of a drift, mainly designed and developed by new media artists to randomise navigation and facilitate unexpected journeys in real environments. Instead of reading such apps in the spirit of the SI's use of walkie-talkies on *dérives* with the intention of opening up alternative phenomenologies of space, they could equally be seen in the context of Brian Holmes's argument as to the redundancy of a psychogeographic aesthetic, situating locative media as 'locational humanism' in which the ideology of drift interpellates the subject into an imperial global infrastructure (Holmes, 2004).

The idealisation of disruptive play, when taken as the free play of signifiers, also leads to the related self-referential ironies, ambient practices (Mulholland, 2003) and discursive games that came to characterise the sardonic and yet ebullient psychogeography of the 1990s around such groups as the London Psychogeographical Association (LPA), Manchester Area Psychogeographic and others described by Stewart Home in his book *Mind Invaders*. In the case of these groups however, play was arguably utilised in a far more critical manner, usefully undermining and disrupting the ontological and ideological fixing of psychogeography and its historical trajectory.

We can now quickly recap the interrelated issues above, issues that become problematic in cases of over-reliance on psychogeography as a negative, critical method without accounting for context.

On the one hand, the retreat into play and participation in much contemporary psychogeography stems from the assumption that in critiquing *one particular* ideological machinery of the urban environment, play and participation are therefore inherently critical and egalitarian. By making this assumption, one may dangerously miss one's own constructive moment, this being the moment in which such practices are put to work against themselves.

In the second case, the danger remains ever present that ironic play may lead to purely aesthetic simulation, becoming the only possible refuge in the absence of any stable ontological ground (to some degree transposing metaphysics with aesthetics, and as such remaining in part affirmative). Here, psychogeography risks becoming preoccupied with autocritique, owing to the apparent impossibility of a wider revolutionary project. Such a tendency is repeatedly parodied by groups like the LPA, through the use of ironic revolutionary language and performed organisational forms, although in the LPA's case, they largely avoid a self-limiting, positive identification with aesthetics.

This leads us onto a third problem, one that perhaps results from the resignation from a political programme into autocritique, or individualised and individualising experiences, a problem to be found in a parallel focus on decomposing the subject. Whereas the advantages of psychotropics, automatism and devices such as dowsing or algorithms for bypassing conditioned spatial consciousness are suggested by a certain reading of situationist psychogeography, there, the altering of perception was arguably conceived as a tool in a wider programme, something akin to Brecht's distancing effect, rather than a limit in itself. In many more recent practices the social conditions become less something that can be understood, let alone reunited with the subject in some Hegelio-Lukácsian fashion. Instead, they become the locus of sublime otherness and this decomposing of the subject less about subjectivation and more about a quasi-mystical encounter with the numinous.

Though admittedly in much less of an occultist vein than some other recent psychogeography, the example of contemporary British author and journalist Will Self's fictional and non-fiction treatment of the psychotropic is illustrative. Whilst echoing this earlier characteristic of psychogeography, it also suggests a shift from a methodology of subjective disorientation for the purpose of ideology critique and better understanding of wider social conditions into individualised narratives. Such an approach potentially risks becoming a nihilistic criticality, having lost faith in totality, and without the ontological ground of a political programme on which to stroll.

After one has rejected a certain metaphysics, the question of a contemporary psychogeography posed by these 'negative' practices indeed becomes: on what ontological ground do we walk? Debord, after a Hegelian Marxism, claims that history, that is to say practice, proves the truth of a theory amongst theories, separating what he decried as 'farcical literary revolutions' from effective social transformation (it is this that founds his understanding of the realisation of art in life) (Debord. 1955: 11-12). The question of whether an emancipatory political programme is possible within psychogeography perhaps becomes one of whether, and how, such a programme is possible at all.

From multiple cul-de-sacs we might broadly categorise as (at least nominally) orientated towards 'negation,' we observe that psychogeography is also prone to wander in the opposite direction, towards an affirmative ontology – be that distinctly metaphysical, or indeed, positivist. These iterations often treat psychogeography as a scientific practice for gaining affirmative knowledge of a territory or 'objective' (i.e. experimentally verifiable) insights into human psychology. Whether such affirmation is founded upon a programme of an overly teleological dialectical materialism or the self-perpetuating logic of capitalist technical innovation, it tends towards an enclosure of such practices within reified forms.

Arguably Engels was an early proponent of an 'objectivist' psychogeography, using comparable methods to better understand urban revolt and to conduct radical ethnographic fieldwork in service of a revolutionary programme (Engels, 1895: 14). Yet his endeavours are not normally understood as psychogeography precisely because they are so firmly rooted in his overarching dialectical materialist perspective which instrumentalised and subordinated such practices to a pragmatic and programmatic framing. In this sense, his approach also leads away from psychogeography, in that these practices cease to be understood as such. When stripped of a certain 'artistic' indeterminacy, psychogeography is quickly instrumentalised into the more conventional academic terrain of anthropology, psychological, behavioural or cultural geography, sociology and environmental psychology. These practices could trace an alternative genealogy to Kevin Lynch's 1950s speculations on cognitive mapping, and later developments in this line at Clark University in the 1960s from David Stea, where the term 'psycho-geography' was coined independently as a branch of academic geography (Wood, 2010: 186).

It should also be noted that yet a third genealogy of the term is possible, in the Freudian psychoanalytical theory of geographical representation developed by William G. Niederland and Howard F. Stein. Their psychoanalytical approach casts psychogeography as the symbolic externalisation and projection of an individual's psychology onto their environment, an understanding ultimately emerging from Niederland's work on river symbolism, again in the mid-1950s, making for the broadly concurrent emergence of all three uses of the term (Stein and Neiderland, 1989).

These more 'scientific' branches of psychogeography are antecedents of various contemporary practices, both within the academic social and biological sciences and at their margins, for example the neuroscience approach taken by Hugo Spiers of UCL involving MRI scanning navigating subjects, or the biomapping of Christian Nold. Ultimately, the interpellation of such work within capitalist schemas of technical innovation configure it as predisposed towards increasing possibilities for capital accumulation. Psychogeography's existence within the academy as such is more ambiguous, containing both this inherent instrumentalisation, but also a certain space of criticality. Likewise, psychogeography's academicisation, in art history, literary studies, performing arts, humanities and social science, whilst serving to broaden interpretations of psychogeographic practice, situates it on an ontological ground that prefigures the possibility of its reification within the logic of accumulation.

Such is a brief summary of the cul-de-sacs that we hold face much contemporary psychogeography, something that the practice of the SI never really resolved, instead preferring a tenuous dialectical gloss over these contractions between poetic and scientific, critique and affirmation, teleology and event. At any time this tension is resolved one way or the other, the practice appears to suffer and stultify. In this sense we might see psychogeography as mirroring a distinct politics of a certain kind of art in the unresolved tension between self-dissolution into life and attempting to retain an autonomous, non-instrumental space, where 'aesthetic experience is effective inasmuch as it is the experience of that and' (Rancière, 2002). In this sense, perhaps we arrive at a notion of psychogeography's place as an art form, if that is not, once more, to enclose it in metaphysics.

This leads us to now explore a different approach to this problematic, perhaps a more conciliatory one, but one nevertheless closer to our own practice as Ernest. When Mark Fisher expresses a dissatisfaction that the 'zine anthology *Savage Messiah* by artist Laura Oldfield-Ford has attracted the label 'psychogeography,' preferring instead to approach it via the notion of 'hauntology' (Fisher, 2011: xiv) he indicates one way forward. This is a term he appropriates from Derrida's considerations on Marxism, to express something that evades a simple dichotomy between presence and absence, affirmative ontology and criticality. Perhaps this is where we might investigate a 'northwest passage' - to use Debord's 'own' de Quincean metaphor - out of the cul-de-sacs of contemporary psychogeography, between a method of negation and a positive concept.

The street in tides of images, along lines of text. Moving on

The ways in which historical and contemporary psychogeographies have attempted to traverse these cul-de-sacs can be gleaned from how they attempt to make records of their practice. It is this, more than any other aspect, that causes the irresolvable shift between negation and affirmation, absence and presence, to shimmer most starkly into view.

This is where we place our own investigations, into this shifting, spectral context; the fungal blossoming of a new psychogeographic underbelly that cannibalises and clings to the decaying, bloated corpses of its undead predecessors, haunting back alleys and libraries, seething streets and flickers of microwave radiation. This perhaps gives us a perspective from which to approach our own work as part of Ernest, and the relations and returns to psychogeography this explores. The remainder of our considerations coalesce around this more methodological avenue, attempting to situate our own experiences within a historical psychogeographical tradition as it relates to the use of various recording methods.

To pick a fairly recent example as a way to approach this, in Iain Sinclair's filmic collaborations with Chris Petit, or in the juxtaposition of his prose with the photography of Marc Atkins in *Liquid City* (Atkins and Sinclair, 1999), it is the interplay of image and text that suggests the inherent tension in creating a psychogeographic 'artistic' record. Here Sinclair stirs the experience of *dérive* through text, alongside suggestive, symbolic image-poems, ghost-images with textual descriptions, and images as descriptions themselves, of urban banalities stopped on photographic paper, in black and white.

The black and white image of the city, largely absent of human presence, yet paradoxically attesting both a presence and absence of the photographer, has also been posthumously associated with psychogeography and its stirrings in surrealist photographic explorations of the city. Taking the city as arena of chance encounter and alienation, these images attain a haunted quality, attempting to bleed the hidden presence of an imagined totality, hovering only as a horizon glimpsed in flickers of loaded, metonymic fragments. De Chirico's influence is evident, as is an ancestry in Romantic invocations of the *genius loci*. The meticulous practice of documenting an empty Paris that Eugène Atget pioneered, which Breton and Man Ray acknowledged by publishing his photographs in *La Révolution surréaliste*, and that finds its echo in Bill Brandt's portraits of a blitzed London, can also be seen as fringing psychogeography. Likewise it appears in the noir dreamscapes of George Brassaï, or what we might venture to call the 'profane illumination' of Ilse Bing's lyrical urban monochromes. Jacques-André Boiffard's photographic illustrations for Breton's *Nadja*, or Man Ray and Brassaï's for *L'Amour fou* were described by Walter Benjamin as making 'the streets, gates, squares of the city into illustrations of a trashy novel,' drawing off 'the banal obviousness of this ancient architecture to inject it with the most pristine intensity towards the events described' (Benjamin, 1978: 183). In other words, to invest a unifying psychic presence in image fragments, fragments that show up only its absence, to reach for the horizon of a totality that the indecipherable and mysterious fracturing of the modern city occludes.

When Breton begins *Surrealism and Painting* by championing the affective immediacy and phenomenological primacy of the image as a means to short-circuit reason, he approaches its frustrated psychogeographic appeal. Yet we recall that he himself was a poet and writer and Surrealism's central orientation was textual. Later in the same text Breton laments on 'the stabilizing of dream images in the kind of still-life deception known as trompe l'oeil' (Breton, 1972: 70). This is what the SI drew upon in casting images as mediation, exploring this dialectic between immediacy and distance that can likewise be recast in the primary shift we have identified, between affirmation and negation.

These images themselves perhaps disrupt this in a more hauntological manner however, something that Debord perhaps gestured towards in his early films. We might understand the flow of such practices into current psychogeography via Debord's own interrogations into this ontology of representation.

From static, to moving images, the *unheimlich* black and white scenes, replaced by black screens of unbearable duration.

This negation of the image, a strangely hauntological cinema, was something Debord had taken from his precursor and later, sworn enemy – the founder of Letterism, Isidore Isou. In his film *Treaty on Venom and Eternity* (1951), Isou approaches the image in a way worth revisiting. The current restored version of the film (110 minutes from over 4 hours) has a series of warnings at the outset, from the note that it allegedly produced rioting audiences when shown at Cannes Film Festival, to the pragmatic warning that tickets will not be refunded. However, as Andrew V. Uroskie argues, rather than a *jeune rebel* film, Isou's and other Letterist films are 'better understood as a series of complex constructions: admixtures of proposition and cancellation and re-combinations of pre-existing audiovisual material into new assemblages for thought and experience' (Uroskie, 2011: 26).

Isou wrote, directed, composed the music and acted for this film, which opens to a black screen lingering for five minutes, accompanied by the sound of the 'Letterist Choir.' During this five minutes, in the current restored version, a scrolling didactic text, aimed at its American audience, reads: 'Dear Audience: The film you are about to see differs radically - to put it mildly - from any film ever made any time, any place. It is the work of Jean-Isidore ISOU, founder of LETTERISM. ISOU and the letterists responsible for this film are a group of artists working in Paris.' This audience is also warned, through a note at the end of this insert, that: 'In fact, the neighbourhood of St. Germain-des-Pres is an invention of the author, and represents nothing but the road of the author's Calvary.' These warnings, overlapping the Letterist choir not only distort the immersive experience of the black screen and the sound associated to it, but are perhaps a form of acknowledgement that the image alone should be intervened upon, disrupting its filmic presence.

Strikingly enough, the next image is that of a typical Parisian road sign, 'Rue Danton', which the character Daniel passes on his way out of the cine-club. On his way out, walking the streets of Paris, Daniel speaks, image and sound unaligned, we hear his thoughts, perhaps from the cine-club, the crowds rejecting his propositions in rows of insults: 'I want to destroy the picture from the speech... to do the opposite of what has been done...[...] Who said that the Cinema whose meaning is movement... must be movement of image and not movement of speech? *Idiot! What will happen to photography?*'

To this, the answer is that one should go further than photography, go beyond its meaning; the film stock needs to be approached directly, in its materiality. Its documentary purpose, its supposed visual immediacy or presence has been stained by its ambitions to become artistic, and therefore distant, representational, from its clarity to its *clair-obscur* and further, into its uselessness.

Furthermore, the classic unity image-text should be overcome: 'The first apoc-alyptic sign of disjunction ... the rupture of this bloated organism called Film. [...] To conquer, one must divide. [...] In relation to sound they [image and text] must be incoherent.' Isou's is a critical image, one whose ontological refuge is to show and speak of its making, thus its viewing. Its production directly linked to its reception, part Brecht, part Artaud, not in the indexical but the critical - do-ing away with any associated artistic debris. Following a lineage from Baudelaire to Rimbaud and Mallarmé, Isou sought a dismantling of form, a stripping down of both the image and language in search of an essence. As the Letterists sought to strip language to the letter, the cinematic image too must be dismantled, call-ing for direct intervention on the film strip. His answer to the ontological aporia he approaches is the very materiality of the image, experience de- and re-mate-rialised, working it against itself in the play of its affirmation and negation, the absent possibility of indexical identity with the world, transposed onto a critical self-identity, something that attempts to rediscover a presence, through itself in the letter or the celluloid frame. Likewise, by negating its audience through the boredom of the blank screen, it attempts to realise them, through their ac-tivation – making spectators participants. We can thus see this strategy as an attempt to resolve the dialectic of form and essence, yet one disrupted by a spec-tral quality of the inability of a full negation, a lingering presence that cannot be eradicated that is yet an absence that haunts these attempts to found a new ontological presence for the image.

This is foregrounded in the juxtaposition of image and text, where the text produces a distancing effect upon the image and vice versa, each highlighting the irreducibility of one to the other, or each to itself, exposing the way that each necessarily exceeds itself in the irresolvable resistance of this dialectic to its own closure.

We propose that this informs later International Letterist experiments in psychogeography, in which the tension between aesthetics as an affirmation-al ontological ground and as a critical deconstructive tool haunts the practice, precisely in its resistance to adequate documentation. Psychogeography is ap-parently haunted by the failure of its own prosaic documentation to live up to the poetry of its practice, yet the two remain inseparable, co-contaminated but utterly irreducible to the other.

In the projects that we have undertaken with Ernest, the use of images has been equally problematic for us. More usually the image is deferred into its oth-er, becoming text, becoming map, becoming another mnemotechnical method, yet somehow remaining image. Images and events are also co-constituted and yet irreducible to each other. Our general flight from documentation is more accurately recast as the creation of documentation never to be presented (for example lengthy recordings of conversations that will never be replayed, re-pre-sented or transcribed, photographs not to be viewed). This forms a futural horizon of an absent audience in what Boris Groys has called a 'spectacle without spectators' (Groys, 2009) in reference to the text/image culture of self-exhibitionism that reached a sort of hegemony with the proliferation of web 2.0 user-generated content. What we might be tempted to call a 'post-audience performativity' can better be understood as a '*pre*-audience performativity' and in this way, a reflection upon the generalised collapse of a spectacle-participation binary identified by Claire Bishop as characteristic of contemporary neoliberalism (Bishop, 2012b).

In this way our psychogeographic experiments, such as the project *#pigeonsdontriot*, were punctuated by textual and imagistic projections onto imagined future contexts, moulded both by a library of the residual visual and literary psychogeographic references that dog our steps, as much as the mnemotechnical retentions of the architecture itself. The projections made explicit their orientation towards, and haunting by, a premonitory presence: an absent audience that constitutes the continual dialogue between affirmation and critique that we find in our engagements and encounters with the city.

#pigeonsdontriot explored the performative dimension of spatial encounter and the imaginary, projected totality suggested through this self-exhibitionism in social media. In exploring this interface of subjective and collective, that both street and tweet evoke, we wanted to examine the fetishisation of social media in the liberal discourse around recent social unrest. The project attempted to make use of a self-critical, collectively voiced, geotagged twitter account with no followers to explore this. It was self-critical in the sense that we conceived it in dialogue also with the ubiquity of uncritical deployments of locative media within much contemporary psychogeographic practice.

Tweeting highly 'subjective' tweets, such as details of intimate relationships, from a collective voice both presented and yet distanced these experiences, foregrounding their representation insomuch as they manifested interspersed with half-remembered and unattributed quotes from a psychogeographic 'canon', exposing them as already hauntological. At points our voices became indistinguishable not only from each other, but from the literary residue hovering in our heads, and in the city itself, comprising our subjective experience in the environment at each moment, projected onto an absent audience as the condition of its aesthetic immediacy.

These tweets were not only textual, but often also visual, comprising a range of poor quality phone images. Again the hauntological status of these images was their severance from indexicality, as they were geotagged in locations that often did not correspond to their subject matter. Their 'poor-image' status, to echo Hito Steyerl, recalled Isou's attacking of the film stock, in both foregrounding their presence as an attempt at self-identity, whilst at the same time undermining it through their drift.

The spatialising of the tweets served not as a navigational diagram, but rather to approach and frustrate the dialectic that Debord establishes in his commentary on Hegel in thesis 161 of *The Society of the Spectacle*, between the necessary temporal alienation that founds subjectivation, and the spatial alienation that characterises the fragmentary nature of contemporary urban experience. Subjectivation, as the dissolution of the subject in the objective, and its re-emergence transformed is figured here. Arguably, this absent horizon of audience, is precisely the spectacle, an apparently objective totality that circumscribes our subjectivation as only occurring in and through it, concealing the spatial fragmentation of experience that makes such temporal subjectivation impossible in other, alternative ways. The psychogeographic is here that which disrupts this process, by undermining 'false' presences.

What could stand for a conclusion

When Balzac - himself somewhat psychogeographically - says: 'Paris is an ocean; heave your lead, and you will never find the bottom' (Balzac, 2005: 15) perhaps the analogy could be drawn with psychogeography itself. Here we could only cast a cursory glance across its shifting surface. Earlier we speculated that for contemporary psychogeography, one 'northwest passage' out of its many potential cul-de-sacs was by intervening as a spectral third term in an apparent dialectic between negation and affirmation. Debord's dialectical critique of Surrealism was that it attempted to realise art without abolishing it, i.e. that Surrealism failed to exceed the realm of art, affirming it without negating it – life became spectacular but creative subjectivation did not become life. Debord saw the SI's programme as an attempt to overcome this historical cul-de-sac, bringing Surrealism's psychogeographical encounters into the realm of everyday life by transcending art and engendering a more participatory form of subjectivation, via the notion of the 'situation'. Yet as we have seen, the collapse of spectacle and participation is troubled once more by this spectral undecidability of art, and the ghosts of psychogeography that hover around the very limits and possibilities of politics and aesthetics, and the unanswerable question of course, of whether psychogeography is in fact art at all.

Does this offer us an understanding of psychogeography as an emancipatory practice? Not really. A rejection of programmatisation leaves psychogeography's deployment as a directly political tool clearly weakened. Yet this programmatisation, as we have explored, should one adopt it, would leave one not doing psychogeography as such any longer, but some other of the myriad, more institutional disciplines that overlap its territories. In this respect psychogeography is to some degree still avant-garde, albeit a curiously backward-looking, hauntological one. In this sense, its route out of the cul-de-sac is via the corpse road of art, and its own indeterminacy. Yet this does not mean we should spend all our time tying ourselves up in ontological knots and spooky Derridean metaphors with a sell-by date of Halloween 1993. To arrive at such a road does not necessarily mean a resignation, but perhaps a redoubling of our efforts, psychogeography as militant research, discovering reasons to go on in the fragments we encounter.

It is perhaps in psychogeography's opening of the fragmentary encounter onto the negative horizon of totality, that potentially we are dealing with an inversion of what Breton labelled 'objective chance.' Rather than the encounter illuminating flashes of a totality, this horizon of negativity, reveals instead the situatedness, preciousness and precariousness, of the encounter. Maybe then Breton is half right, when in the opening of *Nadja* he famously asks: 'perhaps I am doomed to retrace my steps under the illusion that I am exploring, doomed to try and learn what I should simply recognise, learning a mere fraction of what I have forgotten' (Breton, 1928: 12). Perhaps too he is unwittingly correct when he speculates that we are ghosts, best defined by who, or maybe what, we haunt. Perhaps the question now then is not how we escape psychogeographical cul-de-sacs, but rather how we might return to them, haunt them, in better, more effective ways.

References

Atkins, M. and Sinclair, I. 1999. *Liquid City*. London: Reaktion Books.

Balzac, H de. 2005 [1835]. *Père Goriot*. Translated by Katherine Prescott. Whitefish: Kessinger.

Benjamin, W. 1978. 'Surrealism: The Last Snapshot of the European Intelligentsia,' in *Reflections*. Translated by Edmund Jephcott. New York, NY: Harcourt Brace Jovanovich.

Bishop, C. 2012a. *Artificial Hells: Participatory Art and the Politics of Spectatorship*. London: Verso.

_____ . 2012b. 'Participation and Spectacle – Where Are we Now?' in Thompson, N. (ed.) *Living as Form: Socially Engaged Art from 1991-2011*. New York, NY: Creative Time, 34-45.

Breton, A. 1972. *Surrealism and Painting*. Translated by Simon Watson Taylor. New York, NY: Harper & Row.

_____ . 1999 [1928]. *Nadja*. London: Penguin Books.

Coverley, M. 2006. *Psychogeography*. Harpenden: Pocket Essentials.

Debord, G. 2006 [1955]. 'Introduction to a Critique of Urban Geography' in Knabb, K. (ed.), *Situationist International Anthology*. Berkeley, CA: Bureau of Public Secrets.

Derrida, J. 1997 [1967]. *Of Grammatology*. Baltimore, MD: Johns Hopkins University Press.

Engels, F. 1934 [1895]. 'Introduction' in Marx, K. *The Class Struggles in France, 1848-1850*. New York, NY: International Publishers.

Fisher, Mark. 2011. 'Introduction' in Oldfield-Ford, L. *Savage Messiah*. London: Verso.

Groys, B. 2009. 'Comrades of Time.' *E-flux journal*. 11:12. Available: http://www.e-flux.com/journal/comrades-of-time/. Last accessed 30/01/2013.

Hanson, S. 2007. 'Mind the gap: psychogeography as an expanded tradition.' *Street Signs*, Autumn.

Holmes, B. 2004. 'Drifting Through the Grid: Psychogeography and Imperial Infrastructure.' *Springerin* 3/04.

Home, S. 1998. *Mind Invaders: A Reader in Psychic Warfare, Cultural Sabotage and Semiotic Terrorism*. London: Serpent's Tail.

Mulholland, N. 2003. 'Bill Posters is Guilty (On the cultural logic of ambient)'. *Mute magazine* 1:25.

Rancière, J. 2002. 'The Aesthetic Revolution and its Outcomes: Employments of Autonomy and Heteronomy.' *New Left Review* 14, March-April.

Sinclair, I. *Once Upon a Time in the Fields*. Vol. 3, London Fields Radio. Available: http://www.londonfieldsradio.com/podcasts/. Last Accessed 14/3/2011.

Stein, H. F. and Niederland, W. G.1989. *Maps from the Mind: Readings in Psychogeography*. Norman, OK: University of Oklahoma Press.

Uroskie, A.V. 2011. 'Beyond the Black Box: The Lettrist Cinema of Disjunction.' *October* Winter: 135, 21-48.

Wood, D. 2010. 'Lynch Debord: About Two Psychogeographies.' *cartographica* 45:3.

Filmography

Treaty on Venom and Eternity. 1951. Film transferred to DVD. Directed by Isidore Isou. France: Films M.G. Guillemin.110 mins.

II. Feral Youth

5

THE REBEL WITHOUT A CAUSE AS PROTAGONIST OF UNRULY POLITICS

Femke Kaulingfreks

Several occasions of protest leading to urban riots have disrupted public peace and reclaimed the streets, in both 'Western' and 'Eastern,' or 'Arab,' cities, over recent years. These events have led some to conclude that we increasingly live in a time of riots (Badiou, 2012). The Arab Spring, Occupy, the Gezi Park protests in Istanbul and the demonstrations instigated by the Free Fare Movement in Brazil are recent events of uprising involving large masses of young people who lost their trust in more traditional instruments of political participation. These youths took (to) the streets to demand a change of governance, since in their eyes existing political institutions fail in the areas of representation, accountability and transparency. The widening gap between state institutions of governance and the interests of common people is not only noticeable in autocratic societies. Progressive theorists like Simon Critchley (2007, 7) and Chantal Mouffe (2005, 4) speak of a 'democratic deficit' in politics. Since the universal acceptance of a neo-liberal model of democratic governance, politics has ceased to be the platform for ideological debate. It is not surprising then that politics does not touch upon people's concerns at a crucial internal level, it is reduced to a mere organizational strategy for society that regulates people's lives from the outside. Those who should be represented in democratic institutions find themselves at an increasingly large distance from the political process.

Protests, which address this issue, have differed largely from one another, involving different actors, ignited by different circumstances and taking place in different countries. Nevertheless, these recent uprisings are generally distinguished from other events of violent disorder in the streets, which seem to lack political significance. Unexpected riots like the ones which took place around Paris in 2005,[1] in Amsterdam in 2007,[2] in Copenhagen in 2008,[3] in London in

---

[1] See 'Timeline: French riots; a chronology of key events'. *BBC*. November 14, 2005. Available: http://news.bbc.co.uk/2/hi/europe/4413964.stm. Last accessed 05/08/2014.

[2] See 'Moroccan-Dutch youth riot in Amsterdam following fatal incident'. *Digital Journal*. October 16, 2007. Available: http://www.digitaljournal.com/article/240329. Last accessed 05/08/2014.

[3] See 'Danish youths riot for 7th night, several arrested.' *Reuters*. February 17, 2008.

2011,[4] and in Stockholm in 2013[5] were perceived by politicians and media commentators as striking blindly, without any motives except for criminal intent, and without any signs of a legitimized revolt. These riots were instigated by predominantly male youngsters with an immigrant background from deprived urban areas. In all cases violence erupted after a confrontation with serious, often fatal, consequences took place between the police and an inhabitant from a stigmatized neighbourhood. Following these events, representatives from the institutional domain showed a lack of recognition for the grief of those surrounding the victim, and a lack of respect for those expressing their frustration and discontent regarding the events. These ingredients sparked off an enraged reaction which spread to other areas, involving thousands of young people in street riots and looting, who did not necessarily share the specific frustration and experiences of injustice that initiated the first emergence of rioting. Such events differ from the actions of pre-organized, politically conscious social movements or pressure groups because no communiqués are spread, no spokespeople are put forward to address the press and no banners are carried. Unlike uprisings associated with movements like Occupy, the Arab Spring or the Gezi Park protests, these events seem to lack a clear political goal and a strategy aimed at constructive and effective alternatives. Commentators and political representatives tend to analyze such events not in relation to, but in opposition to society as lawless deeds, inspired by personal frustrations or the desires of abnormal young people who do not know how to behave as good citizens. Their abnormality is seen as being caused by social and educational deficiencies, alcohol and drug abuse, criminal tendencies and/or an aggressive, antisocial youth culture. Such sudden attacks on civil peace are a clear cause for moral panic and are met with a strong and undisputed condemnation of the events in both the public and the political debate (Cohen, 2011).

The reaction of Nicolas Sarkozy, then French Minister of Internal Affairs, to the Parisian riots in 2005 and the reaction of David Cameron, English Prime Minister, to the London riots in 2011 are exemplary in this respect.[6] Sarkozy described the youth involved in the French riots as criminal gang members

---

Available: http://in.reuters.com/article/2008/02/17/idINIndia-31995320080217. Last accessed 05/08/2014.

[4] See 'UK riots: London in lockdown, but violence flares across UK'. *The Guardian.* August 10, 2011. Available: http://www.guardian.co.uk/uk/2011/aug/09/uk-riots-police-tough-lockdown. Last accessed 05/08/2014.

[5] See 'Stockholm sees fourth night of rioting'. *CNN.* May 24, 2013. Available: http://edition.cnn.com/2013/05/23/world/europe/sweden-rioting. Last accessed 05/08/2014.

[6] See: 'Inflammatory Language'. *The Guardian.* November 8, 2005. Available: http://www.guardian.co.uk/news/blog/2005/nov/08/inflammatoryla. Last accessed 05/08/2014.; 'England riots: Broken society is top priority - Cameron.' *BBC.* August 15, 2011. Available: http://www.bbc.co.uk/news/uk-politics-14524834. Last accessed 05/08/2014.

and scum [*racaille*] from whom the country should be liberated. English Prime Minister David Cameron analyzed the London 2011 riots as a sign of the 'moral collapse' of a 'broken society.' By stating that this moral collapse is manifested by a lack of parenting skills in 'troubled' families, and that an 'all-out war against gangs and gang culture' is needed, Cameron sought the origin of the riots in deviant socio-psychological behavior, youth culture and youth delinquency. He explicitly stressed that the riots were a matter of gang culture and not of poverty, discrimination or unequal social chances. Such reactions clarify how these riots are not analyzed as a political act, but rather perceived as the product of violent and uncivil behavior in urban youth culture, which generally threatens the public sphere in Western European cities[7] (Decker and Weerman, 2005). A gang mentality, macho and narcissistic attitudes and eagerness to seek physical or verbal confrontations are all characteristic of an image of street culture, which is seen as counterproductive to good and accepted citizenship and devoid of any socio-political awareness. A continuous emphasis on the 'pointless violence' in the actions of young urban 'troublemakers' places them outside of the body of 'normal' citizens, and inside a frame of deviant exponents of a dangerous street culture. This street culture seems to collide with the dominant, civil culture in society (Van Strijen, 2009). As a consequence of this dichotomy young rioters are easily placed outside of the moral structure and political rules of society. Civil disturbances and riots instigated by youth of immigrant descent, like the cases mentioned before, are not seen as an aspect of the social dynamics within society, but as a threatening destabilization of society by those who do not merit to be seen as fellow citizens.

The culturalization of citizenship

This interpretation of the behaviour of 'young urban troublemakers' has consequences for their citizenship status. It is exemplary for a way of thinking in which deviant behavior is not imagined as a contested part of society, but rather as external to society. Citizenship becomes 'virtualized' in this context, according to Dutch sociologist Willem Schinkel (2010). The meaning of citizenship has shifted from the formal and juridical status of those who rightfully live within the borders of the nation state, to a status of moral and cultural acceptance, which can be gained if sufficient integration is shown. This shift is influenced by a globalization process which, according to Schinkel, makes Western societies increasingly ethnically heterogeneous. One can be in the possession of a formal citizenship status, but this does not automatically imply that one is seen as a 'good' citizen who is accepted as a part of civil society. Citizenship is 'turned into a possibility instead of an actuality, and… a virtue. This way citizenship,

---

[7] See http://efus.eu/en/topics/risks-forms-of-crime/collective-violence/efus/2567/. Last accessed 05/08/2014.

which is increasingly problematic as a mechanism of in- and exclusion of the nation-state, becomes a state-controlled mechanism of in- and exclusion of society' (Schinkel, 2010). Since citizenship is seen more and more as an ideal of citizen-participation or a virtue, it becomes a prescription, meant to guide one's attitude and behaviour. The virtualization of citizenship signaled by Schinkel is complemented by what other social scientists characterize as a 'culturalization of citizenship' (Duyvendak, Hurenkamp & Tonkens, 2010). It is not only a certain level of self-sufficiency and active participation in the area of employment, housing and social security that determines one's successful realization of good citizenship, but also one's adoption of the mores of the dominant culture. Issues, which were previously explained in terms of class dynamics, are now analyzed in the context of what Slavoj Žižek calls 'the culturalization of politics,' in reference to Wendy Brown. Brown defines the culturalization of politics as 'the reduction of political motivations and causes to essentialized culture' (Brown, 2006: 20). Under the influence of this reduction, an emphasis on cultural origins dominates the analysis of political inequalities and injustices. Looking through a culturalizing lens, such inequalities and injustices are presented as consequential to certain cultural identities and therefore as insolvable by any possible change to the political organization of society. If cultural identities are seen as pre-constitutive of social interactions, political inequalities have to be tolerated as a given, inscribed in the logics of the distinction between the authentic political community and its outside (Žižek, 2008).

In the case of the aforementioned riots involving the youth of immigrant descent, it is not only a culturalization of citizenship that contributes to the stigmatization of the instigators. In addition, the culturalization of politics contributes to a framing of the riots as originating from a deviant street culture, while possible political motives are not acknowledged. Frustrations in relation to discrimination, ethnic profiling, poverty and isolation are not recognized as valid incentives underlying the disruptive events and are consequentially not seen as issues of injustice and inequality which could be tackled within the political arena. This depoliticization of the riots becomes possible when political participation is defined within an institutional context. One acts politically if one either remains within the framework of political institutions by the practice of voting or through membership of a political party, or if one aims to deliberately reform this framework of political institutions, by adopting social movement strategies such as demonstrations and strikes. The actions of young rioters like the ones who turned parts of London upside down in 2011, do not fit into this representation of politics. I wish to contest this exclusion from the domain of citizenship and politics of young urban troublemakers, by stating that their disruptive interventions in urban space can be seen as a form of unruly political agency. Despite the fact that they are less articulately linked to specific political goals than the uprisings I mentioned at the beginning of this chapter, these events also address the democratic deficit in the various European countries where these riots took place. In the act of rioting, young urban troublemakers make themselves visible as citizens who are not sufficiently represented in the formal practice of politics. Their disruptive actions therefore have a political sense, even if they express themselves in unconventional ways, even if they operate outside of the domain of the law and even if they do not share a dominant culture, which is imagined as the foundation of good citizenship.

The Rebel without a Cause

The moral rejection of the 'uncivil' behaviour of young troublemakers, and their consequent disqualification as 'outlaws', placed outside of the accepted citizenry, is no new phenomenon. Already in the 1950's representations of derailed adolescents and their deviant youth culture, caused both scandal and excitement through mass media. 'Counter' culture was perceived as a social context in which youngsters developed a dangerously rebellious identity, which conflicted with standard expectations of a teenager's personal development (Roszak, 1995 [1969]). The imagination of such counter culture within expressions of pop culture easily lead to moral panic. James Dean as 'Rebel without a Cause' is an iconic image in this respect. Dean plays the role of teenager Jim in the movie *Rebel without a Cause*, who feels misunderstood and undervalued in his family home and looks for recognition and companionship outside, on the streets. There he engages in a competition with other recalcitrant teens, which leads to various minor and major disasters, amongst which an illegal car race with a dramatic ending. In this role Dean personified a generation adrift in the 1950's, estranged form its family and local community. The initial and most obvious reception of the film narrative focuses on mindless teenagers acting violently out of despair, caused by parental neglect, psychological insecurities and capitalist alienation. This presentation of the hidden causes behind the seemingly erratic anger of the protagonist, seems to be derived from a classical pathologization of adolescent, delinquent behaviour (Bowlby, 1944). Such an interpretation assumes a lack of social engagement and political awareness in the actions of the protagonist, who is depicted as a rebel, but his revolt seems to be missing the point. The behaviour of the rebel without a cause seems to be standing alone, without an embeddedness in a certain rational or emotional context, which could serve to explain its origin or end. He is indeed an 'outlaw', a barbarous outsider, who is untouchable in the referential framework of accepted civic participation, which therefore places himself outside of the domain of the law, the community and the mores of his time.

This characterization of the rebel without a cause is symbolic of the fear, and consequent condemnation of various generations of deviant teenagers. The rebel without a cause is not recognized as a political agent who is involved in a legitimate form of social or political resistance. A legitimate revolt consists of an interaction within a social context, which is deliberately criticized in a conscious reflection, with the aim of changing it for the better, or replacing it with a new social structure. Clear demands for change are formulated and expressed and a program or agenda is formed, which indicates the route to take in order to make the envisioned change happen. In the case of rebellion without a cause, such a deliberate articulation of demands and the setting of a deliberate political agenda seems to be absent. This absence forms a clear cause for moral panic; fear emerges for the dissolution of society under the devastating impact of violent outlaws who strike at random. It is exactly the inexplicability of senseless violent behavior, which seems to spring out of nowhere, which makes the appearance of the rebel without a cause in public space all the more threatening. Stanley Cohen already noted that the less a social phenomenon makes sense in the light of generally accepted social norms, the more reason there is to panic. The greater the unpredictability of the events and the strangeness of the actors involved, the more chance there is that concerns for a certain social problem will evolve into moral panic.

Since the release of the movie *Rebel without a Cause* the paradigm of the disenchanted youth, along with the socio-political context in which it emerged, has undergone various shifts. James Dean is nowadays perceived as an icon of brave and youthful civil criticism, aimed at the narrow-minded conventions of post Second World War Western society. It is now other young people who are seen as dangerous and deviant rebels without a cause. These are no longer the middle class white adolescents resembling Dean's character in the movie, but rather lower class youngsters from immigrant families, who feel discriminated and stigmatized in various other ways. They are easily marked as natural outsiders, not only because of the opposition between street culture and civil culture, but also because of racist tendencies such as ethnic profiling by the police, and so-called post code discrimination, already placing them in the position of outlaw because of their area of residence. Despite the fact that those designated as rebel without a cause look different and have other experiences to fifty years ago, they are still the object of exclusion. We see that the designation of rebels without a cause is still rooted in the de-politization of so-called senseless violent behaviour. This mechanism of exclusion became yet again apparent around the London riots in the summer of 2011. However, these riots and other similar cases of seemingly senseless public disturbances caused by young inhabitants of deprived neighborhoods could also be perceived through the lens of unruly politics.

Unruly Politics

Unruly politics is about the actions of people who do not play by the rules of the game of institutional politics. It is a name used to describe the interventions of those who disrupt the framework of institutional power relations, because they are in a position which leaves them no other option in order to influence the organization of society. One could think of various examples, ranging from the occupation of public squares and churches by undocumented refugees, to the development of alternative community-structures and housing without property ownership by travellers and indigenous peoples. Here I focus on riots instigated by young urban troublemakers, because the perceived senseless and violent nature of the events and the perceived incivility of those involved indicate how much unruly politics can differ from accepted forms of political agency.

> Unruly politics, as we define it, is political action by people who have been denied voice by the rules of the political game, and by the social rules that underpin this game. It draws its power from transgressing these rules – while at the same time upholding others, which may not be legally sanctioned but which have legitimacy, deeply rooted in people's own understandings of what is right and just. This preoccupation with social justice distinguishes these forms of political action from the banditry or gang violence with which threatened autocrats wilfully try to associate them (Khanna et al., 2013: 14).

The way in which we have come to understand legitimate and meaningful political agency is defined by formal political power structures. Unruly politics withdraws itself from the dominant logics of formal politics. It explicitly voices the experiences of those who are not heard within this formal domain, and who refuse to abide by the logics of formal politics. We should not evaluate the political sense of unruly politics by the standards of formally structured governance. Unruly politics is not univocally aimed at overthrowing the old government and installing a new one, gaining a better position for a certain part of the population within the parliamentary system, or other goals, which can be easily understood as productive, accountable and profitable in the light of mechanisms of formal governance. Unruly politics demands 'a new mode of political enquiry which spills outside of traditional notions of politics, and in which the relevance of acts and events is not reduced to the effect they have on formal structures of the political establishment' (ibid, 11).

Those who express unruly politics engage with the state, but on their own terms. (ibid, 12) Expressions of unruly politics do not let themselves be translated into the language of negotiated demands and interests, within a setting of parliamentary mechanisms. (ibid, 10) They do not abide by the logics of representative politics, but rather enunciate a political meaning which is unmediated, which does not let itself be represented or translated in another context, in another moment, or for the benefit of other people. Unruly politics is always situated in a specific time and place, engaging specific people. It cannot be reduced to fit to general procedures, which are designed to bring a plurality of people together in one body of manageable citizens. At the same time, expressions of unruly politics evoke a universal wish to live a dignified life, and to be treated justly by state representatives, regardless of the particular envisioning of what a dignified life might contain in each different situation, for every different person. Unruly politics is always temporary, and effective in its surprise. It is not carefully designed as a party-political campaign, but rather emerges in unexpected events. It does not only take place at the sites which are deliberately designed for public and political debate, but it also politicizes spaces which are meant to be neutral or private, like the streets, abandoned houses and virtual social network sites. It does not originate in the recognition of people who have always shared the same identity, but it forms a site of solidarity for people who recognize a similar precarious situation in their lived experiences, despite their possibly completely divergent identities.

Unruly politics has a clear informal character. Those who lack a formal citizenship status, or feel impaired to make use of their formal citizenship status, literally gain space for their lives in informal ways. Through these same informal channels they sometimes have considerable impact on the formal domain of politics. A variety of scholars have studied the emergence of informal politics in different contexts, often focusing on non-Western countries. Informal political struggles are here clearly opposed to hegemonic systems of governance, which can be colonial or post-colonial, religiously grounded and/or anti-democratic, and are often dominated by a neo-liberal, capitalist agenda (Gibson, 2011; Bayat, 1997; and Naples and Desai, 2002). Many of these studies investigate how the struggle of the poor and marginalized to make a living in the underground economy is a political act in itself. Informal politics and informal economy is thus intertwined (Cross, 1998; De Neve, 2005; Fernandez-Kelly and Schefner, 2006; and Neuwirth, 2011). Unruly politics is not only informal, but also explicitly contests the political process as it takes place within the formal sphere. Within a Western context, studies which focus on what could be named unruly politics, often focus on deliberately anarchist and/or anti-capitalist movements, applying a conscious strategy of direct action, opposing state authorities (Katsiaficas, 2006; Graeber, 2009). New Western social movements often operate within an urban context to reclaim the right to the city for those who do not fit into the city branding strategies of marketeers (Harvey, 2012), and occupy urban space in order to protest against the political dominance of capitalist financial institutions (Blumenkranz, Gessen, et al., 2011). However, here I wish to focus on forms of unruly politics, which are less deliberately organized to directly confront the state, but which emerge in struggles of every day life, and can culminate in a revolt on the streets.

Street Politics

To further illustrate the notion of unruly politics I turn to the work of Asef Bayat, who writes about the politics of everyday life in the Middle East. Bayat's description of 'street politics' highlights the importance of the domain of the streets in the emergence of practices of unruly politics. (1997) Bayat explores the political agency which is expressed by those who have no 'institutional power of disruption' (ibid, xii), but rather disrupt institutional power constellations with their day-to-day struggles to, sometimes literally, gain a place in society. In a movement of street politics the urban poor and marginalized look for ways to gain access to those material and social goods, and economic opportunities, which lie out of their reach in an official or legal trajectory. In this endeavour they literally take the streets, they re-appropriate parts of public space and public resources of which they have been deprived, sometimes stealthily, sometimes out in the open and by force.

Those who are concerned here are poor, ordinary people living in precarious circumstances, looking for ways to make a living, feed and educate their families, to create a home basis and to freely express their religious or cultural traditions, while suffering from a 'lack of an institutional mechanism through which they can collectively express their grievances and resolve their problems' (ibid, 9). These people live perforce without support of official state institutions and at the same time often deeply distrust any state interference in their lives. Out of fear of regulation, control or discipline by formal state procedures, they search for alternative ways to sustain themselves and gather in informal communities in which they are free to mind their own business. They illegally tap water and electricity, they set up stalls on the side walks of shopping streets, they claim abandoned parcels of land and they occupy vacant houses. The streets are the domain where they meet and form occasional alliances, where shared actions can emerge from a coincidental encounter between different people who happen to find themselves in a similar precarious situation, happen to have common interests, or wish to defend themselves against a common threat (ibid, 17). Bayat illustrates this form of politics with the stories of poor people's struggles for a worthy living in Iran around the period of the Islamic Revolution of 1979. These urban poor are not the political heroes who became known as the ones who carried forward the movement of the revolution. Their struggles were not recognized as making a large contribution to the major political upheavals of their time, but nevertheless had a significant effect on the development of society during and after the revolution in Iran.

Informal politics as understood by Bayat originate in ordinary practices of everyday life, and are not organized in a structured or programmatic way. Community formation in light of this informal politics emerges spontaneously and often develops in very quiet and discrete ways. People who are involved in this kind of informal politics are first and foremost concerned with their individual interests and do not oppose state politics in a direct and public way, as would be the case with a protest movement. They often feel the need to stay under the radar of state officials because of their clandestine activities and prefer their personal safety and wellbeing above the sharing of knowledge and experiences with other precarious groups. They do not feel an urge to achieve publicity for any claims of general interest or to recruit allies with the perspective of a general transformation of society. Nevertheless, their actions are aimed at achieving social progress, and often also manage to establish significant social changes. The urban poor are not only fighting against the injustices inflicted upon them by the dominant classes, but are also pro-actively creating their own opportunities for a better life, which can restrain the privileges of these same dominant groups. In this sense, the direct actions of such precarious groups are not only defensive, but also highly offensive (ibid, 6).

According to Bayat it is important to acknowledge the force of this 'quiet encroachement of the ordinary' in the light of social change, since in times of political transformations such as the Iranian Revolution, the power to establish social change is often undeservedly fully ascribed to general, organized political campaigns and pressure groups.

> A totalizing discourse suppresses the variations in people's perceptions about change, diversity is screened, conflicts are belittled, and instead a grand/united language is emphasized. This suppression of difference by the dominant voice of the leadership has usually worked against the discourse of the ordinary, the powerless, the poor, minorities, women, and other subaltern elements (ibid, 5).

It is precisely by looking at the everyday actions and interactions of a group of people in a precarious position: the urban poor, that Bayat aims to move the understanding of the notion of politics past the options of either well-organized state structures in relation to which the poor are mere victims of their life circumstances, or the promise of a totalizing revolution in relation to which the poor are the promised heroes of absolute change. What brings people together in a movement of street politics is not necessarily consciousness of a collective identity, world view or political dream, but rather the shared determination to overcome singular hardships and develop a self-chosen mode of survival.

> Fundamentally, it is the will to survive and a strong resilience in the face of hardship that motivates the poor to change the pattern of their lives. By doing so, they also change the social environment in which they live and hence the nature of politics. It is true that often, though not always, they proceed individually and quietly, but these individual and quiet actions entail collective and noisy consequences, involving issues of power and politics (ibid, 44).

Other than social movements the urban poor do not form a coherently structured collective around clearly formulated, shared political claims or a collective ideology. In the informal politics of the urban poor 'action' prevails over 'meaning'. (ibid, 7) Conflicting convictions and agenda's are common in the domain of street politics and strong leadership is absent. In general, established political pressure groups like workers unions, political parties or activist organisations do not influence the actions or strategies of the poor who look for ways to get by 'Doing It Yourself', outside of any institutional structure. The actions of the urban poor could be mobilized for the support of a more developed general political programme, but in that case the spontaneous character and the force of direct and unpredictable interventions would be lost. In such a case the political agency of the urban poor could transform into the construction of a social movement, but would lose its self-productivity and unarticulated dynamics.

Partially quoting Gramsci's *Prison Notebooks*, Bayat describes the movement of the urban poor as follows:

> … an open and fleeting struggle without clear leadership, ideology, or structured organization, one that produces significant gains for the actors, eventually placing them in counterpoint to the state. By initiating gradual 'molecular' changes, the poor in the long run 'progressively modify the pre-existing composition of forces, and hence become the matrix of new change' (ibid, 7-8).

However, distancing himself from Gramsci, Bayat states that the activities of the urban poor are not part of a conscious political strategy, but are rather born out of necessity to survive and live a dignified life (ibid, 8). An opposition to state powers can be part of the struggle, but is not a goal in itself. It is in the moment when outrage emerges because of injustices caused by state authorities, that people join forces to resist a common enemy. On the other hand, deals or coalitions with institutional partners are not seen as morally despicable, as long as they serve the practical goals of those looking for improvement in their daily endeavours. Street politics is first and foremost a movement of ordinary people who wish to secure the necessary means to make a living for themselves and their close ones, while the fact that many people struggle simultaneously for their personal survival makes it possible for a shared political sense in these singular struggles to emerge. It is not a deliberate, intentional choice, which is made from the start, to change society in favour of precarious groups. However, it is rather the similar, undeniably pressing circumstances of the moment and the situation, which can be traced in a variety of daily challenges that make political sense.

According to Bayat, the urban poor who are involved in street politics develop their own community structures parallel to the structures of society from which they are excluded, or which they deliberately denounce as unjust or worthless. At the same time, their informal community structures interact with, and sometimes actively counteract, the broader framework of society. State authorities display an ambivalent attitude towards such informal communities. Governments often simultaneously support self-sufficiency and responsibility for the social welfare of citizens, but at the same time carry out disciplinary and restrictive policies in order to monitor the permissive participation of citizens in society. The interaction of informal communities and formal structures is therefore characterized by 'a combined and continuous process of informalization, integration and reinformalization' (ibid, 12). The fact that the urban poor do not form a deliberately organized political movement, which envisions a total revolution, but rather act out of a felt necessity to survive, makes the relationship between formal and informal politics complex and pluriform. It is not a clear cut opposition between state institutions and the people's movement which is at stake here, and therefore one can not simply speak of the 'destructive behaviour of the dangerous classes' in relation to street politics (ibid, 4).

Precarious political agency

Bayat is describing street politics as it takes place amongst the urban poor in developing countries, which are often ruled by undemocratic regimes, but the characteristics of the informal politics, which he describes, can also be found in a Western context and a democratic setting. Also in Western European societies a lack of institutional representative mechanisms can lead certain groups to feel the need to find a solution to their problems in unruly ways and through informal community structures. The voiceless in the institutional domain also generate pressure on the streets in the West, when they do not gain access to established political organisations or social movements. Especially in the recent period of economic crisis, the increasing inequalities between privileged and precarious groups lead to a renewed visibility of revolting urban poor on the streets of European cities, especially in Southern countries like Portugal, Spain and Greece. In the uncomfortable and disturbing act of street nuisances and rioting, it can become apparent who is excluded from the political game, as it is played in the conventional way.

Riots instigated by youth with an immigrant background in various European cities form one of the examples of how marginalized citizens lacking political representation and economic means turn to unruly politics in order to make their grievances public. The lack of programmatic and clearly articulated demands, the focus on the individual interests above the general interest and the ambiguous and sometimes instrumental relation towards state institutions, which Bayat describes, can be related to the uncivil protests of Western European 'rebels without a cause'. The situatedness of their actions, the spontaneous and non-thought out character of their organisation and their precarious life circumstances can be recognized. They can be seen as the young urban poor within a European context, who also form their own informal community structures in the shadows of the larger society. However, in the case of young urban troublemakers in European cities, their encroachment upon authorities can become less quiet and more destructive than the cases described by Bayat. Other than the urban poor who are primarily looking for shelter and means to make a living, and try to build up a satisfactory life, these 'rebels who are denied a cause' often publicly seek recognition of their right to existence as dignified participants in society. It is the right to be noticed as a worthy person, the right to make use of urban space, the right to find access to formal education and jobs, the right to be justly treated by the forces of law, and the right to be respectfully addressed by fellow citizens, which plays a part in their often disruptive and destructive presence in the public domain.

The unruly politics of young urban troublemakers should be understood as this uncivil fight for recognition, rather than as an efficient revolutionary project, aiming at radically new forms of governance. Not only the life circumstances of young urban troublemakers, but also their political agency is precarious. The actors involved in this struggle use unruly political means in order to indicate their state of exclusion, but do not propose structural alternatives to the dominance of neoliberal governance and capitalist economy, for example. Young urban troublemakers do not propose an effective, alternative model for the political organisation of society, they rather try to claim access to the existing structures of society. In this sense, their unruly politics indicates a problem, but does not offer a solution. They are no deliberate radical militants or transformers, despite the fact that their agency can assume militant forms and might be an incentive for political transformation.

The unruly politics of young urban troublemakers is also not about creating a state of total anarchy, but rather about creating 'subversive ruliness'. The translation of justice into a system of laws is not dismissed as useless or unnecessary altogether, it is the functioning of existing laws which is questioned. By operating outside of the domain of legally accepted civic participation, and by sometimes deliberately breaking the monopoly on violence of the police, young urban troublemakers demonstrate a political 'inoperativeness' (Belhaj Kacem, 2006). Their actions are testimonies of exactly those aspects of the political system that do not work, at least not for them. It is a lack within the system of political representation, which becomes painfully clear in their actions of public disturbances, uncivil interactions, or street violence, without an immediate proposal as to how to fill this lack. Such unruly agency can be seen as an enraged and frustrated reaction to the painful distance between an officially recognized political discourse and the complicated social reality in which people living in precarious circumstances find themselves. This is a fundamentally different mode of expression than that of a traditional political insurrection. It is not organized in a structured and programmatic way, no conscious political claims are expressed. Nevertheless, it makes political sense, precisely as a result of its inoperativeness, signaling the flaws within the political system.

We should merit the political sense of unruly political actions, like riots and public disturbances, as acts in themselves, without immediately demanding an effective outcome. In a situation in which structural social changes are hard to imagine for a young generation growing up in times of crisis and polarization, one should not measure their political conscience to their ability to propose alternative models for society, but to their ability to open our eyes for the flaws in the existing political model of representation. The fact that young urban troublemakers are expressing their frustration about the current situation, without a vision of clear-cut alternatives does not make them a-political. It merely shows that one has to start somewhere to express dissent, even if one is not yet sure of the direction one should take. Maybe in our time we should turn the old 1960s mantra of political militancy around. It is not the end of a utopic political dream which justifies the means of a violent uprising, it is rather the means of spontaneous violent riots, which might eventually lead us in the direction of a justified end; a more just and equal political organization of society. This form of spontaneous unruly politics, could eventually provide the inspiration for more revolutionary forms of unruly politics, since it opens up a critical attitude towards the applications of the law, which could lead to new ways to fight for justice outside of the limits of 'civil' and legalized political participation, as a coalitional effort.

References

Bayat, A. 1997. *Street Politics: Poor People's Movements in Iran*. New York, NY: Columbia University Press.

Belhaj Kacem, M. 2006. *La psychose française; Les banlieues: le ban de la République*. Paris: Gallimard.

Blumenkranz, C., Gesse, K. et al. 2011. *Occupy! Scenes from Occupied America*. London and New York, NY: Verso.

Bowlby, J. 1944. 'Forty-Four Juvenile Thieves: Their Characters and Home Life'. *International Journal of Psychoanalysis*.

Cohen, S. 2011 [1972] *Folk Devils and Moral Panics*. Abingdon: Routledge Classics.

Critchley, S. 2007. *Infinitely Demanding; Ethics of Commitment, Politics of Resistance*. London and New York, NY: Verso.

Cross, J. 1998. *Informal Politics: Street Vendors and the State in Mexico City*. Stanford, CA: Stanford University Press.

Decker, S. and Weerman, F. (eds) 2005. *European Street Gangs and Troublesome Youth Groups*. Oxford: Altamira Press.

Duyvendak, J.W., Hurenkamp, M. and Tonkens, E. 2010. 'Culturalization of citizenship in the Netherlands'. In Chebel d'Appolonia, A. & Reich, S. (eds) *Managing ethnic diversity after 9/11: integration, security, and civil liberties in transatlantic perspective*. New Brunswick, NJ: Rutgers University Press, 233-252.

Fernandez-Kelly, P. and Schefner, J. 2006. *Out of the Shadows: Political Action and Informal Economy in Latin America*. University Park, PA: Pennsylvania State University Press.

Gibson, N. 2011. *Fanonian Practices in South Africa: From Steve Biko to Abahlali baseMjondolo*. Scottsville: University of Kwazulu Natal Press/Palgrave Macmillan.

Graeber, D. 2009. *Direct Action: An Ethnography*. Oakland, CA and Edinburgh: AK Press.

Harvey, D. 2012. *Rebel Cities: From the Right to the City to the Urban Revolution*. London and New York, NY: Verso.

Katsiaficas, G. 2006. *The Subversion of Politics: European Autonomous Social Movements and the Decolonization of Everyday Life*. Oakland, CA and Edinburgh: AK Press.

Mouffe, C. 2005. *The Democratic Deficit*. London and New York, NY: Verso.

Naples, N. and Desai, M. 2002. *Women's Activism and Globalization: Linking Local Struggles and Transnational Politics*. London and New York, NY: Routledge.

Neuwirth, R. 2011. *Stealth of Nations: The Global Rise of the Informal Economy*. New York, NY: Pantheon Books.

Neve, G. de 2005. *The Everyday Politics of Labour: working lives in India's Informal Economy*. New Delhi: Social Science Press.

Schinkel, W. 2010. 'The Virtualization of Citizenship'. *Critical Sociology* 36: 265-283.

Strijen, F. van 2009. *Van de Straat: De straatcultuur van jongeren ontrafeld*. Amsterdam: SWP.

6

'WE HATE HUMANS': SOME PROBLEMS IN READING THE 2011 ENGLISH RIOTS WITHIN A RECENT HISTORY OF WORKING-CLASS VIOLENCE

J.D. Taylor

> People aren't scared ...You locked us up, we get stopped and
> searched every day, there's nothing to lose.
> Jaja Soze on the August 2011 riots in his area, *The Grime Report*.

> It is an incontestable fact that if men have found themselves in the
> streets, armed, in a mass uprising, carrying with them the tumult of
> the total power of the people, it has never been the consequence of
> a narrow and speciously defined political alliance.
> Georges Bataille, 'Popular Front in the Street' (1936).

Brixton resident Jaja Soze had his own explanation for the cause of the four days of rioting which spread across English cities across August 2011. Despite 5 people dying and over 4000 arrested, the UK government chose not to hold a public enquiry into the disturbances, with UK Prime Minister David Cameron dismissing the disturbances as mere criminality. Such accusations of violent law-breaking have menaced reports of riots throughout the latter half of the twentieth century, yet in each instance the particular riot itself is cited as being relatively unique for its atypically criminal character. This glitch in contemporary reportage reflects the political response to undermine the validity of the rioters' dissent, and additionally an unease about how 'the streets' themselves become temporarily weaponised and controlled by rioters, often young working-class men in this analysis, who deploy violence as a feature of their protest.

In the rush to fill this void and analytically stamp the August 2011 riots with a digestible explanation, the LSE and Guardian newspaper's *Reading the Riots* report and other analyses have explained causes including revenge against police harassment, unemployment, cuts to benefits, youth services and access to further and higher education and, more tentatively, a new culture of materialistic opportunism as causing the riots. Of course, this begs the question, is there a need for yet another exhaustive analysis of the August 2011 riots, in the wake of so many recent examples? This paper does not provide more evidence regarding the causes of the riots themselves, but instead offers a critique of contemporary riots reporting, and its failures to first, clarify the fundamental element of social class in these disorders; and second, assume the retrospective inevitability of the rioters' behaviour as victims of straitening circumstances. Instead this paper contends that a historical analysis of the riots through the problem of violence and privatisation of public space can contribute to a more nuanced understanding of the August 2011 riots. Additionally, it directs attention to the under-researched enjoyment of violence and 'attitude' using the subculture of English skinheads, with reference to a wider history of working-class aggression and disturbances in the UK. Central to this analysis is alienation in urban areas, and how alienated populations struggle for control and power, through a law-breaking violence which asserts itself both in and on 'the streets'.

The streets, as both a topological and cultural location, has been celebrated for its opportunities of self-expression and escapism from stifling norms of control of the bourgeois family parlour or the industrial factory-owners. From Laura Oldfield Ford's recent *Savage Messiah* artwork through Iain Sinclair, Jonathan Raban, the Situationist International, Walter Benjamin, Charles Baudelaire, down to Thomas de Quincey and many others, a line can be traced in the rich 'psychogeography' and urban '*flâneur*' literature that cites and sites the city streets as a locale for seditious and unruly styles and desires that come to life in the competing bustle of urban identities and ideas. The market, the carnival and the riot have all separately been analysed as locations that facilitate such seditious and unruly styles. Yet outside the eccentricities of rare individuals or the conspiratorial and alcohol and hashish stained ramblings of fringe quasi-political groupings, a deeper historical analysis is needed to explain how alienation works in urban spaces, and how streets are the site of struggle for expression and power for different, conflicting urban populations. After all, 'the streets' is also a synonym for a certain kind of urban authenticity, an unvarnished and unpretentious expression of how things really are or profess to be. In order to explore such a vast interdisciplinary field of study, I use the recent attraction of the August 2011 riots to explore a longer and more ambivalent history of urban disorder in England since the late 1960s. I read the riots within a late twentieth century history of working-class youth violently reclaiming alienated, often privatised, spaces, and examine this problematic of reading resistance and violence using two tools: the phenomena of British skinhead style from 1967-81, and the development of skinhead violence into football hooliganism, to propose how style and attitude provide opportunities to express power, and to be criminalised by the powerful; and the recent concept of 'unruly politics' being developed at the Institute for Development Studies. Reading ambivalent and complex events like the August 2011 riots as 'resistance', where overtly lacking a political nucleus, requires reflection on which accounts of 'resistance' are valorised, and the role of class in making judgements on unruly violence. It finally asks whether criminality and violence can or should be separated in a sanitised sociological reading of contemporary class revolt.

'There's nothing to lose'

A summary of the August 2011 riots themselves will help to begin this investigation. Violent civil disturbances took place from Saturday 6 August to Tuesday 9 August 2011 across English cities, with the majority of offences and disturbances taking place across London, with lesser disturbances taking place in Birmingham, Manchester, Liverpool and elsewhere. They began in Tottenham, North London, following a local protest at a police station against the police shooting of Mark Duggan, a young black man, which led to a street battle between local residents and outnumbered police forces. The spectacular failure of the police to regain control of the streets of Tottenham, symbolised in a burnt-out police car and images of hooded men throwing projectiles and burning materials at a beleaguered police force, distributed by photos and eyewitness-reports rapidly across social media, gave encouragement to other people across the country to occupy the streets and retake power, and desirable consumer items, in the vacuum of control.

Though the rioters did not universally conform to a specific profile, generally they tended to be young men, neither largely black nor white, many of whom had previous criminal records, and came from urban areas suffering high multiple deprivation, as the Guardian-LSE's *Reading the Riots* report and others demonstrate (see Home Office, 2011:3-5; Williams and Cowen, 2012:1-2; Ministry of Justice, 2012, Guardian-LSE, 2011). Of those arrested by October 2011 nationally – which only provides a limited understanding of who actually participated in the riots – 91% were male; 72% were aged between 10-24; ethnic profile tended to be mixed with 40% white, 39% black (though only 32% of arrestees by Metropolitan police described themselves as of white ethnicity); 76% had a previous caution or conviction; and of adults arrested, 35% were claiming out-of-work benefits, and of young people arrested, 64% lived in the 20 most deprived areas in the UK (Home Office, 2011:3-5). Over 5,175 offences were recorded by the police, 68% by London's Metropolitan Police; of these, around 86% of recorded crimes were for burglary and criminal damage, with a total of 4,105 arrested by October 2011 (Home Office, 2011: 3-4; Ministry of Justice 2012). When analysing those arrested – who must not be taken as a wholly representative sample, given that those arrested tended to have previous convictions, and were therefore much easier for police to identify than first-offenders - the rioters shared a common profile: disaffected young men from deprived areas, likely to be unemployed, have criminal records, and facing very limited opportunities regarding education, employment, and housing.

Beyond the crime and arrests statistics, the Guardian and LSE found a discrepancy between the commonly-reported causes of the riots, both in the press and in government reports – gangs, criminality, lack of morality – and those causes which rioters themselves have reported – the death of Mark Duggan, revenge against perceived police harassment through recurrent street stop-and-searches, unemployment, poverty, and a wider sense of betrayal by government unwilling to tackle MPs expenses scandals and bankers bonuses whilst reducing access to further education by cutting the Educational Maintenance Allowance, increasing university tuition fees ninefold in the same number of years, as well as cuts to youth services, benefits, and so on (Guardian-LSE, 2011). Yet the feelings of having nothing to lose, and taking to the streets to express one's anger, consistently recur in English working-class urban neighbourhoods from the late-twentieth century onwards. Instances include: Notting Hill 1958; Lewisham 1977; Chapeltown 1975, 1981, 1987; Toxteth 1981; Brixton 1981, 1985, 1995; Handsworth 1981, 1985, 1991; Broadwater Farm 1985; 'Poll Tax riots' of 1990 which led to the collapse of Margaret Thatcher's Conservative government; London Mayday riots 2001; race riots in Oldham, Bradford and Harehills 2001; the Student Anti-cuts protests 2010-11; and the August 2011 riots more recently (Jefferson, 2012:8-9; Thomas 2012:121). This list of events overlooks the regular disturbances and battles on streets surrounding football grounds across the UK over this period; and those played out in the sectarian contexts of Belfast and Derry in Northern Ireland. Disobedience, a collective no-saying, takes place in the streets, which are transformed from their daily function of places of residence, shopping, and transit, to become politicised, militarised battlegrounds.

The August 2011 riots were noted to be unusual by Guardian-LSE reports firstly for their disproportionate geographic focus, and secondly for the focus on looting (Guardian-LSE, 2011:8). Yet a study of headlines and perceptions following the riots in a location featured in August 2011, Brixton, thirty years previously, details that fears of 'criminality' and looting were also then used to reduce and dismiss the grievances of urban protesters, though with less notable racial subtext than with previous riots (Van Dijk, 1991:91-95; Murdock, 1982:108-109; Thomas, 2012:114-120). The effect of the riots was further amplified by the previous lull in civil disturbances during urban protest, which had since Mayday 2001 been defined by their largely polite, peaceful and predominantly middle-class nature, as was the case in the long series of anti-war protests from 2002 onwards, or the fizzling out of the 'anti-cuts' movement among trade unionists and students over the summer of 2011. The backgrounds of unemployment, previous criminal records and urban marginalisation correlate with other youths involved in criminal disturbances in overtly politicised contexts elsewhere, such as in the case of the riots in Paris' largely racially-segregated working-class *banlieue* neighbourhoods in 2005; or in the profile of young men who used street disturbances and self-immolation to challenge their lack of opportunities and local government harassment and corruption across various North African states in 2011.

Again, as with previous English disturbances, the rioters did not offer or conform to any political message or grouping: their protest consisted of angry conflicts against police and destruction of police property; and disturbances began in response to the death of one or several young men, usually led by other young men of the same social and ethnic background. Rioters acted largely together in union, often abandoning gang divisions, with the effect of scaring the police, government, and wider middle-class society (see interview in Guardian-LSE, 2011:23). They were dismissed as criminals and treated seriously by national governments, which mobilised security forces against them (though slowly – an effect later blamed on low police morale and cuts to police forces). Rioters reported a sense of freedom in taking to the streets, and taking control through attacking policemen, streets and buildings belonging to local councils and businesses – usually chain stores – as well as the general possessions of older working adults and, as I speculate, the symbols of conformism to an alienated and disempowered state of being – cars, small local businesses and houses. This elated feeling of taking power by damaging specific targets reflects what is perceived to manage these urban spaces ordinarily – urban local governments, chain superstores, violent and discriminatory police forces, and their technologies of surveillance. Such an analysis might explain the consistent choice of targets and the pleasure often reported in attacking them, with one rioter interviewed by the Guardian describing it as 'the best three days of my life' (Guardian, 2012). The disturbances simultaneously reflect a lack of obvious political idealism, with rioters themselves citing 'revenge' against police, rather than fairer policing; and attacking the government, rather than fighting for alternative forms of political organisation, as reasons for taking to the streets.

This lack of idealism had made them compelling fodder for subsequent academic analyses by largely middle-class voices not directly involved in the riots or having any personal contact with those caught up in the disturbances (see the somewhat reactionary introduction to Badiou, 2012: 1-6). These accounts are usually written with the purpose of revealing one looming socio-economic or political cause of the riots of which all rioters were seemingly in silent agreement on, be it criminal acquisition or a protest against the public spending cuts of the Coalition government. Instead however, the anger evident could be categorised with other seemingly nihilistic acts like not voting during general elections, as cases of working-class protest, demonstrating at once the futility of striving to be 'listened to' or recognised by authorities, when daily discrimination occurs, yet failing to assent to the common rules of everyday life. This would explain why the community debates held in largely black urban communities, advocated for in the conclusion of the Guardian-LSE's 2011 *Reading the Riots* often failed to reach any agreement about the cause of the riots or the solution going forward, in that their base assumption was an intrinsic problem within the culture and morals of young black men (my view is based on my own observations as a charity coordinator working with disadvantaged young men in inner London, where I was often invited to participate at meetings and radio debates). Based on the data of those arrested, the ethnic profile of the average rioter was mixed, though his social class was not: the *Guardian* found 59% of those arrested came from the 20% areas worst in multiple deprivation (Guardian-LSE, 2011:14). Class and masculinity have been clearly more substantial factors for young people from deprived urban areas in expressing dissatisfaction, dissent and revenge against a discriminatory system of police, politicians and businesses that seem to have barred all access to a better quality of life, be it through education, employment, housing, and a life not trapped in self-perpetuating poverty and welfare dependency.

The challenge for both rioters and the wider democracy is to fully understand the causes of the riots in the first place, which are decades-entrenched in the neoliberal project; and secondly, how to channel and direct the dissenting voice of the young and the poor to deliver substantial structural change. By analysing how the behaviour and dress of rioters have been criminalised – think of the 'masked' 'hoodies' of 'feral underclass' 'chavs', to borrow some of the various popular pejorative terms for young people from deprived areas of England – one can gain a better understanding of how alienation is formed and reacted by style, attitude and identity by marginalised working-class subcultures, and how these subcultures have been analysed and criminalised by governments and media outlets. Skinheads, a violent and defiantly working-class youth subculture of the streets, operative in the UK from the late 1960s up until the early 1980s, present a good place to begin analysing how accusations of criminality and violence conceal a masculine oppositional subculture that attacks middle-class norms, symbols of mainstream power, and enjoys the unruliness of its collective activities.

'This is England! And they don't live here'

The skinhead style emerged as a subculture belonging to mostly (though not exclusively) white working-class youths under the age of 18 living in urban areas. (Filkin, 1969: part 1). It emerged in England during the late 1960s, at a time of growing public media discourses of violence among youth subcultures, preceded by mods and rockers, punks and goths after, and before that teddy boys (Hall & Jefferson, 2006; Mungham & Pearon, 1976). Like these, it combined both a strict fashion style with a 'way of life', in enjoying Reggae and Ska music from the West Indies, football, a certain pride in asserting your own national identity, an endorsement of masculine values, and a pleasure in fighting. Skinheads tended to come from new housing suburbs built during a time of great social upheaval for the working-classes: from the late 1960s and early 1970s, working-class urban communities were intensively demolished and relocated in suburban estates as part of an intensive housing and social improvement programme. By the 1970s however, as recession, power shortages, strikes, inflation, wage freezes and unemployment began to beleaguer the UK economy, frustration, boredom and a sense of abandonment by government was felt by a young generation sick of being told that they'd 'never had it so good', to use Prime Minister Harold Macmillan's 1957 phrase. As one skinhead put it in 1969, in a BBC interview where he reflected on his failure to become a journalist and the lack of opportunities in his neighbourhood, 'it just don't work' (Filkin, 1969: part 2). The style was a response to alienation in space and time, of having both a sense of future and past displaced, out of reach, and requiring reinvention.

Aside from the specificity of their appearance and their greater proclivity to violence, the skinheads were similar to these other subcultures in that they tended to be dominated by young men, and adopted distinct styles of dress, music, identity, and associations with violent fracas. Unlike the rioters discussed earlier, skinheads dressed and associated with each other as a way of life rather than coming together for specific disturbances. Perhaps the rioters might themselves be better understood as belonging to an existing youth subculture – an urban underclass of 'hoodies' facing similar problems to skinheads like unemployment, lack of opportunities, social marginalisation, and conforming to a similar way of life, such as associating in gangs – who came together in the riots, but existed before and after as a subculture. The viability of this hypothesis will be explored in the sections below.

Skinheads were from the outset associated with violence and physical intimidation, of roaming the streets seeking out violence. Their stark stylistic conformity, perhaps like that of the hoodie, reflects a collective posturing that marks both an anti-establishment appearance and the alienated reclamation of streets as politicised territory of authentic life. Nick Knight photographed the skinhead revival in London's East End over 1980-81, a style that combined hardened Mod fashion with West Indian rudeboy influences from 1968 on, during a time of relative prosperity. Skinhead was a style based on a strict adherence to a very specific combination of influences, amongst which, were: American 'preppy' button-down shirts, chinos and slim Sta-prest trousers; slim tailored overcoats and suits derived from UK Mod fashion; a love of Ska, Reggae, as well as odd touches of aristocratic fashion flair, like pork pie hats and silk handkerchiefs in breast pockets, derived from black Caribbean migration to the UK since the Windrush voyage of 1948; as well as polished work boots, and cropped hair – a more straightforward rejection of middle-class hippie fashion and its 'drop-out' anti-work ethos (Knight, 1982). The skinhead style could identify young men from disparate working-class backgrounds, providing a conformity to otherwise bored and alienated young men.

This was closely matched by the importance of territorially grouping into firms around football. A contemporary observation from a football match in 1968 gives a sense of this unusual stylistic and social conformity: 'They all wore bleached Levis, Dr. Martens, a short scarf tied cravat style, cropped hair. They looked like an army and, after the game, went into action like one' (in Knight, 1982:11). Football violence begins from early 1960s, made possible in part by the relative affluence of working-class youth who could afford not just to go to home games, but to travel to away fixtures too. As Nick Knight puts it in his 1982 votive to the subculture, *Skinhead*: 'Football was the major event of the week. It offered all the excitement of an adventure with *"yer mates,"* the chance to display fanatical loyalty to your club, to prove your hardness and win the admiration of your friends. Clashes with the police and opposing supporters, and taking part in the ritual songs and chants of the football ground, together with the opportunity to get drunk and run amok, provided the sort of power and excitement which is normally denied to working class youth' (Knight, 1982:17). Football became not just a tribal hierarchy and social bond among young men, but a kind of battle, not just between the players, but between fans too, providing both an agency for working-class men to take actions into their own hand; a safe space to break social rules that they felt fettered by in their work or unemployed lives; and most importantly, an opportunity to physically vent anger and frustration by fighting other fans present for the same purpose.

Specific strategies over the last thirty years have made skinhead violence more difficult: police surveillance easily identifies known offenders; more regular police patrols and anti-social behavioural orders physically restrict and disperse hostile gatherings; its appearance has become synonymous with racist aggression and is therefore incompatible with mainstream social conformity and employment; and the skinheads too have grown up, and the look largely gone out of fashion, as with other subcultural style of the time. During the early 1980s football violence became a 'moral panic' of the time, and like with 'muggings' and 'youth knife crime' following it, facilitated the introduction of intensive new police powers like banning individuals from certain areas, routine stop-and-searches, the mass introduction of police and local government CCTV surveillance in public areas (Hall et al., 1978; Taylor, 2013:89-91). Notably it also became associated with working-class male behaviour and their perceived lack of morality being the cause of any barriers to employment, opportunities, fair treatment by public authorities, employers and police (Jones, 2011:94).

By the time of the Hillsborough Disaster in April 1989, during which 96 football fans were crushed to death and a further 766 injured following a stampede, the apparatus of working-class alienation was being established. Although caused by overcrowding grounds and, argued the 1989 Taylor report, a fundamental lack of 'police control' (Home Office, 1989:49), it led to the introduction of all-seater ticketed stadia, and a marketised family focus into football which in effect pushed fandom into pubs and into the home, increasingly the most meaningful setting of social interaction and engagement. It was only a year after the 1989 Disaster that Sky Television was set up, with The Sports Channel offering live England football to the nation, at a price, establishing the gradual domestication and suburbanisation of leisure from football grounds and city centres first into pubs and out-of-town retail parks built en masse from the early 1990s across England, then followed by well-equipped home entertainment systems, broadcasting every conceivable type of entertainment into the home, often paid for with cheap credit. All this fits within a privatisation of public space to manage this potentially dangerous alienated youth. One can note that the televisions and games consoles being looted in scenes from the August 2011 riots would be used to play violent video-games like *Call of Duty: Modern Warfare 3* and *Battlefield 3*, where young men can gather together and fight each other online, from the comfort or alienation of their bedrooms, or even that most anti-social and addictive of all hypermasculine video-games, *Football Manager*.

Hoodie horrors

Commentators on the August 2011 riots cited the new use of social media as a cause of the riots, particularly their speed: Blackberry Messenger, Facebook and Twitter have each been cited as aiding the rapid organisation of gathering points for rioters (Guardian-LSE, 2011:30-33; Economist, 2011, para. 2). Although important as aids, it is unlikely that the rioters would not have organised without these, nor that they had no other unique identity. Social media might have benefited a skinhead gathering, but is unlikely that it would have significantly altered the profile of dress, music or attitude that skinheads were able to adopt in general conformity with each other. Instead, what linked the appearance and dress of rioters was the 'hoodie', a sweatshirt with an attached hood, which in the last ten years has become a symbol for the criminal urban underclass youth who have become associated with wearing it.

The outcry that followed David Cameron's more sympathetic call in 2006 for support for young offenders (leading to the 'hug a hoodie' quote wrongly attributed to him) symbolises the great distaste and associations of criminality a garment has with the 'feral underclass', as another Conservative, Ken Clarke, described them (Clarke, 2011, para. 1). And just as skinheads and bikers were exploitatively written about in pulp fiction paperbacks by the New English Library in the 1970s, so hoodies have been 'exploited' as a genre in recent film. Johnny Walker has recently written about British horror's recent demonisation of working-class youth in the 'hoodie horror'. Exemplified by films like *Summer Scars* (2007), *Eden Lake* (2008), *The Disappeared* (2008), *Harry Brown* (2009), *Heartless* (2009), *F* (2010), *Shank* (2010), and *Cherry Tree Lane* (2010), they place hoodies against well-to-do, middle-class citizens who they hunt down, torture and kill (Walker, 2012: 447), mirroring social anxieties about the atavistic violence disenfranchised working-classes might pose, their plots reflecting anxieties around an intrinsic evil in working-class children produced by a morally lax upbringing. Owen Jones has analysed how class explanations over the last thirty years have increasingly used explanations of moral collapse blamed variously on maladjusted immigrants, single-parent mothers, violent video games and other contemporary bogey-men to account for a 'Broken Britain' and its 'social recession', as David Cameron termed it in 2010 (Jones, 2011:78-83; 194). All this serves to provide a conveniently moral rather than socio-economic account of widening wealth inequalities.

Yet whilst Jones analyses the demonisation of the working-classes as a completed process, the skinheads were eschewing the polite passivity of the Victorian notion of a 'deserving poor' which many Conservatives then and now subscribe to. Their use of violence was a deliberate gesture of revenge and rejection of a society which they felt had locked them out. Skinhead violence around football would continue throughout the 1980s, abandoning cropped hair for a more work-friendly 'Casuals' laddish style of the later 1980s and 1990s. Yet football violence and hooliganism became further separate from the fixtures themselves as fans arranged fights away from grounds, with violence rather than sporting success being the focus of interest. Violence and fighting became the weekend attractions of a frustrated working-class masculinity, which felt marginalised from employment and social recognition. Occupying and disrupting the streets was a political expression of communal identity and frustration by working-class young men who felt isolated and trapped by their lives, by their lack of power and opportunities to live a different life and lifestyle to their parents' generation. The streets which had themselves come under increased control by technocratic urban planning by local government from the early-1960s onwards. As an expression of identity, it needed to draw on and invent certain traditions of authenticity and Britishness in order to base its 'proudness' and 'common cause', terms which one young skinhead interviewed in 1969 used to describe his choice of dress and lifestyle (Filkin, 1969: part 2).

Dick Hebdige, whose studies of youth subcultures have become classics of cultural studies to the point of cliché, also wrote about skinhead culture in an article for Nick Knight's eponymous collection. For Hebdige, the skinheads emerged from a specific disempowerment, which they sought to overcome through the adoption of a style that created new rules for its own logic and identity, hinged around authenticity and Britishness: 'skinheads are playing with the only power at their disposal – the power of having nothing (much) to lose. … Contrary to the media stereotype of the mindless skinhead thug, it has its own logic, its own rules and reasons'. Two obsessions dominate the style: 'being *authentic* and being *British*' (Knight, 1982:28).

Yet Hebdige's insight falters where much of the commentators of the August 2011 riots also fail to consider: firstly, the specifically class-defined nature of this alienation at the heart of skinhead identity; secondly, the frequency of violence and civil disturbances in the streets by young working-class men, in various guises and contexts. When the skinhead dressed in an aggressive style and got together with his mates to start fights on hippies, other football fans, groups of Pakistanis, whoever they deemed 'other', they were reacting in an antisocial and aggressive way to a society that didn't provide sufficient access to different types of employment, the culture to engage in further and higher education, and what might give them an independence and stability to develop their own identity. Their reaction was antisocial perhaps because social standards in turn expected them to peacefully and liberally abide with what seemed like an unacceptable and unfair establishment. Hence the hatred of hippies could be read as a reaction against middle-class culture and humanism which sanctioned a peaceful and inoffensive 'playing by the rules' which the skinheads, and later football firms, all dominated by white working-class men, came to reject. Glimpses of these appear in popular football chants by different fans of the 1970s, and since: 'no one likes us, and we don't care' of Millwall; and more curiously, 'we hate humans', a Manchester United fan chant of the 1970s, in response to being labelled by the press as 'animals' (Robbins, 1984:74).

Their behaviour is not a political response to circumstances, and it eschews political reasoning in favour of the efficacy of actions and emotions like revenge and violence. As Hebdige puts it, 'Though they may be, at times, loosely allied to a particular kind of politics, that alliance is uneven and transitory. … Most skinheads (like the majority of young people in Britain) couldn't care less about organised politics of *any* kind' (Knight, 1982:33). Yet it would be a mistake to describe the unruliness of skinheads or hoodie rioters as wholly anti-political, given that they constituted a profound challenge to the order and consensus of the *polis*. It is a challenge that stems from a politics of alienation and oppression/control against police and government by a section of working-class and unemployed males. What can be made then of a political understanding of these disorganised, unruly displays of violence?

Unruly politics

Making critical sense of something as atavistic and incoherent as urban riots or an aggressive youth subculture that lasted little over 15 years is often incompatible with the assumptions of liberal political thought: the voices caught above often willed violence and anger for the pleasure of their expenditure alone, sometimes without a greater political or social intent. This problem of imposing political definitions on the streets correlates with new research on 'unruly politics' at the Institute of Development Studies (IDS) since 2011, which has sought to understand the kind of ambiguous political acts of groups which do not conform to traditional definitions of 'political' actions by the state, international NGOs, or the old left. As Mariz Tadros puts it, unruly politics marks a new global political phenomena which sees 'the masses engaging through spaces outside state and civil society and through a different new form of agency' (Tadros, 2011: para. 1). Whilst it can threaten to damage police and government forces, it is not intrinsically attached to a democratic or 'progressive' goal (in the Western liberal sense, as Tadros uses it), nor is it representative of the population at large, and is often led by reactionary movements. An example of unruly politics would be the mobilisation and organisation of the 'Arab Spring' democratic protests, which refused to engage existing political parties and civil society bodies, choosing to form new assemblies instead.

As Tadros (2011: paras. 1-3) defines it, unruly politics involves creating new political spaces for contestation where these have been lost or removed by states or civil society. However in the case of young working-class men in inner-city England, there had not been any loss of political space to speak as a civic voice – rather, it had not existed to begin with. There is a sense of abandonment compounded by decades-sustained unemployment, poor community relations with police and local government, inflammatory reportage of immigration levels in the mainstream press, and a frustration at a basic lack of employment and education opportunities. The riots of August 2011, like previous English riots, did not conform to any existing political message and so might be termed 'unruly politics', breaking the rules of the status quo and, in their event, narrating a political message of anger and frustration at socio-economic problems that are generations-deep. Disorder and violence obscure this narrative however, which leads to the pessimistic probability that such riots will occur again as benefits and public spending cuts continue to be targeted at working-class, largely northern, constituencies from April 2013 on; and that these riots will again be dismissed as atypical events of criminality and moral collapse, with any racial characteristics inflated.

Can a politics therefore be developed out of this unruliness? Yes, argues Alex Shankland, another member of the IDS in his account of the #OccupyLSX movement in London, provided it abandons the 'scariness' of its mere unruliness in favour of a 'subversive ruliness' that tackles authorities directly. The subversive efficacy of OccupyLSX (and as he implies, other peaceful disobedience groups like UK Uncut) lies in that 'it challenges the claims of the powerful to rule by right, by unmasking the unruliness with which they have used their political and financial power' (Shankland, 2012: para. 10). A more polite form of dissidence could be more effective in highlighting unemployment and police discrimination by detailing how these broke the written rules of the establishment. But such a response assumes that, if exposed, authorities will have to 'play by the rules', an unusually optimistic view of political management. Long after

OccupyLSX was evicted, neither bankers nor politicians had introduced any structural transformations to prevent a future credit crisis, collapse of banks, abuse of parliamentary privileges, or independent regulation of the press. Secondly, it would require formal and organised social assemblies among working-class youths themselves, which at this stage feels like a remote probability. As Shankland argues, such a political movement could emerge out of communication between the older, middle-class and less unruly #OccupyLSX movement and similar anti-cuts activists, and the youth involved in the riots. But neither social side has so far managed to organise together, despite common political objectives, perhaps because of base assumptions about the propriety and ethics of unruliness, violence and civil disobedience, as well as more general divides in terms of cultural language, class and age. Shankland is correct to warn that 'mobilisation that challenges the state but leaves streets unsafe and refuse uncollected will rapidly lose legitimacy' (Shankland, 2012: para. 11). But the advocates of 'subversive ruliness' offer somewhat feeble success stories that have since been outmanoeuvred by larger political and military forces, like the indigenous people of Acre State, Brazil (Shankland, 2012: para. 12), or the democratic movement Tahrir Square (Tadros, 2011: paras. 7-8).

Ultimately, what might be gained from the two instances of youth-led violence above, with their seemingly nihilistic and diverging ends? In the first case, that class is a key factor for analysing civil disturbances, and should be considered even where a dominant racial motif may appear (cf. Foucault, 2003:60-62; 80-83). Secondly, that 'unruliness' and 'revenge' are central expressions of riots through damage of property and attacks on police on the streets. Third, that in being unruly, such disturbances do not serve a purpose or set out a goal, nor do they make a singular demand, say compared to the more traditionally-understood 'protests' of mass-marches and petitions. As such, making definitions or divinations of its politics is only to impose one's own inferences based on agenda. Given the real probability of such riots recurring soon, the challenge for liberal, socialist and anarchist academics is to address how this problem of unruliness can be harnessed by future democratic political movements in the streets, beyond either nihilistic window-smashing or inoffensive protest placards.

References

Badiou, A. 2012. *The Rebirth of History*, trans. by G. Elliot. London and New York, NY: Verso.

Bataille, G. 1986. *Visions of Excess: Selected Writings 1927-1939*. ed. and trans. by A. Stoekl. Minneapolis, MN: University of Minnesota Press.

Clarke, K. 2011. 'Punish the rioters, but address our social deficit too', *Guardian Comment is Free*, 5 September. Available: www.guardian.co.uk/commentisfree /2011/sep/05/punishment-rioters-help. Last accessed 29/07/2014.

Economist, The. 2011. 'The Blackberry Riots'. 13 August.

Filkin, D. (dir.). 1969. 'Man Alive: What's the Truth about Hells Angels and Skinheads?', *BBC*, transmitted 10 December. Excerpts of documentary available: http://www.youtube.com/watch?v=EYJ_ThM0Ffk [part 1, last accessed 02/01/2013]; http://www.youtube.com/watch?v=xxlEXd4fx9U&NR=1 [part 2, last accessed 02/01/2013].

Foucault, M. 2003. *'Society Must Be Defended': Lectures at the Collège de France 1975-76*. Trans. by David Macey. New York, NY: Picador.

Guardian, The, and the London School of Economics (LSE). 2011. *Reading the Riots: Investigating England's Summer of Disorder*. 14 Dec.

Guardian, The. 2012. 'Reading the Riots: "I have no doubt the riots will happen again" – video'. 2 Jul. 2012. Available: http://www.guardian.co.uk/uk/ video/2012/jul/02/reading-riots-video. Last accessed 02/01/2013.

Hall, S., et al. 1978. *Policing the Crisis: Mugging, the State, and Law and Order*. London: Palgrave.

Hall, S. and Jefferson T. (eds.). 2006 [1975]. *Resistance through Rituals: Youth subcultures in post-war Britain*. Second Edition. Abingdon and New York, NY: Routledge.

Home Office. 2011. *An Overview of Recorded Crimes and Arrests Resulting from Disorder Events in August 2011*.

_____ . 1989. *The Hillsborough Stadium Disaster 15 April 1989: inquiry by Rt. Hon. Lord Justice Taylor. Interim Report*. London: HMSO.

Jefferson, T. 2012. 'Policing the Riots: from Bristol and Brixton to Tottenham, via Toxteth, Handsworth, etc'. *Criminal Justice Matters* 87:1. 8-9.

Jones, O. 2011. *Chavs: The Demonization of the Working Classes*. London: Verso.

Knight, N. 1982. *Skinhead*. London, New York, NY and Sydney: Omnibus Press.

Ministry of Justice. 2012. *Statistical Bulletin on the Public Disorder of 6th-9th August 2011*. Last updated 13 September.

Mungham, G. and Pearson G. (eds.). 1976. *Working Class Youth Culture*. London, Henley and Boston MA: Routledge & Kegan Paul.

Murdock, G. 1982. 'Disorderly Images'. In Sumner, C. (ed.) *Crime, Justice and the Mass Media*. Cambridge: Institute of Criminology.

Oldfield Ford, L. 2011. *Savage Messiah*. London: Verso.

Robbins, David. 1984. *We Hate Humans*. London: Penguin.

Shankland, A. 2012. 'OccupyLSX, Unruly Politics and Subversive Ruliness' *Our*Kingdom, 19 Jan. Available: http://www.opendemocracy.net/ourkingdom /alex-shankland/occupylsx-unruly-politics-and-subversive-ruliness. Last accessed 02/01/2013.

Soze, J. 2011. 'London Riots – Jaja Soze talks about Brixton riots 2011', *Grime Report TV*, 9 August. http://www.youtube.com /watch?v=04kqYW2PN30 . Last accessed 02/01/2013.

Tadros, M. 2011. 'The Politics of Unruly Ruptures', *United Nations Research Institute for Social Development*, 5 November. http://www.unrisd.org/80256B3C005BE6B5/%28httpNews%29/6CACEA99340950AAC125795D00581C33. Last accessed 02/01/2013.

Taylor, J.D. 2013. *Negative Capitalism: Cynicism in the Neoliberal Era*. Winchester: Zero.

Thomas, S. 2012. 'A War on Babylon 1981'. In Briggs, D. (ed.). *The English Riots of 2011: a Summer of Discontent*. Hook: Waterside.

van Dijk, T. A. 1991. *Racism and the Press*. London and New York, NY: Routledge.

Walker, J. 2012. 'A Wilderness of Horrors? British Horror Cinema in the New Millennium'. *Journal of British Cinema and Television* 9:3. 436-456.

Williams, N. and Cowan, N. 2012. 'Manchester Riots 2011 and the Index of Multiple Deprivation'. *Radical Statistics* 106. 30-48.

7

BLACK OUTBREAK

Dhanveer Singh Brar

I. 'The Whites have become Black'

Friday 12th August 2011. The BBC's *Newsnight* programme convened a panel to reflect on the five days of rioting that had taken place on the streets of England over the previous week. Chaired by Emily Maitlis, the invited guests passed judgement on the events which began in Tottenham with a peaceful protest over the shooting to death of Mark Duggan by the Metropolitan Police as part of Operation Trident. The most memorable intervention on *Newsnight* that evening came from David Starkey. Taking up the role of caricatured right wing historian, Starkey revelled in diagnosing the causes of the riots. With his appeal to Enoch Powell sliding between romanticism and hysteria, it became clear that more was at stake than Starkey conducting a clinic on the health of the nation. Watch the *Newsnight* episode again and it is possible to see that he is exhibiting some strange symptoms of his own. Starkey has come down with a case of something quite serious. It might be that he is suffering from the very thing he is trying to diagnose.

Starkey's performance as both clinician and patient is encapsulated in his infamous announcement: 'the whites have become black'. In arriving at this formulation, Starkey was attempting to isolate the specific substance which he believed had set off the rioting. But as he looked to identify that substance he reached fever pitch, producing the lyrical melancholy – dressed up as plain speaking British historicism – of his performance. The substance Starkey was pursuing on *Newsnight* was marked in all the intellectual energy he used to make the claim that 'the whites have become black'. He described how this substance had caused the dissolution of an apparently previously secure racial and colour distinction, but only in order to reify the natural order that distinction seemingly represents. For Starkey the type of social, material and psychic breakdown evidenced in the riots had been on the horizon for some time. It had been on the cards because poor whites – or 'chavs' (Jones, 2011) – have been exposed to a substance made by black culture. This substance is 'violent', 'destructive', 'nihilistic', and all of its characteristics can be ascribed to its inherent blackness.

This black substance, which lives out on the street and within black culture, had gone to work like a foreign pathogen on 'chavs'. Its infectious qualities represent a threat to the coherency of the country. The way it has invaded and divorced 'chavs' from their whiteness is indicative of the way Starkey's white Britain is now in exile, foreign to itself.

During his diagnosis Starkey pinpointed where he thinks this violent, destructive and nihilistic black substance is concentrated. It is black music which is the problem. To be more specific, it is a form of street music Starkey places under the heading 'rap'. The dysfunctionality of black culture in Britain manifests itself as a dysfunctional substance within rap music. It is through prolonged exposure to the substance, which in many ways *is* the music, that anyone, no matter their colour or racial category, can be transformed into a black. For Starkey becoming this type of black is a precondition for the social breakdown which leads to rioting.

Starkey was not making these claims in isolation. His appearance on *Newsnight* was the most spectacular apex of a general discourse which collapsed rioting, black culture, blackness and black music into the production of an anti-social substance. Writing in *Prospect* magazine, David Goodhart ascribed the causes of the riots to two mutually generative factors. The first was 'an angry, destructive, self-limiting background thud' which is inherent to rap music (Goodhart, 2011). There is for Goodhart something at work within the sonic qualities of the music he chooses to call rap, which renders it incompatible with proper modes of social comportment. All that is carried in the 'thud' operates in tandem with a 'more combustible material in the black, or rather African Caribbean culture of the inner city' (Goodhart, 2011). According to Goodhart not only is there something inherently unstable in inner city black music, but that culture and the people who operate within it are equally erratic. Whilst he is not clear as to whether it is the thud of rap which creates the combustibility of the culture, or if the music is a transmission device for a material which makes certain types of black culture and black people more combustible, the result is the same: 'the twitchiness of the black street' (Goodhart, 2011).

The diagnostic language used by Goodhart was also in evidence in Paul Routledge's piece for *The Mirror*. The riots for him were a result of the damage rap music has done to the textures of everyday life, or what could be called street life, in the city. The 'pernicious culture of hatred around rap music' creates entities who bubble away, constantly perched on the cusp of violence: 'Tension is always there. You see it in their eyes, hear it in their voices, and it can break out over the most trivial issues. I've been on the receiving end, threatened on a number 12 bus to Peckham for no apparent reason' (Routledge, 2011).

Before addressing the discourse on rioting, race, blackness and music as exemplified by Starkey, Goodhart and Routledge, it is important to clarify some of the genre related terms being used here. When each of these commentators cite 'rap' music they are deploying a generic term which does not account for the degrees of differentiation between the forms of black music in Britain which could be placed under the loose heading 'rap'. For the purposes of this piece I am going to work on the assumption that when they speak and write of 'rap', what Starkey, Goodhart and Routledge are referring to – to the extent that they have any clue – is grime. The reason for making this assumption is that in the decade preceding the August 2011 riots grime was the leading iteration of black music in London and across the UK.[1] These commentators appear to be tapping into a moral panic which accompanied the music over that same period (Hall et al., 1978). The diagnosis Starkey et al. give of grime does not position the music as a form for depicting images of violence, destruction and nihilism which are generally considered to be inherent aspects of black culture. The music is not thought to be reflective of black pathological tendencies. Instead they work on the basis that grime *is* pathology. Grime *is* pathology because the black people who make it and the areas of the city they live in *are* pathology. It is this conceptual assumption within the discourse on race, riots and street culture which allows these commentators to claim there is a black substance at work in grime which was the underlying cause of rioting. Starkey, however, added a further dimension to this moral panic. The black pathogen which is carried in grime does represent a set of social problems which are racially and colour specific. But for Starkey this pathogen is not restricted to the black people who generate it. The blackness, which is to say the pathology, that is grime can traverse the racial dynamics of biological, cultural and colour difference. What Starkey is saying is that that which makes grime black, and therefore pathology, has incubated for so long on the streets in certain parts of Britain, that some whites are white no longer.

Over the course of this chapter, I want to take up a position with regards to the discourse on the 2011 riots, blackness, grime and pathology which is counterintuitive. Although it might be counterintuitive, it is a necessary move to make in order to address what is at stake when race, colour, street culture and law are invoked in this way. The position I want to take up is as follows: Starkey, Goodhart and Routledge are in many ways right. Much of what they had to say in the aftermath of the 2011 riots is correct. It is just that they are right for all the wrong reasons. I would go further and state that they have no idea if their diagnoses are right or wrong, or why they might be both right and wrong. By running a clinician's eye over black culture in Britain, and issuing a

---

[1] Emerging in the early 2000s out of the Bow, E3 area of East London, Grime is considered to be part of the range of musical iterations which make up the Hardcore Continuum (jungle, UK garage, 2step). The major pioneers of the sound included MCs and producers such as Wiley, D Double E and Dizzee Rascal. After gaining an underground following, Grime achieved mainstream critical recognition with Dizzee Rascal's album *Boy in Da Corner* winning the 2003 Mercury Music Prize. See Dan Hancox, *Stand Up Tall: Dizzee Rascal and the Birth of Grime* (Amazon Media, 2013).

series of statements on grime as the generator of a highly dangerous mode of street comportment, Starkey, Goodhart and Routledge tuned into a particular set of frequencies. These are frequencies which they were never really prepared for, because of the constraints they use to flatten out the perceptions of black culture and grime.

What the degrees of intimacy and distance between their pronouncements on grime and the lived experience of the music reveals is the way these commentators put into play the very possibility they are trying to annul. This is especially the case with David Starkey. His performance on *Newsnight* opens up, in the process of trying to shut down, the fact that there is a substance at work in grime, as the music of London's black streets, which makes blackness generalisable. Blackness - a racial condition which is supposed to be the problem of those who have the colour black, for whom blackness is their problem and renders them problems - can be passed on. It can be passed on to those chavs for whom the street is also a fundamental grounding point, through a substance transmitted in and as the music. This is why it becomes necessary to state that Starkey et al. were both right and wrong. Grime is violent, criminal and black, but only in the sense that it is self-weaponising, fugitive and encounters and escapes the constraints of a discourse on black pathology. The music steals away, spreads into the streets like an infectious outbreak, and as Starkey says, but in ways he will never fully comprehend, turns whites into blacks.

The process of working with and against the reduction of blackness and black music to criminality is shaped by four questions: What is the substance that black people have which makes them a street problem? Is this the same substance which makes grime a black street problem? What is the problem with the idea that whites can become black? How does grime conduct this transformation out on the streets of London?

II. Form 696

Whereas Starkey, Goodhart and Routledge would claim to be producing social commentary, it would be more accurate to describe it as moral panic. But to stop there when addressing the post 2011 riots discourse misses the point of giving someone like Starkey such close attention. The type of moral panic he and others exemplified is too easy to dismiss as unsubstantiated hot-air. Instead I want to argue that their diagnoses form part of a larger circuit which has a more concrete and pernicious relationship to black music, and as a result black social life, in cities such as London. Moral panic dressed up as informed pronouncements on black social life can be situated along a sliding scale of activity which includes the production of social policy about, and the everyday policing of, those forms of life we choose to call black. The point here is not to claim that Starkey and those like him are the product of an atmosphere created by policy and policing, or that their public announcements directly influence policy. What I am reaching for is the way all of these activities form part of a circuit which encircles and contains black life, whilst at the same time black life, by way of its existence, constitutes a reticence which resists containment.

In terms of naming grime as the black pathology which caused rioting amongst blacks and former whites, Form 696 operates as part of this containment circuit. Form 696 was a risk assessment exercise introduced by the Metropolitan Police force in 2004. It was designed to address the 'risk' of criminal activity and violence at any music event across the city. The form allowed the Met to pre-emptively gather information about performers and audiences from the promoters of a music event. Failure to comply would lead to its closure, with a £20,000 fine and possible jail sentence for the license holders. Journalist Dan Hancox, writing in *The Guardian*, *The Daily Note* and *Woofah* has raised the profile of this issue, detailing the effects it has had upon grime and other related genres of black music in London. At first there was a blanket enforcement of the form across all music venues and events. Amongst its most disconcerting elements was the request that license holders provide information about the racial make-up of the audiences expected at their event, and if any performers held criminal records. Added to that was the need for promoters to detail the genres of music to be played at their event. The suggested examples listed on this section of the form would generally be regarded as black, such as bashment, R'n'B and garage.

The Met initially were heavily criticised over Form 696. The most vocal opposition came from the established elements in the music industry which considered themselves safe, legitimate and resented the additional administrative complications the form presented. Alongside this there were also accusations levelled at the Met of racially profiling music fans and performers. The decision was made to produce a second version of the form, which as Hancox reports, was more subtly crafted:

> They went away. They came back. They announced that actually, sorry chaps, they would stop bothering live music fans across the board, instead narrowing their focus to 'large promoted events between 10pm and 4am which feature MCs and DJs performing to recorded backing tracks'. Or 'grime nights', as they are sometimes known (Hancox, 2010).

He continues:

> It's no exaggeration to suggest that the period 2004-09 represents a systematic and deliberate attempt by the Metropolitan Police to remove music performed largely by young black men from the public sphere. [...] It's bureaucracy as a weapon. (ibid).

Form 696 was more or less successful in excluding grime from public space in London. Its success was not necessarily a direct result of the technical procedures laid out by the Met. Rather the very existence of the form generated an atmosphere of suspicion around grime. Venues became increasingly nervous about putting on grime nights and even went to the extent of self-policing by banning the music entirely. The fact that some performers did have criminal records, however minor, gave the Met licence to stop and search them as they arrived at or left shows. The Met even went as far as to intervene in charity organised events featuring grime artists (Topping, 2012; Hancox, 2009).

Hancox's likening of Form 696 to a bureaucratic weapon is apt, in that a music which was designed for large gatherings in nightclubs was restricted to having a pirate radio presence. As I will go on to argue, this did not initially place a bar on the rate of sonic innovation in grime, but it was clear evidence of how the music was deemed to be to too volatile to exist in London's public spaces, primarily because it was considered to be too black.

From examining the case of Form 696, it is possible to understand how the discriminatory policing of grime operates from within the same system of logic as the pathological discourse produced by Starkey at al. They constitute different intensities of that system. The response from those looking to defend grime from this logic has generally involved taking up two positions. The first is exemplified by the journalism of Hancox. This entails, quite correctly, pointing out that there is little rationale for devices such as Form 696. The evidence of increased likelihood of violence at grime nights was minimal at best. The problem is that something like Form 696 does not require much in the way of evidence. It becomes a self-justifying measure for the Met police. Once its processes are set in motion, it is designed to reproduce, in the eyes of the law, the very social problems it is meant to police. In this respect Form 696 is an iteration of the Met police's continued use of racial profiling when deploying stop and search methods (Akwagyiram, 2012; Townsend, 2012).

The second response from those defending grime is aimed at the types of media commentary produced by Starkey, Goodhart and Routledge. The counter argument runs that those who think grime is a direct cause and therefore a manifestation of inherent black criminality, are severely misguided. The music is not a generator of the pathology which lead blacks and former whites in rioting. Instead grime reflects an environment in which there are a number of social problems. It is more accurate, so this line goes, to think of grime as a form of reportage from areas of the city where poverty and crime are concentrated. In this respect it is merely the representation of a bombastic worldview, the hyper-reality of those who are often unaccounted for except when they are considered socially problematic.

Whilst I can understand why the second type of defence of grime is felt to be necessary, it is a somewhat dissatisfactory position to take. The dissatisfaction stems from the way the defence of grime as reportage often reads like an active misinterpretation. It takes on the appearance of an alibi for someone whom you suspect might be guilty of the charge after all. What is often bypassed in this instance is the phonic materiality of grime. There is a lack of attendance to the way the music is made, the way it works, and the effects it produces. This inability to listen to grime whilst defending it means there is no troublesome encounter with what I call its self-weaponisation, fugitivity and blackness. Neither is there any troublesome encounter with the trouble it causes Starkey and the Met's pathological constraints.

III. The sonic ecology of Grime

In order to tune into grime's capacity to cause – or rather to be – trouble, it is best to turn to music journalism on the genre. Writers in this field were concerned with what made grime the latest iteration of black music in Britain, and as such they were attentive to its innovations in sonic form and content. Music journalists though are not musicologists. They do not study the sonic activity of music as a set of technical exercises in isolation. Instead there is a sociological tendency in music journalism to situate a new genre within extra-musical fields of reference. Although the defence of grime as reportage did emerge through music journalism, I would argue there was also a tendency within the field to take a more ambivalent attitude towards its social effects. In the case of grime, writers placed an emphasis on geographical and social environment. Although it is not always made explicit, there are moments where the analysis switches from addressing grime as the product of an ecology, to thinking of grime as a means of producing that ecology.

Writing in *The Wire* magazine, Simon Reynolds opened his primer on grime with an account of its geographical setting:

> Its absolute heartland consists of a few square miles in that part of East London not served by the Tube. In truth it's a parochial scene, obsessed with a sense of place, riven by internecine conflicts and territorial rivalries (the intense competitiveness being one reason Grime's so creative) (Reynolds, 2009).

Reynolds plays on a sense of grime's isolation. Not only did the music emerge in a detached part of the city, but that detachment gave it its unique qualities. Initially with little or no relation to an exterior world, the music was severely inward looking, determining its own patterns. The resulting tensions, according to Reynolds, gave grime its hyperbolic productivity.

Martin Clark, in his grime and dubstep column for *Pitchfork*, extended the combination of isolation and tension in Reynolds account. He did so by describing grime as a 'microcolony within a city so culturally insular vast swathes of Londoners are oblivious to its way of living' (Clark, 2005). This incisive synthesis of biological language from Clark lends itself to a conception of grime as self-generative and potentially infectious.

Discussing Lethal B's 'Pow!', Dan Hancox makes a direct link between ecological setting and the sonic content of grime:

> 'buss' meaning to fire a gunshot, bust a move, or strike out, express yourself – find space and freedom. Grime in its first flash of youth was thrilling because it was claustrophobic, a hectic cacophony of beats and synth stabs, channelling the high-rise tension of tower blocks, the limited horizons and possibilities. But just like real claustrophobia, it demands freedom – and space (Hancox, 2011).

Hancox destabilises the line between geography and class to argue that grime's isolation and restrictions gave it a sonic potency which was violent yet productive.

Whilst it might not have been a conscious feature of writing on grime, there was certainly a particular approach taken to the music in this field. Music journalism on the genre seemed to collapse its emergence in a specific part of the city (East London), terrain (housing estates, high rise tower blocks), social and economic conditions, and the myopia of the scene, into the phonic materiality of the music. All of these elements seemingly fed into the way it functioned sonically. From this perspective it becomes difficult to sustain the idea that grime is only reflective of these ecological factors. There is a trace, in the writing of Reynolds, Clark and Hancox, of the music as an active entity. Grime does not necessarily report on but makes a mode of social comportment.

If grime makes a mode of social comportment, it is one which is widely considered to be black and pathological. This was certainly the case for Starkey, Goodhart and Routledge when they cited grime as the cause for rioting amongst blacks and former whites. A similar logic applied to the Met's policing of grime through the use of paperwork. Form 696 criminalised grime by working on the assumption that the music was already criminal and would thus only attract violent, anti-social, black elements. To repeat, the task here is not to defend grime by countering this logic, but to counter-intuitively complicate it. This means engaging with this pathological discourse as one which is correct, but also so out of sync that it misses the point.

This requires attending to the accusation that grime is violence. To rephrase that sentence, it requires attending to the ways in which grime is violent. Writer and deputy editor of *The Wire*, Derek Walmsley addressed this issue in a paper he delivered at the University of East London in November 2011. Basing his paper on what he referred to as grime's prime period in London (2003-2007), Walmsley examined the relationship between violence in the form of the music and its cultural associations with violence. He did this by drawing on the content of grime lyrics, the structural organisation of those lyrics, and the way they operated as part of the soundscape of grime.

For Walmsley the music's lyrical content was shaped to a large extent by the available forms of delivery. Over the 2003-2007 period grime MCs predominantly used the AAAA/BBBB rhyme scheme. This was determined by the sonic composition of grime riddims. As opposed to the standard form of U.S. hip-hop, grime operated at a much higher beats per minute rate (usually 140 bpm). Due to the greater time and space, in US hip-hop rappers were able to embellish their lyrics and rhyme structures. The sonic content of grime's more claustrophobic 'coldness and rigour' meant MCs in East London had much less room (Reynolds, 2009). Thus their lines needed to fit within this structure but also carry the necessary drive to develop a unique vocal style or flow.

The AAAA/BBBB rhyme scheme was taken on within a grime scene which was determined by the ecological factors set out above. Hyper localisation, intense rivalries, and a musical community defined by reputation, all fed into grime's adoption of the competitive Jamaican soundsystem culture style of MC battles as its main performative mode. Walmsley argues that although the chosen rhyme scheme mitigated against the use of the word 'violence' itself, the combination of tight soundscape, social environment and performative setting, meant MCs used their lyrics as 'synonym engines' for violence (Walmsley, 2011). Grime of this period became notorious because MCs packed their bars with references to guns, knives and general violent acts. Added to this many riddims were built around samples of ammunition being loaded or fired.

The question of violence in grime, according to Walmsley, is not necessarily connected to the violence of these lyrical allusions to weapons. Due to the way in which the soundscape siphoned the MCs delivery, the references to guns and knives arrived so frequently and at such pace as to become almost meaningless. Rather he argues that what took place was the weaponisation of the lyrical delivery itself. MCs were not so much producing relentless attacks in terms of lyrical content, but instead overloading themselves with gun and knife references in order to fire off their lines like ammunition. At stake in grime was not just the choice of language, but the delivery of what Reynolds calls 'word bullets' (Reynolds, 2009).

At its peak between 2003-2007 grime was violent. There were violent operations at work in the music. Grime was designed to weaponise itself and its protagonists. But the violence Walmsley maps out is not the equivalent of the pathological discourse of violence, of black violence, of black as violence, that became attached to the genre. Within this pathologisation there was a refusal to listen carefully to the phonic materiality of grime and the ways its soundscape is determined by its own internally negotiated set of terms. When Starkey or the Met inadvertently tune into these 'word bullets' they only hear a confirmation of what they suspected all along: a violence, criminality and nihilism inherent to the black things that make this music, which if not contained, is in danger of breaking out and infecting whites.

IV. Pirate radio, audio virology and pathologised blackness

The relationship between violence and weaponised form, grime as a product and productive of an ecology, and the pathological discourse of racial disorder, outbreak and control, are the central features of the genre set out so far in this chapter. In order to consider the conceptual significance of these features, it is worth turning to the work of Steve Goodman. In his *Sonic Warfare*, Goodman maps out what he calls an 'audio virology', which lends itself to the ways weaponisation, ecology and pathology are at stake in grime (Goodman, 2010, xix). He does so by paying close attention to the phonic materiality of music produced in certain types of modern urban environments. The case Goodman makes for audio virology is that the music produced in these settings animates collectivised forms of violence and fear which are already present. The way an audio virus moves across this terrain in the form of 'dread' both induces and frustrates the attempt to pathologise these forms of music (Goodman, 2010: xiv).

Audio virology is the product of a 'contagious nexus' generated by the ubiquity of housing estates, ghettos, slums, favelas and shantytowns under the conditions of global capitalism (Goodman, 2010: xx). Within these settings there is a proliferation of sound system cultures which develop unique modes of rhythmic organisation. Goodman zooms in on the moment where this contagious nexus of urban environment and sound system rubs up against capital. For him it is in this friction that an audio virology is set loose. What takes place during these antagonistic moments is that the fear and violence already attached to the setting is sonically reorganised in a way that allows it to cut through and reorder the environment:

> The production of vibrational environments that facilitate the transduction of the tensions of urban existence, transforming deeply engrained ambiances of fear and dread into other collective dispositions, serves as a model of collectivity that revolves around affective tonality and precedes ideology (Goodman, 2010, xx).

Goodman points to a reorganisation of populations that is fundamentally rhythmic. Ahead of ideological doctrine, it is the vibrational practices of a given sound system culture which animate new dispositions. The resulting 'model of collectivity' is difficult to identify for those not in sync with the new rhythmic propositions. The key is the way fear and violence are reformed into collectivity through the use of 'bass materialism' (Goodman, 2010: 28). As a generator of the nexus, bass materialism offers a 'more basic power of organised vibration'

(Goodman, 2010: 172). This power is, for Goodman, 'subpolitical' in that it does not appear to offer a coherent program (Goodman, 2010: 172). Yet its vibrational qualities allow populations to 'attract and congeal' in ways which are customarily ascribed to formal political ideologies. The way Goodman maps out audio virology seems to conceive of populations within urban sound system environments as collective organisms. The phonic materiality of these cultures operates like a contagion. It reorders violence and fear into a form of 'dread' which rather than repelling, congeals groups in ways which do not always register.

Goodman brings audio virology to bear on grime, and in particular the use of pirate radio as a broadcast technology for the music. With the enforcement of Form 696, pirate radio became increasingly important to the productivity of grime. Pirate radio sustained the genre and played a vital part in its popularity. Even in this format grime operated in a problematic relationship to the law, with stations deploying a range of tactics to avoid a combination of broadcasting license authorities and police (Mason, 2008). Goodman argues that in this respect pirate radio was a perfect medium for grime. It allowed the music to enhance its virological qualities. As a result grime became involved in a phono-biological conflict with the attempt to police broadcast systems. Goodman describes the conjunction of grime and pirate radio at its peak as the formation of a 'sonic war machine' (Goodman, 2010: 11). In response to the practice of 'monitoring outbreaks' on the airwaves, the grime-pirate radio machinery used the 'logistics of infection' to reproduce itself and evade capture (Goodman, 2010: 178). Using his model of audio virology, Goodman argues that the way in which grime plugged into pirate signals also marked an attraction and congealing of populations:

> Instead of merely making connections between individual cells, an audio virology probes the mutational potential of pirate media, asking what aesthetic transformations, what new modes of contagious collectivity, and what rhythmic anarchictectures such microcultures might provoke (Goodman, 2010: 179).

In its provocation of the law, grime similarly provokes an audio virology which goes to work on transforming singular units into a collective organism. This is due to the way grime is a receptacle for and reorganises the ecology of its East London environment.

It is possible to see how Goodman's account of audio virology interacts with the post-2011 riots discourse on grime. In particular his take on the music's virological capacities confirms and interrupts David Starkey's *Newsnight* performance. During his analysis of the contagious nexus that is grime though, Goodman does not directly address the question of race. He does not attend to the ways in which grime's status as black music formed part of its conflictual phonomaterial operations. Lewis Ricardo Gordon and Fred Moten's work on the discourse of black pathology can be used to bridge this gap. There is a synchronicity between Goodman's understanding of audio virology as a phe-nomenon which induces and frustrates the law, and their respective takes on blackness and criminality.

Gordon and Moten take their lead in this area from Frantz Fanon. They both respond to Fanon's designation in *Black Skin, White Masks* of blackness as a zero-degree non-status. In terms of a discourse on black pathology, this means theorising the overbearing reduction of blackness to criminality. Gordon, in tracing this reduction from slavery, through Jim Crow, to the prison-industrial complex, takes up with Fanon's self-diagnosis:

> Blacks here suffer from the phobogenic reality posed by the spirit of racial seri-ousness. In effect, they more than symbolise or signify various social pathologies – they become them. In our anti-black world, blacks are pathology (Gordon, 2000: 87)

He argues that black social life is conditioned by the assumption that it is inher-ently criminal, or rather that it is crime. There is no possibility of avoiding this verdict. According to Gordon, any attempt to live in a way which might counter this logic is understood as a breach of the law, which only confirms that appar-ent self-evidence of the charge of black criminality.

Moten looks to push beyond the delimitations that Gordon, by way of Fanon, sees working on black social life. For him there are a series of conflations at stake in the background to a discourse on black pathology. This discourse is con-ditioned by the inability to mark the distinctions between three triangulating categories. These categories are: a) blackness as a concept or force; b) the colour black and its modalities; c) blacks or the people we choose to identify as black. Although these categories are always operating in relation to each other, and do come into contact and merge, the distinctions between them are collapsed when blackness is fixed as pathology.

Moten steps into this conflation and complicates it in ways which also com-plicate Gordon and Fanon. He argues that whilst there is a 'brutal history of criminalisation' which renders black life pathology, it is necessary to draw a distinction between criminality and lawlessness (Moten, 2008: 187). This is a distinction which black social life animates. Black social life is considered to be criminal because the very blackness of blacks is evidence enough of a flawed inability to live lawfully. It is the function of the law and the police to monitor this inherent criminal tendency. In the fact of its very living Moten concurs with Gordon that black social life can do nothing other than induce self-justificatory measures which render blackness the crime. But he argues that such 'reticence' is more than a means of self-incrimination. Black reticence is also always a law-lessness (Moten, 2008: 179). It is a 'fugitive movement' which both escapes the law and through escape occasions law enforcement (Moten, 2008: 179). In this respect to claim that blackness and blacks are pathology is misplaced. Instead blackness is a 'dangerous' but 'constitutive supplement' to the law, a constraint which occasions and troubles pathological discourse (Moten, 2008: 180).

This is a necessary distinction for Moten. Collapsing blackness into pathology is not just brutal for what it does to the black. It also involves indexing the colour black and the concept blackness solely to the people we choose to call black. It locks all three into place. What the lawless, fugitive, breakaway reveals is that blackness is mobile. The fugitive movements of black people shows blackness is not strictly the property of those we identify as black:

> What Fanon's pathontological refusal of blackness leaves unclaimed is an irremediable homelessness common to the colonised, the enslaved, the enclosed. This is to say that which is named in the name of blackness is an undercommon disorder that has always been there, that is retrospectively *located* there, that is embraced by the ones who stay there while living somewhere else (Moten, 2008: 187).

What Moten is reaching for with 'undercommon disorder' is the generalisability of blackness. It is something black social life *has* but does not *own*. He is not saying that there is a desire amongst black people to escape blackness as some kind of limitation on their lives. Instead blackness is a constraint which conditions the pathological violence of law against it, and goes in lawless flight from the law as blackness. Marked in the fugitive trouble it causes is the possibility of blackness being passed on to those who also lived under conditions of brutal criminalisation. There is in Moten's approach to black pathology an undercommoness with Goodman's audio virology, which also means Moten enters Starkey's world, if only to mess with him. Blackness is a pathogen which insistently confirms and breaks out from the logic that fixes blackness, black and blacks as violent, destructive and nihilistic. It goes in flight through the very heart of the claim that it is fundamentally anti-social in order to attract and congeal populations who are in tune with its underground movements. This is how it decolonises whites.

V. Jammer's birthday, Deja Vu FM, 2003

The combination of Goodman and Moten does more than point back to David Starkey's hyperbolic lyricism. It also points back to the questions which are the motivation for this chapter. These are questions regarding the 'problem' of blackness out on the streets, the 'problem' of grime as black street music, and the 'problem' of whites on the streets becoming black. In order to bring all of these elements together it is worth zeroing in on an instance of grime being produced as the self-weaponising, fugitive, black problem Starkey came into contact but could never quite live with. The instance in question is Jammer's birthday bash on Deja Vu Fm, filmed in 2003.

A camera opens in the storage room on what might be the rooftop of a block of flats. The room is run down at worst, functional at best. Off-white walls marked with streaks of black paint, exposed piping, tiny air vents and bars over the windows. But the room is packed. There are around ten men and one woman gathered in there, all responding to music being played on a set of speakers. The men constitute a roll call of the leading grime MCs of the moment; Wiley, Crazy Titch, Dizzee Rascal, Kano, D Double E and Escobar. Off screen, it is Mak 10 on the decks. This is the nerve centre of the pirate radio station Deja Vu Fm. Mak 10's role is to set the terms of the show, but he is also having those terms dictated to him. The MCs are all listening, observing, poised to grab the mic and talk back to the riddims he selects. He is not the focal point of the makeshift studio though. The MCs are all also sparring with each other, even more so given that there are at least three major grime crews represented in the room. There is an internal battle going on here, but it is also much more and less than that. As the mic is passed around from MC to MC, something else is being shifted around the circuit that has been put together in this room.

To repeat, this ecological arrangement constitutes a pirate broadcast system for grime. But it could also be thought of as a laboratory, one set up in the heart of the microcolony. What is being manufactured here is a phono-material substance with weapons capabilities. As each MC steps up to deliver his bars, what we see taking place on screen are different iterations of this phono-biological war machine. The MCs are turning themselves into weapons in order to battle with all the other hardware pulsing around the room. But this conflict goes into the collective production of an unstable, virological, infectious, violent, criminal substance being sent out on the Deja Vu signal. A signal which anyone can pick up on.

Each MC uses a combination of roll and flow, which in parts attracts and in other parts repels the rest of the occupants. Take D Double E. Hunched, head down, locking himself off. He is detached and calculated. There is an economy to all that he does, which gives him greater control and the sense that he has more time within the intense 140 bpm rate. The others in the room step off, giving him space, in what appears to be a sign of respect.

Escobar has to work much harder. Eyes closed tight in concentration. Rocking from side to side. He has both hands on the mic as the over-amplified gun blasts and metallic drips of the riddim threaten to run him over. Sensing this the others in the studio crowd around him, either detecting a weakness or as a show of support. The relief when Mak 10 cuts the sound for a pull up is clear, as Escobar's lines ease and he can hand over to Crazy Titch.

It is with Titch's intervention that we get the most spectacular manifestation of the phono-material substance being sent out over the Deja Vu signal. Unlike Escobar or D Double E, Crazy Titch steps into his bars and faces off. Shoulders back, head up, he swaggers and shudders his way through the gun blasts. In

Titch's weaponisation we see and hear all the ways in which Starkey was both right and wrong about grime, rioting and blackness. Despite the obvious distance between Starkey and Titch, there is a nearness, an intimacy between the two of them. Titch is hysterical. Titch is violent. Titch is criminal. Titch is black. As he performs on Deja Vu, he produces all of these markers, but not simply in confirmation of Starkey's pathological diagnosis. Instead Titch's intervention produces a substance which rubs up against Starkey and caused the historian to make his own hysterical criminally misinformed pronouncements about the inherent flaws in black people and black music. Rather than Starkey diagnosing Titch as the problem, it is the MC, as he plugs into and becomes part of the Deja Vu system, who is generating Starkey's racial melancholy. Titch resonates with and becomes a transmission device for a black virology which is undercommon (in that it is his but not his property), fugitive (in that it renders him lawless) and lives out on the street. It is a black operation which Starkey, as he watched the 2011 riots, was terrified had now become a general operation. Something had been breeding in the music and sent out on its pirate signals. Eventually this substance broke out like a black outbreak on the streets. Starkey was right, over exposure to grime had generated a new entity in the riots - the former white or the new black. The question remains: is there anything wrong with that?

References

Akwagyiram, A. 2012. 'Stop and search use and alternative police tactics'. *BBC News Online*. 17 January. Available: http://www.bbc.co.uk/news/uk-16552489. Last accessed 05/12/2012.

BBC News Online. 2011. 'England riots: "The whites have become black" says David Starkey'. 13 August. Available: http://www.bbc.co.uk/news/uk-14513517. Last accessed 05/12/2012.

Clark, M. 2005. 'The Month in Grime/Dubstep'. *Pitchfork*. 22 June. Available: http://pitchfork.com/features/grime-dubstep/6073-the-month-in-grime-dubstep/. Last accessed 05/12/2012.

Gordon, L. R. 2000. *Existentia Africana: Understanding Africana Existential Thought*. New York, NY and London: Routledge.

Goodhart, D. 2011. 'The riots, the rappers and the Anglo-Jamaican tragedy'. *Prospect* 185. 17 August.

Goodman, S. 2010. *Sonic Warfare: Sound, Affect and the Ecology of Fear*. Cambridge, MA: MIT Press.

Hancox, D. 2009. 'Public Enemy 696'. *The Guardian*. 21 January.

_____ . 2010. 'The Outsiders'. *Daily Note*. 11 February.

_____ . 2011. 'Pow!: anthem for kettled youth'. *The Guardian*. 3 February.

_____ , 2013. *Stand Up Tall: Dizzee Rascal and the Birth of Grime*. Amazon Media.

Hall, S. Critcher, C. Jefferson, T. Clark, J. & Roberts, B. 1978. *Policing the Crisis: Mugging, the State and Law and Order.* London: Macmillan.

'Jammer Birthday'. 2007. Uploaded 3 December. Available: http://www.youtube.com/watch?v=8UdBSxZ067k. Last accessed 05/12/2012.

Jones, O. 2011. *Chavs: The Demonization of the Working Class.* London: Verso Books.

Mason, M. 2008. *The Pirate's Dilemma: How Youth Culture is Reinventing Capitalism.* New York, NY: Free Press.

Moten, F. 2008. 'Case of Blackness'. *Criticism* 50:2 (Spring).

Reynolds, S. 2009. 'The Wire 300: Simon Reynolds on the Hardcore Continuum: #7 Grime (and a little Dubstep)'. *The Wire* 300. February.

Routledge, P. 2011. 'London Riots: Is rap music to blame for encouraging this culture of violence?' *The Mirror.* 14 August.

Topping, A. 2012. 'Police accused of discriminating against urban music scene'. *The Guardian.* 8 January.

Townsend, M. 2012. 'Stop and search "racial profiling" by police on the increase, claims study'. *The Guardian.* 14 January.

Walmsley, D. 2011. 'Welcome to Violence'. Paper delivered at *Music, Politics and Agency in the Digital Age: East London.* 16 November. University of East London.

III. Public Service Announcements

8

POLITICS (AND MIME ARTISTS) ON THE STREET

Paulius Yamin

A survey conducted in 2008 asked the people of several Latin-American cities to choose which public figures and institutions they trusted and which ones they did not.[1] Not unlike the other Latin-American cities surveyed, 64% of the people in Bogotá said that they trusted teachers (the highest percentage, followed by the Catholic Church and the Army), while only around 10% said that they trusted public servants and only 4% politicians (the lowest two percentages).[2]

Figure 1. Bogotá, picture taken by the author on 24/01/2013.

The specific context I want to present here concerns an 'experiment on political theory' (Dalsgaard, 2009) which was conducted by the local government of the city and started around 20 years ago. During Professor Antanas Mockus'

---

[1] *Encuesta de Cultura Ciudadana* [Citizenship Culture Survey]. 2013. Corpovisionarios.

[2] The institutions and figures included in the survey are (in descending percentage of people claiming to trust them): Teachers, the Catholic Church, the Army, the Radio, Priests, National Government, Television, Press, Police, Mayor's Office, Regional Governments, Judges, Pastors, Religious Organizations, Syndicates, Congress, Public Servants and Politicians.

first term as Mayor of Bogotá, mime artists were used as a pedagogical tool to re-interpret and change people´s behaviour in the city. And in doing so, they managed to introduce a new relationship between politics and the street. A relationship that is not based on supporters or contradictors of specific causes that come together in the public spaces of the city to hear a speech or to attend a protest or a march, but rather on individuals that just happened to be there and were involved for some seconds in a charade about political ideas in their most quotidian and banal dimension: that of dealing with people´s everyday behaviour on the street. As an article in the *Harvard Gazette* reported, this experiment consisted on turning the city into 'a 6.5 million people classroom' (Caballero, 2004). It is a context that manages to disrupt the relationship between politics and the street through... mime artists!

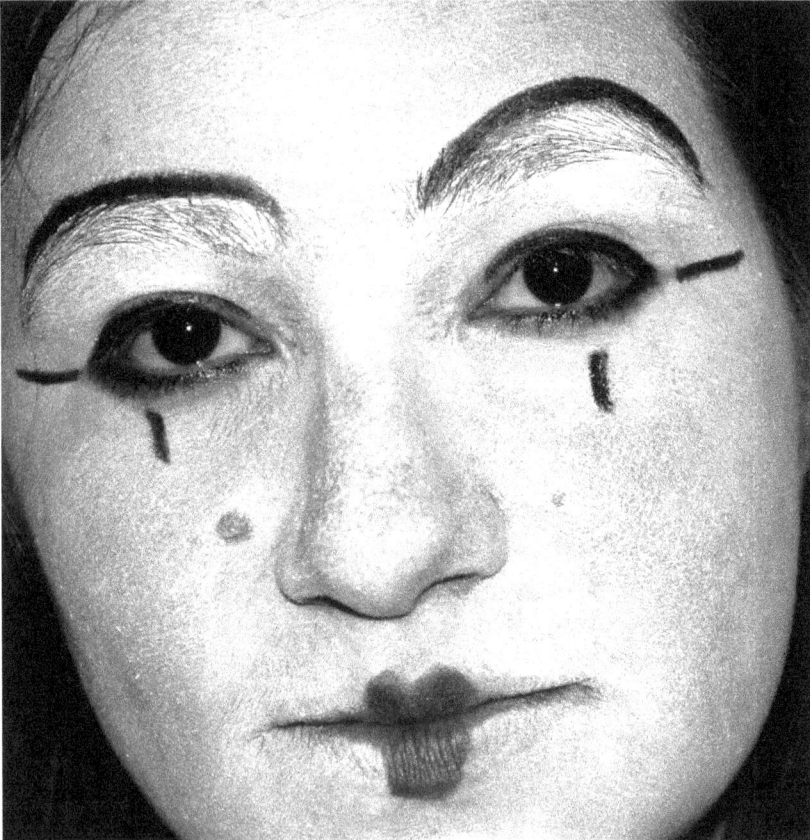

Figure 2. Mime artist, Picture taken by the author on the 23/01/2013.

All the city's a stage...

In 1994 Antanas Mockus, a philosopher and mathematician who had just resigned as Principal of the biggest public university of Colombia, the Universidad Nacional, was elected mayor of Bogotá as an independent candidate, having competed against the traditional political parties of the country. As Lucas Ospina (2012) writes, Mockus' political career started in 1993 when he was still Principal, during a national arts meeting which took place at the Universidad Nacional. There, in a 1500-people auditorium filled with students, 'Mockus tried to speak but he was booed by an immense minority, so he turned his back to the audience, he pulled down his pants and with his hands he grabbed his buttocks' (Ospina, 2012). As Mockus declared several years later, this was an act that aimed to connect two extremes, 'extreme contempt and extreme submission' (Dalsgaard, 2009). The recording made it to the news and the gesture was heavily criticized: the Principal of the biggest private university in the country formally requested the President to remove Mockus from his post, the director of the Museum of Modern Art declared that it was a 'vulgar' and 'unnecessary' gesture and the Director of the National Department for Security called for Mockus to undergo psychiatric testing (Ospina, 2012). After resigning he became a national celebrity, something of a symbol of honesty and bravery (Dalsgaard, 2009). He ran for mayor of Bogotá and won.

Antanas Mockus was mayor of Bogotá twice, from 1995 to 1997 and from 2001 to 2003. His government created specific symbolic interventions staged on the streets of the city with the explicit purpose of shocking people, and through shock to create cultural paradigms that would solve, or help solve, specific social problems. The final aim of the interventions was to show that most of the problems of the city could be solved collectively by the citizens themselves. To quote just a few of the most significant examples, the mayor was filmed taking a shower and turning it off while he soaped in order to encourage people to use less water;[3] a 'Night for Women' was declared and men where invited to stay home and take care of the children while women went out;[4] 'thumbs-up' and 'thumbs-down' cards where distributed so that people could peacefully approve or disapprove other people's behaviour in the city; people were invited to pay 10% more taxes than they owed,[5] and, as will be my focus here, mime-artists were sent to some street intersections to show people the 'correct' way to behave on the street.

According to Doris Sommer (2006) this 'range of social contributions through creative practice' are strategies of cultural agency, which manage to

---

[3] 'In just two months people were using 14 percent less water, a saving that increased when people realized how much money they were also saving because of economic incentives approved by Mockus; water use is now 40 percent less than before the shortage' (Caballero, 2004).

[4] '700,000 women went out on the first of three nights that Mockus dedicated to them' (ibid).

[5] 'To the surprise of many, 63,000 people voluntarily paid the extra taxes. A dramatic indicator of the shift in the attitude of "Bogotanos" during Mockus' tenure is that, in 2002, the city collected more than three times the revenues it had garnered in 1990' (ibid).

'put culture to work' by using the techniques of art as a political practice. 'Social problems' are conceptualized in this perspective as a matter of values and beliefs, as cultural formations. Through pedagogy, then, one can change what is considered 'morally and socially accepted behavior' in order to solve those problems (and the state, with its large resources and reach, is a privileged scenario to actively introduce and support those changes). Following Jon Elster (2007), Antanas Mockus (2002) understands human behavior as an interplay between motivations and regulations. In his view, the way we behave is both a consequence of the *reasons*, *emotions* and *interests* that motivate our actions and the *social*, *legal* and *cultural* regulations that restrict them.

Making stronger laws and sanctions, then, is rarely efficient in preventing certain behaviours (particularly on the streets) for the simple reason that there will never be a policeman or a camera watching every person all the time.[6] We are also capable of following certain rules or behaving in certain ways for other, very powerful, reasons: for example, we might follow certain rules because we think it is the right or wrong thing to do anyways, because others might think it is right or wrong, or because we understand the broader importance of following certain rules. Public policy and government should therefore not be exclusively based on creating or enforcing specific laws, but *also*, and in the first place, on specific pedagogical strategies that change or reinforce social and cultural values and rules. In Colombia - Antanas Mockus often says in his presentations - even if killing is clearly forbidden by the Constitution, in certain contexts it is socially and culturally acceptable, even praised (take the portraits of drug lords on TV, for example). To reduce homicide rates, then, it is not enough to create stronger penalties or to enforce control, but rather to create a cultural 'taboo' around killing: people can be *taught* (and ought to be taught by the state and by other citizens) not to kill, or for that matter to respect other rules as well, such as traffic lights or not throwing garbage on the streets. As the documentary 'Bogotá Change' (Dalsgaard, 2009) puts it, 'People throw garbage on the street because it is morally acceptable, or people act violently because the culture does not condemn it. Mockus wants to change people's morality' (Dalsgaard, 2009). Those interventions relied heavily on introducing some kind of art to the streets, the strangeness and creative possibilities of a consciously created and enacted situation that would revive people's civic spirit, an operation that requires a change to the moral sense of how to behave in the city. The politician is no longer the puppet of its own dark secrets and allegiances, but rather an artist that stages his acts to influence people´s behaviour and finally to change the configuration of society.

---

[6] In a similar way and following the surveys he carried out among some 22000 primary and high school students in Bogotá, Enrique Chaux (2012) argues that this can be seen from an early age: most children know the rules by heart, know what they are allowed to do and what is forbidden, but most of them do not follow those rules.

Through the operations that are displayed here, the calculus of force-relation-ships and distinct spaces of the *strategies* embrace the heterogeneous and im-provised inventiveness of the *tactics* (Certeau, 1988: xix) in order to be more effective in transforming them, on transforming everyday practices. Discipline, which 'breaks down individuals, places, time, movement, actions, and opera-tions' (Foucault, 2007: 56) is suspended by introducing the abnormal, the un-canny and the unfamiliar on the street; but this is done to establish a new 'nor-mation' (Foucault, 2007: 57), an order in which the *norm* becomes 'the final division between the normal and the abnormal' (ibid).

... and all the men and women merely players

The kind of *situations* that were created in Bogotá at that time can be found in different theories of everyday life as creative possibilities that can break alien-ation (like those of Debord and the 'Situationists' [see Debord, 2002], or the 'moments' of Lefebvre [see Lefebvre, 2008]). According to these theories, by cre-ating specific situations that stem from everyday life itself, people should be able to experiment with and regain control of their own everyday lives. The para-lyzing effect of boredom, routine and a life lived as a spectacle (that is, where images are repeated in front of us and we don't have any choice but to passively consume them) are 'cut' or 'interrupted', in the words of the *Internationale Situ-ationniste*, by seeking the 'passionate abundance of life through the transforma-tion of transitory moments deliberately organized' (IS, quoted in Sheringham, 2006: 166). The city and the street are taken here as concrete entities (and not just as abstract or theoretical formations) which can and must be transformed by experimenting with them: as Michael Sheringham (2006) comments, the situationists' activities were mainly a way of engaging with the city. But what happens, then, when those situations are planned and implemented by the gov-ernment in order to change the way people behave on the streets?

One of the iconic actions that Antanas Mockus established as mayor was to hire mime artists and send them to the streets to 'teach people how to live and behave properly in a city' (Dalsgaard, 2009), as the media reported at that time. Taking the idea to the extreme in order to maximize the force of the *shock* that was sought, the traffic police were replaced in a specific area of the city by mime artists. By encouraging and giving examples of 'good' behaviour and by reject-ing those behaviours defined as 'bad' (that is, bad for security, mobility, respect among citizens...), they managed to lead pedestrians and drivers into respecting some fundamental rules that made everyday interactions and coexistence in the city more manageable and with less victims (like the safest time and place to cross the road or to stop the car and so on).

Speaking informally with some people that lived in Bogotá when the initi-ative of the mimes was created, it is quite interesting to note that most of them reported that they changed their everyday behaviour when crossing the street or while driving because they feared an encounter with the mimes that they had previously seen on TV (as their first reason), and also because it was the right thing to do 'anyway' (as their second reason). They say that each time that they were going to cross the street they remembered the mimes and looked around to see if the group of white-faced actors were performing on that particular street. While they didn't fear the mimes, they did want to avoid an encounter (and especially one where the mimes would illustrate with their games the fact that they where not 'behaving properly') because that would be *embarrassing* and *uncomfortable*. The same logic that the staged situations are meant to break by introducing shock, also helps to reinforce their power of changing the way in which people behave: trying to avoid the new and the *uncomfortable*, people change their behaviour. In other terms, the interventions are effective precisely because people avoid an engagement with the new and uncomfortable and try to stick to routine and naturalized behaviours, where mime artists on the streets are quite uncommon. It is precisely because people try to reject the playfulness of the scene proposed that the scene manages to effectively transform behaviours. More than a contradiction, it is the political mobilisation of cultural values and naturalized behaviours in order to denaturalize and thus transform other naturalized behaviours. Rather than being univocal and clear, the discourses that those interventions produce and re-produce are conveyed through an ambiguous turn that accounts in part for their efficacy, because the messages are always *unfinished* and *partial* on purpose 'so that the citizens can complete them as they like'.[7]

To put it in schematic terms, the logic behind those actions is something like this: a 'social message' is created through the performance of the mimes, which is then learned or interiorized by the citizens mostly through the media, and because of this a social (what other people say), moral (what I think is right) and legal (rules and sanctions) forms of control are put in place to reinforce that message (by the institutions and authorities first but then, ideally, mainly by the citizens themselves).

What is imagined here as 'the mimes', was initially just a group of 20 professional artists working on a couple of street intersections. To change the way people behave in a city with a population of seven million, specific interventions at different spots are not enough (that is, interventions in a few streets, where the number of people in direct contact with them will always remain very limited). Being a local government strategy which is targeted to the city as a whole, there has to be a wider audience interpreting (and learning from) those situations: if 'direct contact' in a few streets is not enough, then the images of the street transmitted and repeated on the media might work, just as that initial gesture of Mockus that forced his resignation as headmaster 'worked' politically only

---

[7] Antanas Mockus, personal communication, 2012.

when transmitted on national TV, even if involuntarily and with random results (that is the power of *play* involved here). In the same way, this whole 'experiment' worked because it was built through an image of the street that was widely spread on television, on the news, in newspapers and on the radio.

The point here is the spectacle, the fact that the actions were heavily advertised and commented on (as well as mocked) in the media. What allowed some kind of highly political performance to be created, a performance that in the end favoured some kind of change on a big scale as to how people behave in the city as a whole is not the street itself but its image and its spectacles, the ways in which it produces and recreates discourses within itself and towards the city as a whole, to the point where the street and the scenes performed in it start to resemble the whole city (and vice versa). Politics return to the stage of the street and the street returns to the stage of politics because the street, or rather its image, is where all this is meant to happen. Political engagement and political conflicts take place and are transmitted from the street, which is seen as the 'public place' *par excellence*, where different trajectories of people, of interests, of institutions, of artists come together and eventually act together or against each other.

What the local government wanted, essentially (the mimes are only one of the possible examples), was to give people different *languages* to express themselves in order to avoid violence:

> 'It was a pacifist counterweight," Mockus said. 'With neither words nor weapons, the mimes were doubly unarmed. My goal was to show the importance of cultural regulations' (Caballero, 2004).

The focus of the local government was to increase people's capacity to live together and resolve conflicts peacefully, while the main goal was to save lives. And what is maybe the most compelling thing about this context and the actions undertaken using the 'techniques of art' (Sommer, 2006) to change culture is their efficacy. The Danish documentary 'Bogotá Change' (Dalsgaard, 2009) reports that the week after a specific measure forcing bars to close at 1:00 A.M. was put into place - accompanied by several pedagogical actions that included the mayor himself, dressed in a white gown and with a big wooden clock hanging from in his neck and visiting several bars at their closing time with a group of actors dressed as nuns, indigenous people and mimes, all inviting people to return home - the number of people killed in traffic accidents on weekends dropped from 38 to 18 in one week, while the number of people murdered each weekend dropped from 16 to 4.

And yet, this whole context and its efficacy remains problematic and ambiguous, as do the ideas behind it: while it presents itself as a citizen's movement that uses academic concepts to solve some quite basic social problems that in countries like Colombia are especially urgent, it might also appear as another level of disciplinary 'discursive practices used by the state to direct public thinking' (Foust, 2011: 23). But while surely any means that the state uses to make people obey the law can be seen as the development of governmental control (and this is certainly occurring) this does not exhaust this particular context. Of course the actions are meant to create or reinforce cultural taboos, guilt and social reprobation if one does not follow the law. And yet, Antanas Mockus argues that the Colombian State is quite far from having the capacity to exercise such control, and that at the centre of his actions is what he sees as an anarchist principle, that people should be able to govern themselves to their own benefit along with that of their society. That collectively, through communicative action (Habermas, 1984) that is mainly deployed and shaped through the street, we can reach a certain level of agreement on what shape that 'benefit' is to take. That people should be able to take education to the streets and to create a context where everybody can learn from anybody. Recently, he described the general idea behind his career as follows:

> I will help to make the State stronger in order to make it possible for my children and my grandchildren to be anarchists. When there is a general state of very little obedience to the law, civil disobedience becomes a joke
> (Interview with Mario Mendoza, *El Tiempo*, 3rd March 2012).

What those interventions are aimed at achieving by calling to the revival of the 'civic spirit' is essentially to assure that the law is upheld by influencing moral values and behaviour. The actions that the local government carries out to reinforce specific rules are also and most importantly meant to reinforce the understanding and disposition to comply with the law in general (otherwise there would always be in any given society an infinite number of rules and regulations to reinforce). A 'culture of violence', or a 'culture of taking shortcuts', can thus be changed for a 'culture of legality'. What is to be managed and changed is not chaos or a state of nature, but rather a specific 'cultural formation' which overlaps with the broader culture of the country or the city: a set of rules, regulations and accepted behaviors that must be changed, broken or eliminated.

Commenting further on the context of Bogotá, Doris Sommer argues that 'Culture enables agency. Where structures or conditions can seem intractable, creative practices add dangerous supplements that add angles for intervention and locate room for maneuver' (Sommer, 2006: 3). And it is precisely in the ways in which the operations suggested by this context make use of the street that their complexity and potential can be seen.

The street *is* the theatre

A rather straightforward identification of the street with a political theatre is in a sense possible here, since actors (or the mayor himself *acting* as an actor) are sent to the streets to perform a certain scene. Not the street understood meta-phorically as theatre or its inhabitants as actors, but rather the street *becomes* the theatre and the political space itself in order to make possible a change in the people which traverse it. The street is where politics in the form of cultural change happens, where actors perform and citizens learn (to perform).

It is true that acknowledging the extent to which a term like *citizen* is ambig-uous in a context like Colombia, a 'third world' country with one of the highest inequality rates in the world, is a task which is yet unfinished. And yet, through the 'cultural agency' (Sommer, 2006) that the actions undertaken by Antanas Mockus on his two terms as mayor of Bogotá seem to introduce, this context has the potential to establish a challenging beginning (both in theory and practice) for the task of problematizing the difficult path of *becoming a citizen*. A path that is highly political, and that emanates from the street in the form both of gossip and the electromagnetic waves of television and radio, which transcend even the barriers of gated communities and their closed public spaces where the mime artists of the mayor´s office cannot enter. Physical barriers between public and private spaces become less palpable as the spectacle and its discourses become more acute.

The citizens portrayed in such images of the street, the citizens that vote and get elected, and that learn and teach how one must act in the city, have a special quality. They are not actors or spectators and they are not students: they are passers-by who happened to be there by chance. The pedestrians and the drivers that encounter the mimes are not there to watch a spectacle, but rather to go somewhere else. While passing-by, they encounter politics in a situation in which they are meant to *learn* something. It is not even a matter of individ-uals or of a society versus the State, or of a government against what it seeks to govern, but rather a more intimate relationship between mobile subjects that behave in a certain way and a teaching directed towards their values and beliefs. As Manuel Delgado (1999) argues in a more general commentary, we do not know anything about the protagonists of such street scenes because they are moving, because they are just passing-by. What we *do* know is:

> that they have already left but have not yet arrived, that before or after their passing through they where or they will be fathers, housewives, clerks, union-ized workers, employees, lovers or bakers..., but that they are now, while pass-ing through, pure potentiality, an enigma which gives a sense of uneasiness (Delgado, 1999: 201).

Bogotá itself is made of intersecting routes that come from all over the coun-try. To a great extent due to the violent history of the country and the refugees coming from all over it, Bogotá has now nine times more people living in it than in the 1950s.[8] This movement of individuals and ideas make the city difficult to understand and to manage. Nowadays, the '*desplazados*' (the people who have been displaced from… elsewhere) are quoted in popular, academic and political discourses as the cause of many of the problems of the city. Discipline, which 'analyses and breaks down' (Foucault, 2007: 56), is disrupted by the continual growth which is always changing the nature of the city's population and continuously introducing the uncanny figure of '*l'étranger*' (Kristeva, 1988) to the streets. That is why the relationships of force, defined as strategies are no longer enough to govern it and the random creation of everyday tactics (Certeau, 1988) must also be introduced in the political theatre.

The objective of the cultural politics displayed here is, after all, the 'countless strangers' (Delgado, 1999: 201) that inhabit the streets of the city: the interventions are directed towards *everyone* but at the same time towards no one in particular. Their aim is the specific aspects of culture that are to be changed, towards the values and beliefs that are responsible for the ways in which people behave.

It is from this uneasiness and pure potentiality of the passers-by that politics and a certain possibility for change becomes possible. The power of those operations lies in the shock that they introduce and in the way in which the situations created work on our everyday lives, true, but it also lies in the street itself, because it is on the street that we are all 'countless strangers' while remaining, at the same time, susceptible to encounters with others, to teaching and learning from them, to becoming *citizens* in the sense of reclaiming *some* cultural and political agency.

Through the operations I have drawn on here, the street became the site of politics and cultural change only because it was transformed into a spectacle. But maybe because it originates from a specific (political) situation, it is a spectacle that is not meant to paralyze, but rather to propose a teaching, to encourage action. There are politics on the streets, then, not because there are demonstrations or public speeches (although demonstrations and speeches are still there), but rather because the street has become here the site of performances that manage to break (some of) our assumptions, to disturb the way we behave on it.

If, as both Certeau and Barthes suggest 'our relation to the spectacle of the street is that of the reader' (Sheringham, 2006: 156), what people on the street (and also those watching its image on television) read here is a political message which is aimed at asking questions and proposing changes. The street as theatrical space also becomes much wider that it was meant to be: it becomes the glaring site of everyday politics, where people can (and should) learn and teach each

---

[8] Data from the *Departamento Administrativo Nacional de Estadística* (DANE). Available from the website: http://www.dane.gov.co.

other, where everyone can introduce change by introducing education, where people, ultimately, are challenged with other ways of expressing themselves and are eventually able to find alternatives to the repetition of violence.

References

Caballero, M. C. 2004. 'Academic turns city into a social experiment'. *Harvard University Gazette*. 11 March.

Certeau, M. 1988. *The Practice of Everyday Life*. Los Angeles and Berkeley, CA: University of California Press.

Chaux, E. 2012. *Educación, convivencia y agresión escolar*. Bogotá: Taurus.

Dalsgaard, A. M. (dir.). 2009. *CITIES ON SPEED* - Bogotá Change [Film]. Denmark: Upfront Films.

Debord, G. 2002. 'Perspectives for conscious alterations in everyday life', in Highmore, B. (ed.) *The Everyday Life Reader*. London: Routledge. 237-245.

Delgado, M. 1999. *El animal público*. Barcelona: Anagrama.

Elster, J. 2007. *Explaining Social Behavior. More Nuts and Bolts for the Social Sciences*. Cambridge: Cambridge University Press.

Encuesta de Cultura Ciudadana [Citizenship Culture Survey]. 2008. Bogotá: Corpovisionarios.

Foucault, M. 2007. *Security, Territory, Population: Lectures at the Collège de France 1977-1978*. New York, NY: Picador.

Foust, E. 2011. '1. Word: An Introduction', in Foust, E. and Fuggle, S. (eds) *Word on the Street*. London: IGRS books. 11-30.

Habermas, J. 1984. *The Theory of Communicative Action, Volume 1: Reason and the Rationalization of Society*. Boston, MA: Beacon Press.

Kristeva, J. 1988. *Étrangers à nous-mêmes*. Paris: Gallimard.

Lefebvre, H. 2008. *Critique of Everyday Life: Foundations for a Sociology of the Everyday. Volume 2*. London: Verso.

Mockus, A. 2002. 'Convivencia como armonización de ley, moral y cultura'. *Perspectivas*, 32:1. 19-37. Available: http://grupocisalva.univalle.edu.co/bpr2/esp/Descargas/Memorias/6_Mesa_sobre_convivencia_y_encuestas_Abr_2010/Convivencia_Mockus.pdf. Last accessed 28/07/2014.

_____ . 2012. 'Entrevista con Mario Mendoza.' *El Tiempo*. 3 March.

Ospina, L. 2012. 'Mockus artista'. *La Silla Vacía*, 6 August.

Sheringham, M. 2006. *Everyday Life: Theories and Practices from Surrealism to the Present*. Oxford: Oxford University Press.

Sommer, D. (2006). 'Introduction: Wiggle Room', in Sommer D. (ed.) *Cultural Agency in the Americas*. Durham, NC: Duke University Press. 1-28.

9

ENLIGHTENED STREETS:
PUBLIC ART AND INTERNATIONAL
ANTI-VIOLENCE CAMPAIGNS[1]

Patricia Anne Simpson

Many contemporary cultural theories connect the perception of space to the construction of identity. There are corollaries to the premise that space is socially and historically constructed. Henri Lefebvre's surprising formulation, 'To produce space', stops the reader in her tracks. The assertion that space is 'produced' (2009 [1979]: 186) forces more naturalised images of the street as a corridor into another register. The street constitutes performative as well as a pedagogical space, yielding a constant construction site. In the twenty-first century, the street is a space determined by cultural anxieties as much as by political statement and enactment; virtual and commercial representations along with real bodies are displayed; sometimes damaged. The extent to which multiple agents inhabit, occupy, obstruct, and traverse the street also serves to index the respective agents' status, power, and spatial identity.

Undeniably and historically, the street is also a site of violence on and in which figurative and literal battles occur. As material and ideological thoroughfare, it undergirds the stage of negotiations between difficult dichotomies, among them public and private space, order and chaos, movement and stasis, all governed by implicit hierarchies of power. More local clashes, between political opponents, demonstrators and police forces, and local gangs, for example, concretise the potential of the street for conflict. Some of this violent unconscious spills over into a modern sense of agoraphobia. In modernity, the street as urban space hosts a display of anxieties that blend public and private subjectivities.

[1] I am grateful to the Fulbright Commission in Brazil for my participation in the Fulbright-Hays Summer Seminar (July 2011), which made part of this article possible. I was further supported by a sabbatical from Montana State University, which enabled me to conduct the necessary research in Mauritius and write up the results. I owe a considerable debt of gratitude to the 'Return to the Street' conference organizers, the panelists, and the audience members who engaged us all in a lively and challenging discussion of that revisiting. For their generous assistance in obtaining research materials, communicating with me about their work, and for their efforts on behalf of non-violence campaigns, I also am indebted to Priyadarshni Beegun, Eddy Jolicoeur, and Jane Valls who also permitted the reproduction of figures 7, 8, 9 and 13.

'Space', writes Anthony Vidler in *Warped Space*, 'in these various iterations, has been increasingly defined as a product of subjective projection and introjection, as opposed to a stable container of objects and bodies' (2001: 1). Vidler connects the rise of phobias and anxieties involving public space to the precipitous growth of European metropolitan centres in the nineteenth century, identifying agoraphobia as 'an essentially spatial' and 'equally an urban disease' (2001: 29). The street, I argue in this chapter, is also the site of controlling and 'curing' that urban malaise through the attempted enlightenment effects of anti-violence campaigns. The introjection that stipulates the unease of urban street identity can ostensibly be countered on enlightened streets.

In the early twenty-first century, we can encounter a cartography of the street that inscribes a narrative of identity and difference; that engages discourses of political, economic, and ethnic subjectivities. The map of the New Street insists on citizenship and ownership of public space. The inhabitants affix their signatures to the belligerently local asphalt and simultaneously to global immateriality of virtual networks of representation. Public spaces, however, and the performance of public identities, are often constructed to render the young invisible except as consumers and mannequins for commercial trends. In their introduction to the collection *Cool Places*, for example, Skelton and Valentine address the absence of young people from 'Geography' (1997: 1-2). They keenly observe that public space for the most part has been 'produced as adult space' (1997: 7), and that the street is in many ways the only 'autonomous space' (1997: 7) left for youth to occupy. Part of that occupation involves the positing of a violent young audience that can be enlightened through public art – often sanctioned by adult agency. The street locates a discussion about cultures of violence, but simultaneously serves as palimpsest of pedagogy. As open gallery, it displays the arts of enlightenment that hope to transform and regulate violent impulses through directing the pedestrian or commuter gaze.

Toward understanding the practices that 'enlighten' streets, I examine anti-violence campaigns, both organised and spontaneous (aerosol art, street art and/or graffiti) in three separate locations: Germany, Brazil, and Mauritius. The first two examples serve as an introduction to the more sustained reading of campaigns and public art in Mauritius. In Germany, anti-violence campaigns, municipally sponsored and church-oriented alike, use art to bring the pedestrian or *flâneur* into a space of instruction about drug addiction, prison, and domestic violence. In Brazil, by contrast, the images I analyze are partly state sanctioned, but combine seamlessly with graffiti to add a racially inflected anti-violence message. On the small African-region island nation of Mauritius, officially sponsored anti-violence campaigns are reflected in public murals and graffiti as well. In these three case studies of street art, I examine the rhetorical and visual strategies that define violence by taking a visual and verbal stance against it. The presumptive process of 'enlightenment', however, itself must be problematised. In the individual readings of these three radically different contexts, a common trope becomes legible. Anti-violence campaigns that are publicly sanctioned to 'enlighten' by targeting a specific street culture characterise the violence as a depoliticised, private act which effectively erases socio-economic factors, the effects of global capitalism, and in some cases a colonial history. Traces of this erasure can yet be perceived, as I argue, if we pause to consider the visual culture as street-level critique.

For the most part, these campaigns and artistic articulations share a strategy: they rely on the performative capacity of visual and verbal signifiers to have an effect, persuade, or leave a trace on the larger canvas of the public sphere, in Jürgen Habermas' sense, with regard to violence or the potential for violence that is enacted in private or domestic space. Further, the campaigns are directed at a specific target audience: males between the ages of 12-22. In other words, some campaigns are directed at precisely the demographic that is least included in the geography of public spatial identity. I examine some of the reasons for this contradictory approach.

The Spatial and Optical Unconscious

I have arranged my visual materials in accordance with their location of origin. The focus on three distinct world regions, separate national identities, and target audiences differentiates between publicly and privately sponsored initiatives. I do account, to the extent possible, for religious inflections in the respective visual discourses, primarily to distinguish between civic/municipal appeals and moral enforcement. My examples are drawn overwhelmingly from urban spaces; most are targeted at commuters in high-traffic areas, while some are clearly positioned to draw interest from pedestrians. Most of the public writing that accompanies each image or campaign presumes a moderate level of literacy; some appeals to polylingual agents.

On another level of my analysis in the individual cases, I want to forge a connection between theories of the photographic image and the synapses of the enlightened street. In each of my case studies, location – the site-specificity – of the anti-violence appeal creates a polyvalent context for instruction. The location, the placement of some visual interventions can reveal much about the intended audience, sometimes assuming a level of privilege; at other times attributing a potential for doing damage amongst the target audience. In this sense, the strategies of 'enlightening' as a dominantly, if not singularly, Eurocentric mode of instruction benefit from a more nuanced examination between the assumed universalist and particularizing national or local expressions. The 'radical Enlightenment' (Jonathan Israel), which Nick Nesbitt challenges as a geographic monolith (Europe) through a sustained reading of the Haitian Revolution and the intellectual legacy he identifies as Caribbean Critique effectively deconstructs any notion of Eurocentrism in the enlightenment project. Nesbitt's *Universal Emancipation* identifies the transnational thinkers of the radical enlightenment project who '… constructed a critique of human knowledge and society that affirmed the indivisibility and inalienability of sovereignty' (2008: 2), the instantiation of which he identifies as the Haitian Revolution. Building on this premise, Nesbitt develops a theory of the 'Caribbean Critical Imperative' (2013: 1), by which he discerns the history of this concept: 'From its very first iteration, Caribbean Critique appears concerned not with individuals or with classes but with a series of abstract, universal concepts of relevance to all human beings and not to any specifically regional, racial, or gendered experiences' (2013: 1). In his subsequent examination of key works, by, among others, Aimé Césaire, Maryse Condé, and Franz Fanon, Nesbitt realigns the sense of any geographic or philosophical centrality and displaces the Eurocentric presumption of an enlightenment imperative to acknowledge and extend human rights with true universality to the cultural legacy of the Caribbean basin. In so doing, he effectively delimits the critical concept identified in Theodor Adorno and Max Horkheimer's 'dialectic of Enlightenment' (Adorno and Horkheimer, 1944), which I invoke to suggest the idea of enlightened streets as part of the postcolonial project. In some instances, the street art itself repoliticises the private violence the campaigns are targeting.

The fundamental deterritorialisation of thought Nesbitt's work advances can have significant repercussions for the project of theorizing, through 'enlightening' physical and social territories such as the street, universalised practices of changing everyday behaviour. Fraught with ideological complexity, however, the assumed position of authority always already relies on the hierarchical power to impose standards of behaviour on those whom it perceives to be aberrant. If this is indeed the case, enlightened streets replicate, rather than obvert, the presumably civilising and colonising moment in such scenes of instruction. Beyond contradiction between intent and result, the transnational attempts to teach, speak, and persuade publicly must fail in the process of replicating any hierarchy of knowledge and power. Moments of genuine enlightenment or instruction emerge from the deconstruction of the hierarchies of knowledge that work at the level of street culture.

There is a spatial unconscious at work in many instances of street-level pedagogy. The pedagogical moment emerges, in my case in some retrospect, mediated by the intervention of the photograph itself. An amateur (and not very skilled) photographer, I made an effort to frame my images about anti-violence in as aesthetically composed a way as possible. In the process, the details I planned to crop, the works or campaigns *in situ*, ultimately reveal moments of insight about the strategic planning of the individual projects, sometimes with the effect of inflecting or even undermining the intended message. This retroactive realisation invokes Walter Benjamin's treatise on the work of art in the age of its mechanical reproducibility, and the relative speed of the eye in pho-tography, but also his 1931 essay 'Little History of Photography'. With its over-riding concern for freeing the medium of photography from the comparison with painting and its potentially fetishising abilities, the short history instead reveals ways in which the 'tiny spark of contingency' (1999 [1931]: 511) remains legible in the photograph. With this insight, Benjamin writes of the detail in a photograph from a psychoanalytic perspective: 'Photography, with its devices of slow motion and enlargement, reveals the secret. It is through photography that we first discover the existence of this optical unconscious, just as we discover the instinctual unconscious through psychoanalysis' (511-512). The revelation of that 'optical unconscious' in some of the images I captured and include here invites the viewer or spectator into a critique of the act of looking and photo-graphing, exposing the voyeur in the process. Part of my analysis reflects my own amateurism in photographing, for the 'tiny sparks of contingency' I con-sciously did not edit can serve as apertures through which the strategies of 'en-lightening' presumably violent streets are exposed.

Violence Under Erasure: Nuremberg

My first example (figure 1) involves an anti-violence campaign aimed at allevi-ating human suffering at multiple levels. One image from this campaign instan-tiates an aesthetic tradition that harkens back to an eighteenth-century caveat: it captures the most 'pregnant' moment – prior to the act of violence, thus aligning it with the origins of enlightenment visuality. This campaign was implemented in the centre of Nuremberg (Germany), a city with medieval roots that current-ly hosts a population of approximately 500,000, but serves as the centre of the metropolitan region of 2.5 million inhabitants. In 2010, a Protestant non-profit organisation, the Stadtmission Nürnberg, launched a visual campaign against violence. The organisation is part of Diaconia, which, since 1848, signifies social work of the churches (not Roman Catholic). According the website, it includes 'the regional social welfare services of the 20 member churches, diaconal asso-ciations of other Protestant denominations and approximately 80 specialist or-ganisations working in different fields of social care, health care and education' (Diakonia, 2012). The activities include elder care, support for the unemployed, for at-risk youth, for people with disabilities, and families; they also attend to issues of health care and migration. Different organisations employ nearly half a million people and have as many volunteers. Their services are financed by a combination of public and private funds.

The Stadtmission Nürnberg, one such organisation, designed and imple-mented this campaign. A series of white-out images was painted on temporary walls in the pedestrian zone of the city, and along the historic walking tour. As you can see in the example directed against child abuse, the imminent slap looms over the restrained child. The purpose of this campaign, characterised by the almost Derridean use of the 'erasure' (white space) and defined here by the contours of a violent act (the slap) is to raise general awareness, literally bring to the streets and the forefront of pedestrians the invisible, private acts of violence and anguish that do not feature prominently in the prosperous public sphere of historic city centres. The accompanying texts, long, earnest passages written in German, require the relatively slow pace of the pedestrian or *flâneur* to be read and processed fully. The performativity of these efforts, in other words, demands a high level of commitment, and thus targets a relatively small group of possible donors. In the figure, we catch a frozen glimpse of the audience: next to the evocation of violence is a small poster advertising a Robert Schumann concert. The perhaps random juxtaposition nonetheless speaks volumes about the intended audience. The effectiveness quotient on this enlightened street is calibrated by privilege; it is predicated on the ability of the target audience to care, act, or donate (though donations were not explicitly solicited), once the public art makes the 'invisible' acts of violence, legible on the urban screen.

Figure 1.

Brazil: The Indicting Eye

My second introductory example (figures 2-6) derives from semi-public art and graffiti in Brazil. There is ample material on the elaborate, vibrant, and established culture of public art in Brazil; increasing media attention on *pixação* emphasises the differences between the self-expression of public art in a more figurative tradition and the critical, even revolutionary, impulses of the latter. In *The World Atlas of Street Art and Graffiti*, Rafael Schacter describes the genre as 'militant': 'a local form of parietal writing that since its re-introduction into the city (of São Paulo) in the 1980s has become famed across the world' (Schacter, 2013: 97). The tensions and potential interplay between the two forms have solicited regulatory responses from the state. With the same executive stroke, graffiti was legalised and *pixação*, the São Paulo tag style that remains explicitly political, criminalised (Agência Brasil, 2011). *New York Times* journalist Simon Romero emphasises the underlying issues of social injustice that motivate the runic alphabet, inscribed onto the surfaces of urban decay. The activism of the *pixação* gangs, some of whom use rollers, not spray paint, sets its practices in conflict with public art, which, they accuse, is subject to commercial cooptation. That, however, is my focus here, as I draw examples from visual culture that espouses non-violence, rather than the explicit aggression advocated by *pixação*.

Despite economic growth and centralised government intervention, poverty and profound socio-economic disparities – that do tend to correlate with skin colour, received notions of racial democracy notwithstanding – persist and exist alongside success stories. In contrast to the leading practices of some other rising economies, Brazil is making a concerted effort to lift people from poverty. President Lula da Silva's *bolsa familia*, implemented in 2006 and continued under Dilma Rousseff, provides direct support for 12 million families. Money earmarked for food and education is distributed in the form of cash cards. Moreover, this direct aid coincides with a rising awareness of persistent racism. The government attempted to address the devastating legacy of African slavery in that country with affirmative action in education. The 1988 Centennial celebration of Abolition served as a flash point for marginalised groups, contributing to the passing of Law 10.639 in January 2003, which mandates teaching of Afro-Brazilian history, heritage, identity. Further, 20 November has been designated the official Day of Black Consciousness. The issue of consciousness and public art is located at the nexus of some of Brazil's anti-violence murals.

Recent highly publicised events, such as the 2013 violence and the 2014 protests surrounding the World Cup further emphasise the importance of national identity and radical socio-economic inequalities. In 2013, prompted ostensibly by a relatively modest fare hike on public transportation, a series of demonstrations mobilised the Brazilian middle class and drove them to the streets. The economic growth has enabled the country to lift many from poverty – some estimate 30 million Brazilians (Bowater, 2013); that same growth has fueled not only the hopes but the expectations of the rising middle class, many of whom experienced a renewed sense of politicisation during the protests about transportation and infrastructure. Elaborate preparations for the 2014 World Cup and the 2016 Olympic Games extended the circle of discontent. While football has the potential to contribute significantly to a sense of national identity and pride for many – and to forge bonds across socio-economic divisions – it also has triggered violent protests, to which the police responded decisively, even brutally (Barbara, 2014). The tragic deaths and injuries caused by the collapse of an overpass in Belo Horizonte (3 July 2014), which was allegedly rushed to accommodate the hosting of the World Cup games exacerbated the need for real and permanent investment in Brazil's infrastructure, but also in political institutions.

The controversies funneling around the World Cup have led to headlines such as 'Brazil vs. Brazil' (Barbara, 2014), but have also ignited a commentary in the public sphere, on the urban canvasses, a contemporary open-air gallery. The graffiti artists so engaged in anti-violence activism have responded to the extravagant spending on stadiums, etc., with radical criticism. In a CNN report, two well-known artists from São Paulo, Cranio and Paulo Ito, were asked to comment on the activity and some of the critical images. Ito's image of a hungry, crying child being served a plate with a soccer ball earned him widespread recognition. Even his commentary is careful to acknowledge the enthusiasm for the sport in Brazil, while inhabiting the ironies of the possibly misguided investment of public monies: "'I was trying to talk about football at the moment of the FIFA Cup," said Ito. "I never say (the World Cup) is a bad thing at all but there are problems, like relocating people to live in other neighborhoods and particularly I don't agree with the way FIFA operates'" (qtd. in Macguire, 2014). Brazilian citizens: can be avid football fans and raise critical voices. Public visual culture, critical and careful, reckless and rambunctious, is part of the process of radically enlightening the streets. In light of recent events, the criticism has met with radical repression. In other examples, however, the messages can be disseminated without – but occasionally with – state support.

In Olinda, a city designated a UNESCO World Heritage Site, some murals are openly considered art rather than vandalism. In figure 2, we see the non-violent reference to Bob Marley and reggae, painted on the wall of a school. The image forges a connection between the politics of reggae, race, and education, which posits a motivated, contiguous relationship between the school and the street. Interestingly, above the image, we read the following statement: 'O Governo Do Estado Sauda Toda A Comunidade Escolar' (The state government salutes the entire school community). The endorsement creates an implicit alliance between the efforts of the school community, in choosing non-violent themes for the mural, and the enterprise of education itself, which is a hot-button issue in contemporary Brazil, particularly with regard to increasing access to top-tier public institutions. The next image (figure 3) shows the furthest end of the wall, with the strong imperative 'violencia não!' (no violence!) and the more muted 'paz' (peace), though both remain loudly legible. In figure 4, the next image, we see a self-portrait of a Rio graffiti artist, and I reference it here to establish the connection between personal identity and public statement. Upon first viewing this image, I immediately thought of the illustrious, sometimes self-deprecating tradition of self-portraiture, from Rembrandt to Ernst Ludwig Kirchner and Max Beckmann. In Rio, this legible signature forges a strong link between the aggression of the visual image and the identity of the artist. However, in figure 5, which I took at Cidade de Deus (not where the film *City of God* was shot), we see evidence of a less conciliatory message. The streets of favelas in Rio function off-the-grid; they are far from the public sphere in many ways, and this link to neo-fascist politics effectively dissociates itself from the more supplicant tone of the Olinda school's murals. Only when examining this photograph after-the-fact did the indicting gaze of the young woman sitting to the left penetrate my own intention. In my own retrospective looking, mediated by the snapshot, I caught myself in the crosshairs. Here there is a 'tiny spark of contingency', in this case, the act of shooting the photograph itself indicting me in a kind of poverty tourism, dubbed 'poorism' by some commentators (Schott, 2010). I had strayed from the group to pause before the swastika, only to find myself caught in the indicting glare of a resident whose presence I would have cropped in another context. Finally, in figure 6, I show the street-level view of Rio's first 'pacified' favela. Located near police headquarters, this pocket of urban poverty both exemplifies state mandated intervention to stop violence, but cannot completely escape the cyclical nature of oppression. The relationship between public and private, photographing subject and captured object, is problematised by the presumptive connection between violence and streets of poverty.

Figure 2.

Figure 3.

Figure 4.

Figure 5.

Figure 6.

Mauritius, Men Against Violence, and the Street

The material for the more substantial case study originates in Mauritius. This African-region island nation in the Indian Ocean hosts a population of 1.2 million. With the Indian-Mauritian (and Hindu) majority, and approximately 27% of the inhabitants with African heritage constituting the second-largest group, the island is home to an intensely diverse culture, which is reflected in socio-linguistic, religious, ethnic, and economic pluralities. Still a relatively peaceful society, tensions also persist, especially between the majority and largest minority. Known as the 'malaise kreol', the discontent of the Kreol population was articulated by the seggae singer Kaya. His death in police custody triggered violence that had become unfamiliar to the island nation since independence in 1968. Recent reports point to violence against women as the most serious infraction of human rights. The government has taken steps to address the issue, but NGOs and citizens' initiatives clarify the need to do more - to take prevention to the streets.

Before I proceed with my specific analysis of anti-violence campaigns in Mauritius, I think it is necessary to impart a sense of the media context in which violence, specifically violence against women, is reported. Newspaper coverage is an important indicator of public opinion. In tri-lingual Mauritius, media outlets, including the press and television programming, are state-owned. The same stories appear on any given day in the English-language newspaper, *The Independent*, as well as in a French version, *Le Matinal*. Coverage often corresponds to alarming increases. For example, in a report about the commemoration of the Journée internationale pour l'élimination de la violence envers les femmes, the Minister of Gender Equality noted that there were 1,890 cases of domestic violence within a ten-month period (*Le Matinal*, 2010). More recently, in Radhima Ramdeen's report on forums for victimised women, the article focuses on the work of Forum Citoyen Libre, which organised a workshop (12 March 2012) to give women who are victims of 'moral, verbal and sexual' harassment the opportunity to share their experiences in a safe environment (Ramdeen, 2012: 3). This topic and the articles which foreground the work of activists contribute to a greater awareness of violence against women, on the street or behind closed doors. The reporting itself launches some dramatically 'newsworthy' acts of violence into the public sphere. Some of the coverage in Mauritius holds some surprises for a differently conditioned American reader. For example, some media outlets covered the quest of one woman to bring her fight against gender-based abuse to the public by joining Africa UNITE's expedition to climb Mount Kilimanjaro (Gooraya, 2012: 1). Africa UNITE is a campaign inaugurated by UN Secretary-General Ban Ki-moon, focused on empowering women and advancing gender equality on a global scale. The same edition carried a feature story by the same author, published under the rubric: 'Activist fights violence against women, girls: Roumaan recently climbed Mount Kilimanjaro to raise awareness on issue' (Gooraya, 2012: 3), which provides a fuller profile of Roumaan Issemdar's dedication to social work. She was involved in Men Against Violence (MAV), an organisation whose campaigns I analyze in more depth below; and she participated in the training sessions to raise awareness and change behaviour. By contrast, news stories routinely include information about a victim's sexual activity. The print media evince a public awareness of organised efforts to understand gender-based violence, provide support for victims, and invest in strategies to prevent violence to any extent possible.

While these efforts remain laudable and newsworthy, actual reporting about gender-based violence occasionally replicates preconceived notions about women's involvement, rather complicity, in certain types of assault. Again in *The Independent*, in the News Digest headlines read: 'Adolescent victim of sexual assault', and 'Man accused of sex with minor cousin' (*The Independent*, 2012: 2). In unattributed headlines such as these, the age and gender of the victim factor in the description of violence. Another example invokes a painful tragedy, but again, with reference to a sexually active minor. In the 4 April 2012 edition, front page headlines read: 'Coralie murder linked to affair with 13 yr old', with the article written by Pravind Rughoo (2012: 1). In another case, the *Independent New Service* reported: 'Tenant's lovers abuse 13-yr-old school girl' (*The Independent*, 2012: 1). The story recounts the girl's effort to borrow a pressure cooker from a downstairs tenant. Two men 'proceeded to assault her in turns' (ibid). According to the report, 'Her parents discovered her misadventure on January 3 upon questioning her on what was troubling her' (ibid). She was examined by the police medical officer, 'who noted that the teenager was already a sexually active person' (ibid). On 10 January, the *Independent News Service* authored the article 'Alcohol, sex turn night into nightmare', reporting that a woman was so badly beaten she lay near death: 'A couple had invited two of their friends to a party' (*The Independent*, 2012: 2). As the story unfolds, the reader learns that the husband had passed out from excessive alcohol consumption, and: 'Taking advantage of the situation, the wife took one of the friends to a stable to have a good time' (ibid). The other friend woke the husband and the two of them beat the woman. Again, the guilty phrase is repeated: 'She was having a good time with their friend' (ibid). Though the reports and headlines stop short of 'blaming the victim', publicly revealing age, level of sexual activity, and what is clearly represented as morally problematic behaviour indicate a bias that subtly renders women complicit in their own victimisation.

Prevailing notions about such complicity are targeted by a variety of anti-violence enlightening strategies that activists take to the street. I now turn to the organisation WIN and MAV (figures 7, 8, 9). This campaign specifically addresses human rights violations in the form of violence against women. According to the US Bureau of Democracy, Human Rights and Labor's *Country Reports on Human Rights Practices for 2011* (Mauritius): 'The most important reported human rights problems were violence and discrimination against women' (2011). There is a government Ministry of Gender Equality, Child Development and Family Welfare, which was established in 1982 and currently defines its main objectives as promoting women's rights as human rights, including legal equality with men; to promote the advancement of women economically and alleviate poverty; to advocate for children's rights as human rights, and prevent all forms of violence and discrimination; to promote child welfare and 'family welfare and to combat gender based violence'; and to promote the welfare of citizens in communities toward an inclusive society (Republic of Mauritius, 2012). Thus the Ministry spearheads and joins in the effort to prevent domestic and gender-based violence. Consensus that these efforts need support in civil society is evident in the numerous examples of NGO activity, public awareness campaigns, and religious-based endeavours. In the MAV series, the official slides demonstrate the strategy of 'enlightenment': to disrupt the cycle through parabasis; making sub- or unconscious patterns conscious through context, in order to change behaviour. In other words, the use of readily recognizable references to Facebook (figure 7), Nike ads (figure 8), and the football club 'Manchester United' (figure 9) – social media, consumer culture, and sports – demonstrates a constructed model of behaviour that needs interruption. The strategy is multi-stranded. It is insufficient to encourage the modification of behaviour in one sphere, and the multiple media used, from street signs to workshops and broadcasting, rely on a holistic approach to a pervasive problem. Still, there is a residual enlightenment model at work in the premise that changing thought patterns, even language usage, marks the first step in altering behaviour. How do these additional approaches work with images above street level (figures 10, 11, 12)?

These images and messages discussed above constitute one pillar of many: there was a television special during the thick of the campaign, there are frequent workshops, and also radio adverts. The radio adverts in particular speak in the rushed shorthand of the SMS or text. The speedy male voice rehearses a variety of fairly banal details that need to be 'liked' or 'laughed at' – a nearly automatic 'like' is repeated, followed by 'LOL', 'LOL', 'LOL', for example. The advert vocalises the list and rapid reactions, either 'like' (or not) or 'LOL', without the speaker committing to any depth of decision. This enumerated, conditioned communication via mobile phone is paralleled by the 'slacktivism' of clicking 'like' and the 'thumbs up', without actually engaging the issue in a meaningful way – or raising the question about what type of engagement could be significant. Here it is instructive to recall the highly publicised case of the Kony 2012 film and the ensuing controversy focused on political expression through social media that accords the 'liker' a feeling of having done something. To return to the example of MAV, that mentality is challenged.

Figure 7.

Figure 8.

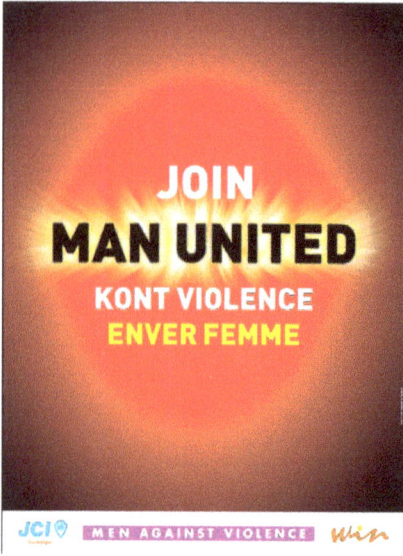

Figure 9.

In the MAV campaign, the purpose is to achieve some positive change in thought and by extension behaviour as a result of disrupting such automated thinking. The approach motivates young men to sign the pledge (figure 13), thereby entering into a contractual relationship. The promise, complete with the performative power of signature, functions as a down payment on future restraint, with the emphasis on training and enlightenment over impulsive anger.

Figure 10.

Figure 11.

Figure 12.

Questions about the efficacy of such campaigns remain difficult to answer. In the case of the Frankfurt am Main campaign 'Gewalt – Sehen – Helfen' [Violence – To See – To Help], for example, the level of recognition among residents of the metropolitan region is used as one metric to indicate public awareness of the organisation's efforts, which include workshops, outreach, and consistent use of symbols in public space, with the latter almost achieving the effect of product placement or 'branding' (Simpson, 2012: 22; 100; 207). It is clear that the question must be answered on a case-by-case basis. In the instance of public art, for example, the message in the graffiti itself is unilateral, unless it generates further commentary. In the efforts of MAV, other metrics are in place. According to Jane Valls, the National Coordinator for Women in Networking, the organisation uses certain measures to gauge the outcomes of the campaign. MAV is among their initiatives, which include running a Women's Leadership Programme (WLP), a campaign for more Women in Politics (WIP), and hosting regular networking events and maintaining databases. She notes that each participant has to attend three sessions; one metric is attendance for sessions two and three. Each participant also completes an evaluation form at the close of the third session. Finally, during sessions two and three, the participants 'share some of their reflections and the small changes they are trying to bring in themselves, e.g., not treating their mum as a maid, making their own bed, better relationship with their sibling, better relationship with their parents, no more disrespectful sms [texts], more respect for girls on the bus, at school, etc' (Valls, 2012). Valls concludes this roster with reference to the commitment observed and recorded from older participants who express a desire to become members of the MAV team and with that, agents of change.

MEN AGAINST VIOLENCE

THE PLEDGE

I pledge to never commit, condone or remain silent about violence against women and girls. I willingly say "NO" to violence against women and girls.

MON ENGAGEMENT

Je m'engage à ne jamais commettre aucun acte de violence d'aucune sorte a l'égard des femmes et des jeunes filles, de ne jamais accepter ni de rester impassible a de tels actes.

MO LENGAZEMEN

Mo fer sermen ki jamais mo pou komet ene acte violence conte ene femme ou ene zene fi et ki jamais mo pou accepté et ki mo pas pou reste trankil lor ca kalité violence la.

Figure 13.

Before moving to the public art against violence, I want to call attention to a religious-based workshop advertised near the billboards with MAV's messages. The images highlight some of the same targets: violence in relationships, but also drug use and alcohol, often factors in tragic acts of violence. This also aims at a type of enlightenment, but with a clearly religious, rather than civic, sense of becoming a good or better (male) citizen. In the anti-violence messages from a local church (figure 14), we have an example of faith-based efforts to alleviate the problems that contribute to violence. At street level, the sign is displayed along with directions to the local beach, an international grocery store, and some real estate agents. From a different perspective, an assumption about local religious practices is implicit. In the next image (figure 15), note the final item in the list: *sorcellerie* [sorcery, witchcraft]. The banner is publicising an event hosted by Light Ministries International, which, according to their website, is a mission 'mandated by God to bring the message of salvation to all nations, starting from our Mauritian nationals and reaching out to the ends of the earth' (2012). The message of salvation assumes certain local religious practices that appear in a list that enumerates the 'other' causes of violence, such as substance abuse and addiction.

Figure 14.

Figure 15.

The next images consist of wall murals from the west coast town of Tamarin, known for the beauty of its bay, its salt flats, and the rising population of ex-pat South Africans who are occupying prime waterfront real estate and largely secluding themselves (figures 16-21).[2] Along the main road, this series of paint-ings addresses violence, substance abuse, and environmental issues. The walls mark the boundaries of private residences. The first actually portrays the cycle of violence; the directive prohibits violence against women, but a careful read-ing of the image reveals a female figure striking back (figure 16). Other messages are positive: in 'parents protect children', we see attention to racial difference in the mother figures, for example, and an almost Madonna-like portrait of that instinct (figure 17). It is significant that the parental figures who serve as the designated protectors are all female, with semi-religious overtones to their de-votion. In the 'no' wall image, the imperative to 'just say no' is rendered lexically through putting the substances and related paraphernalia 'under erasure'. That image (figure 18) portrays more generally the presumed cause-effect relation-ship between drug and alcohol abuse and violent behaviour. With the connec-tion between alcohol and child abuse established, I turn to the next image (figure 19). Here, unlike the raised arm from the Nuremberg street campaign, the adult hand makes contact with the child's body. To the left, a belt is raised. In contrast to the 'protect' message from the Madonna-like images, here both the perpetra-

---

[2] I must add that my many attempts to identify the artist(s) who produced these works and any information about their origins have been unsuccessful.

tors are discernibly male. The slogan also points to the importance of protecting children, who are the future, tomorrow. The frozen moment of impact invokes great ambivalence in the spectator. It brings to mind Sigmund Freud's 1919 essay "'A Child Is Being Beaten'. A Contribution to the Study of the Origins of Sexual Perversions'. Whereas the images before us clearly address themselves to the real threat of domestic violence, Freud's essay dwells with near prurience on ritual punishments inflicted both at school and at home, and the subsuming of this corporal discipline into the realm of fantasy – and because Freud is the source, sexual fantasies. This is not the case in the streets of Tamarin.

Figure 16.

Figure 17.

Figure 18.

Figure 19.

Still, the site-specific location and the streetscape in general contribute to a more nuanced reading of the clear anti-violence message. The placement of much public art by government organisations can itself serve to comment on a somewhat presumptuous attitude toward localities. Some places more than others are perceived to need street-level enlightenment. But these images occupy one tier of space, alongside advertising, landscape, and built environments. A wider-angle view of these visual messages adds another dimension to my reading. In Tamarin, where there is a growing population of white South African expatriates, street-level art and advertising send potentially mixed messages, revealing that there are perhaps different focus groups. The mural images are generated at the local level, but I want to look closely at figures 20 and 21 to examine the intersection with commercial space and international discourses. In this image (figure 20), we see the juxtaposition between the local anti-violence art and the sales space for the 'Out of Africa' experience. With obvious reference to Isaak Dinesen's 1937 memoir, we hear the strategic sale of wild nature and exciting leisure articulated with a specific association: Africa with the wilderness. Mauritius' proudly independent national identity results in ambivalence about its location 'in' or 'on' the African continent. Here, the commercial space, contiguous with both natural wildlife and potential danger, is also contiguous with the social space of violence, evoked in the message to prevent it.

Figure 20.

Similarly, in this image (figure 21), we see barely visible a corner of security, enabled by Island Life Assurance. Two children thrive in happiness and vitality, with the prosperity that permits this insulation from the hazards of life (2012). While these children hover above the pedestrian eye-line, others are victimised below. This streetscape instantiates (unintentionally) the stratification of island society.

Figure 21.

Conclusion

The local, site-specific examples of what I am calling 'enlightened streets' rely on the performative function of language and visual imagery to change or modify patterns of violent behaviour with sometimes unintended consequences. The metonymic relationship between consumer-oriented and pedagogical space is predicated on the contiguity between thought and performance. A strategy of persuasion through stimulated thought underwrites the belief, shared by state, municipal, and ecumenical agencies alike, that all aspects of the human condition can be recuperated through knowledge. This perhaps erroneous assumption links each of these public displays of anti-violence sentiment to a fundamental belief in the rational and reasonable illumination of any aberrant impulses or behaviours. The general aim of enlightening streets, while originating with noble intentions, cannot control the site-specific contexts that posit correspondences between the message and the receiver. For this reason, reading aerosol art, both planned and spontaneous, alongside the commercial codes and cultural corridors with which they share space, becomes imperative. The street sends out many signals, some of which lead to cross-purposes. In each of these case studies, there is an underlying assumption that the reader, viewer, and citizen is excluded, rather than referenced, by the campaigns. That assumption, I believe, makes some streets even more treacherous, through the aura of enlightenment, than we may think. Yet, the street sends out many signals, some of which lead to cross-purposes and sometimes very confusing intersections.

References

Agência Brasil. 2011. 'Lei descriminaliza grafitagem e proíbe venda de spray a menores'. *Terra*. 26 May. Available: http://http://noticias.terra.com.br/ brasil/lei-descriminaliza-grafitagem-e-proibe-venda-de-spray-a-menores, 9e0a0970847ea310VgnCLD200000bbcceb0aRCRD.html. Last accessed 05/08/2014.

Barbara, V. 2014. 'Brazil vs. Brazil'. *The New York Times*. 26 June. Available: http://www.nytimes.com/2014/06/27/opinion/brazil-vs-brazil.html. Last accessed 05/08/2014.

Benjamin, W. 1999 [1931]. 'Little History of Photography'. In *Selected Writings. Vol. 2 1927-1934*. Trans. Rodney Livingstone et al. Eds. Michael W. Jennings, Howard Eiland, and Gary Smith. Cambridge, MA: The Belknap Press of Harvard University Press. 507-530.

Bowater, D. 2013. 'Brazil protests: how the "squeezed middle class" rose up'. *The Telegraph*. 22 June. Available: http://www.telegraph.co.uk/news/worldnews/ southamerica/brazil/10136739/Brazil-protests-how-the-squeezed-middle-class-rose-up.html. Last accessed 05/08/2014.

Diakonie Deutschland. 2012. Website. Available: http://www.diakonie.de/ the-social-welfare-organisation-of-the-protestant-church-in-9306.html. Last accessed 05/08/2014.

Freud, S. 1919. '"A Child Is Being Beaten". A Contribution to the Study of the Origins of Sexual Perversions'. Available: http://www.slideshare.net/341987/ a-child-is-being-beaten. Last accessed 05/08/2014.

Island Life Assurance Company. 2012. Website. Available: https://www.ila.mu/. Last accessed 05/08/2014.

Leena G. 2012. 'Young Mauritian scales Mount Kilimanjaro', *The Independent*, 19 March, 1.

Lefebvre, H. 2009. *State, Space, World. Selected Essays*. Eds. N. Brenner and S. Elden. Trans. by G. Moore, N. Brenner, and S. Elden. Minneapolis: University of Minnesota Press.

Le Matinal. 2010. 'Sheila Bappoo: 1890 cas de violence conjugale'. 26 November. Available: http://www.lematinal.com.

Light Ministries International. 2012. Website. Available: http://light-ministries. org. Last accessed 05/08/2014.

Macguire, E. 2014. 'World Cup: The art of protest. Brazil's graffiti artists tackle Brazil 2014'. *CNN*. Available: http://edition.cnn.com/2014/06/27/football/ gallery/brazil-graffiti-world-cup/. Last accessed 05/08/2014.

Nesbitt, N. 2008. *Universal Emancipation: The Haitian Revolution and the Radical Enlightenment*. Charlottesville, VA: University of Virginia Press.

_____ . 2013. *Caribbean Critique: Antillean Critical Theory from Toussaint to Glissant*. Liverpool: Liverpool University Press.

Ramdeen, R. 2012. 'NGO to hold forum for victimized women'. *The Independent*. 21 February, 3.

Romero, S. 2012. 'At War With Sao Paulo's Establishment, Black Paint in Hand'. *New York Times*. 28 January. Available: http://www.nytimes.com/2012/01/29/world/americas/at-war-with-sao-paulos-establishment-black-paint-in-hand.html. Last accessed 05/08/2014.

Republic of Mauritius. 2012. *Website for Ministry of Gender Equality, Child Development and Family Welfare*. Available: http://gender.gov.mu. Last accessed 05/08/2014.

Schacter, R. 2013. *The World Atlas of Street Art and Graffiti*. Foreword by J. Fekner. London: Quintessence and Yale University Press.

Schott, B. 2010. 'Schott's Vocab. Poorism.' *New York Times*. 13 October. Available: http://schott.blogs.nytimes.com/2010/10/13/poorism/. Last accessed 05/08/2014.

Simpson, P. A. 2012. *Cultures of Violence in the New German Street*. Lanham, MD: Fairleigh Dickinson University Press/Rowman & Littlefield.

Skelton, T. and Valentine, G. (eds) 1997. *Cool Places: Geographies of Youth Cultures*. London and New York, NY: Routledge.

US Bureau of Democracy, Human Rights and Labor. 2011. *Country Reports on Human Rights Practices for 2011 (Mauritius)*. Available: http://www.state.gov/documents/organization/186432.pdf. Last accessed 05/08/2014.

Valls, J. 2012. Email correspondence with the author. 28 July.

Vidler, A. 2000. *Warped Space: Art, Architecture, and Anxiety in Modern Culture*. Cambridge, MA: MIT Press.

10

MOVING FORWARDS, LOOKING BACKWARDS: STREET ART AGAINST AUTHORITARIANISM IN BRAZIL

Holly Eva Ryan

I. Introduction

Brazil's initiatives in the areas of collective memory, truth and reconciliation are welcome but nonetheless late-coming. Whilst neighbouring Latin American states including Argentina and Chile established truth, reconciliation and reparation mechanisms in the immediate aftermath of the return to civilian rule, Brazil's progress in this area has been far slower, prompting some to regard the country as a regional outlier. In this chapter, I suggest that Brazil's authoritarian experience and protracted transition to democracy exhibited a unique combination of features that helped give rise to a pervasive 'culture of amnesia' around the repression and violence of the dictatorship years. Although Brazil's recent institutional initiatives, including the establishment of a Truth and Reconciliation Commission in 2013, are indicative of 'memory's turn' - as coined by Rebecca Atencio (2014) - there remains some distance to travel before the restoration of memory may be considered full and/or complete.

This chapter focuses on the place of street art and street artists in the contested process of 'remembering'. Building on the work of social historians such as Serbin (2006), Chaffee (1993) and Bickford (1999), I argue that, in the absence of (or in addition to) more conventional documentation and accounts of the authoritarian experience, street art may prove to be an expedient source of social history, allowing us to dismantle or re-inscribe dominant narratives. However, in Brazil contemporary street artists and street art commentators have so far failed to take up the theme and call of memory, a fact which attests to the pervasive presence of a 'culture of amnesia' within the cultural industries.

The story of *Grupo Tupinãodá*, São Paulo's earliest known and largely forgotten street art collective is recovered and placed under the spotlight here. *Tupinãodá's* subversive interventions were the very first to adorn the walls of the Beco do Batman and Paulista/Rebouças tunnel in São Paulo - painting zones now famous internationally among street artists, tourists and reporters. The group's work and testimony offer insights into the authoritarian experience and in particular the conditions and risks attached to the expression of dissenting views during the dictatorship. Their art can be considered as politically important in that it offered a sustained counter-discourse and means of re-imagining civic and social life during the dictatorship. Moreover, by appropriating prominent urban spaces and experimenting with large scale abstract designs, their work also set the stylistic and spatial parameters for much Brazilian street art to come.

This chapter proceeds as follows: first, it traces the factors and characteristics of the authoritarian experience that obstructed an immediate 'turn to memory' in Brazil; it then goes on to identify *Tupināoda* as one of the groups that has been pushed out of view or 'forgotten' in the making of a hegemonic memory. Building a case for street art as a valid, if unconventional, source of social history and political power, the chapter then explores the art interventions and experiences of the *Grupo Tupināodá*. It concludes with some reflections on street art, social history and collective memory, including a critical commentary on the political status of street art in today's Brazil.

II. 'Collective amnesia' in Brazil

Tens of thousands were afflicted by the Brazil's period of military rule, experiencing varying levels of censorship, coercion and violence. Social struggles were heavily repressed, thousands of alleged dissidents were imprisoned, tortured or exiled and a number estimated in the hundreds were illegally executed. In spite of these alleged crimes, following the transition to civilian rule in 1985, it took ten years for the state to take its first institutional steps towards reckoning with its violent past;[1] and, a further seventeen years before the inauguration of a truth commission (Atencio 2014). This stands in stark contrast to neighbouring Argentina which established its *Comisión Nacional sobre la Desaparición de Personas*, [National Commission on the Disappearance of Persons or CONADEP] shortly after the collapse of the military regime in 1983 and Chile which created the *Comisión Nacional de Verdad y Reconciliación* [National Commission for Truth and Reconciliation] immediately after the return to civilian government in 1990. Brazil's relative tardiness here prompts further examination. Whilst it is impossible to identify a single cause for Brazil's proclivity to 'forget', it is possible to identify features of the authoritarian experience that made a 'turn to memory' highly unlikely in the immediate aftermath of the democratic transition.

2014 marks the 50th anniversary of the coup that deposed the civilian President Joao Goulart. On the 22 March 1964, over a million Brazilian citizens participated in the *Marcha da Família com Deus pela Liberdade* [March of the Fam-

---

[1] In 1995, President Henrique Cardoso established the Law of the Disappeared (Law 9,140), which made way for families to claim reparations.

ily with God for Freedom], a demonstration against Goulart's proposed social reforms and against the supposed communist threat to the nation posed by his leftist interventionism. Although not all of the marchers necessarily favoured a coup, the demonstration lent a semblance of popular support to the operation that followed shortly thereafter, installing a military regime that would last for 21 years, the longest in modern Latin American history. Upon seizing power, the self-styled 'Supreme Command of the Revolution' instituted a series of *Atos Institucionais* [Institutional Acts or AIs].[2] These were extra-constitutional decrees that reduced the civil service, suspended political rights and established a bogus two-party system that prevented the direct election of presidents and governors.

The regime was not universally popular. However, the military establishment's pronouncements and rhetoric were given credence, amplification and support by many of Brazil's largest news providers. Notably, *Globo, Rede Record, O Estado de São Paulo, Folha de São Paulo, Jornal do Brasil* and *Correio da Manha* have all since been accused of providing a platform for the regime (Coelho, 2013). *Globo*'s complicity - particularly its lack of coverage of opposition movements and police violence against them - has been particularly well-documented. There were, of course, different kinds of interests at stake here. For some journalists, silence was a matter of self-preservation. Fernando Jorge's 1987 publication, *'cale a boca, jornalista'* [shut your mouth, journalist] provides a set of testimonies from dissenting reporters who had survived interrogations at gun-point and the prod of electrodes. Given the unpleasant consequences for those who challenged the status quo, it is perhaps unsurprising that many were reluctant to publicly voice any opposition. However, for some media managers, complicity was less about self-preservation and more about self-promotion. Atencio (2014) describes some of the rewards *Globo* received for their loyalty; including being allowed to pursue an illegal joint venture with the Time-Life Corporation, which cemented the company's leading market position and brought it enormous financial rewards. Whilst publics are not passive recipients of information (Hodkinson, 2010), it is nonetheless important to note the power of mainstream media and its capacity to construct and amplify a hegemonic political narrative at the expense of other versions of events. In the case of Brazil, scant media coverage of the regime's abuses of power helped to project the myth of 'repression lite'; the idea that Brazilian authoritarianism was comparably 'soft'.

---

[2] AI-1 enabled the military government to dismiss 10,000 public servants and suspend the political rights of nearly four hundred citizens, including the deposed president, whilst AI-2 suspended all existing political parties and enabled the regime to created an artificial, two-party system consisting of the government-sponsored *Aliança Renovadora Nacional* [National Renewal Alliance or ARENA] and a sanitised opposition party, the *Movimento Democrático Brasileiro* [Brazilian Democratic Movement or MDB]. AI-5 instituted in 1965 under Costa e Silva, shut down the Brazilian parliament entirely.

Although fewer Brazilians were 'disappeared' than the 2,000-3,000 and 13,000-30,000 estimated in Chile and Argentina respectively, the regime was far from 'soft' in its repression of dissent. Presiding over the bloodiest and most violent period of the military regime, General Emilio Garrastazu Medici gave his security forces free reign to employ torture[3] and inflict terror on 'suspected dissidents' - a group which encompassed broad swathes of the political left including the National Students Union. However, Medici also presided over a booming economy, with growth rates averaging 10.9% between 1968 and 1974 (Skidmore, 1988). His government strategically cloaked itself the glory of the nation's 1970 World Cup victory[4] and embarked on a range of large-scale industrial projects including the construction of the Trans-Amazonian Highway and the world's largest hydroelectric dam in the Rio Paraná, at Itaipu. These projects were lauded by the government and mainstream media as opportunities to lift the hinterland out of poverty and consolidate man's mastery over the intractable rainforest. Bolstered by economic achievements and having managed to successfully tap into a sense of national pride, Medici remained extremely popular, even while intensifying levels of repression in the streets. Strategic moves such as these helped mask the regime's darker side and contributed to the 'collective amnesia' that persisted so long after the transition to democracy.

In Brazil the political opening, known as the *distensão* was extremely protracted. It began in 1974 and finally culminated with direct presidential elections in 1985. Over this period, new political freedoms and higher levels of tolerance towards protesters were seen to emerge incrementally. Notably, the *distensão* featured a range of carefully calculated gestures. Prominent among these was the passing of Law 6,683, popularly known as the Amnesty Law. This law had been eagerly anticipated by a growing movement that called for the pardoning of activists, exiles and political prisoners. However, the final version of the bill that was passed by President João Figueiro in 1979, pardoned *all* political crimes committed between 1961 and 1979, thus legalising impunity for Brazil's military and security officers (Schneider, 2010).

---

[3] In an article for Al Jazeera, Picq (2013) translates the testimony of filmmaker Lucia Murat who was tortured for years during her early 20's. During the Medici era, Murat was arrested and subjected to 'intense beatings followed by sessions of electroshocks while hanging naked and wet from a metal bar. Her naked body was covered with cockroaches, and for months, she spent nights tied up enduring what her interrogators called "sexual scientific torture"'.

[4] The Medici government published and distributed posters linking sporting success to governmental prowess and national progress towards industrial development. In one of these posters, the footballer Pele was featured scoring a goal, alongside this image the following slogan: 'Nobody can stop this country now'. For more details on the regime's political use of the World Cup, see Levine (1980) and Flynn (1973).

Furthermore, commentators have noted the high degree of *continuismo* that characterised the transition.[5] It is no hidden fact that military officials and collaborators secured key positions of influence within the new administration. The first civilian President, Jose Sarney, had long-standing connections to the outgoing regime, having previously led the government-sponsored party ARENA. Atencio (2014:13) highlights how unsurprisingly 'Brazil's first civilian President in more than twenty years took no meaningful steps toward reckoning with such crimes during his administration; to the contrary, he made a practice of pointedly ignoring the question...'. Strikingly, even in the wake of the 1985 *Nunca Mais* Report, which compiled thousands of classified documents detailing the use of torture during Médici's government, the 1979 political consensus held (Skidmore, 1988). Whilst '[t]he report shocked millions of Brazilians who had been unaware of (or had chosen to ignore) the extensive use of torture in the 1970s' (Snider, 2013), the civilian government, conceding to entrenched interests and failed to take steps to address the past violence. It was not until a whole decade after the publication of *Brasil: Nunca Mais*, that the armed forces finally admitted that acts of torture had taken place.

Collective remembrance is only possible to the extent that events and processes from the past are revisited and publicly validated through representative and communicative practices within society. Indeed, '[o]ur impressions yield to the forms that social life imposes on them' (Hawlbachs, 1992:49), such that our memories begin to converge around the versions of events that are given the greatest recognition. Crucially, in the years following the formal transition, sequential '...democratic governments chose to confront the authoritarian past through avoidance' (Goes, 2013:90), upholding an amnesty law designed to foreclose on calls for justice and remembrance and repeatedly conceding to the demands and interests of the military establishment. Drawing attention to the length of the dictatorship too, João Vicente Goulart (son of the deposed president) suggests that the institutional steps taken by the regime succeed-

---

[5] Several scholars have commented on the *continuismo* [continuities] that characterised the democratic transition (See Mainwaring 1986; Linz and Stepan, 1996 and Zaverucha, 1994; Arturi, 2001; Gugliano and Gallo 2013). Mainwaring (1986) for example explains that there was an intention to use the party system reforms of 1979 in such a way as to maximise ARENA's chances of victory in the 1982 elections. The strategy of the military masterminds was to split the opposition into several parties, anticipating either fragmentation, or the emergence of a large and somewhat acquiescent centrist party. This plan in fact backfired as viable and strong centrist and leftist parties emerged in the PT and PDMB respectively. In reaction though, in 1981, the military government once again manipulated the system in its favour, instituting a law to prevent the new parties from forming alliances in the run up to the elections. By 1982, participation in urban popular movements was once again in decline, '...a result of the economic crisis, the attention commanded by the political parties and the government's ability to marginalise these movements. In many rural areas, especially frontier regions, private and public repression remained rampant' (ibid: 11).

ed in transforming the public's consciousness and political expectations. 'The dictatorship raised a whole generation showing them that *that* was democracy, resorting to a number of stratagems to make it look legitimate' (Goulart cited by Bocchini, Lourenço and Virgilio, 2014, emphasis added). 'Nation-building' projects combined with the co-optation of the mainstream press succeeded in building popular support for the regime. The surge in criminal behaviour and violence that accompanied the democratic transition too meant that a decade after the return to civilian rule, less than 50% of Brazilians stated that democracy was their preferred form of rule (Latinobarometro, 2014).

To claim that Brazil has suffered from a 'collective amnesia' unfortunately risks downplaying the efforts of those who worked tirelessly to bring the violence of the dictatorship into public view. However, the notion of 'collective amnesia' does draw Brazil's comparably late entry to the Latin American 'memory boom' into sharp focus. Examining the authoritarian experience more closely, it is possible to underline a confluence of factors that have pressed for the convergence of memories around certain versions of events. In this *hegemonic* memory, the brutality of the regime, the plight of its victims and its contenders were pushed out of view.

III. Remembering? Street art and its forgotten forebears

Collective memory is today an increasingly contested terrain in Brazil. There have been important signs of change in official state discourse since 2005 (Schneider, 2010). For example, the Federal Government under the new leadership of the *Partido dos Trabalhadores* [Workers Party or PT] began to push a harder line on Human Rights and actively promote a new 'culture of memory' around the dictatorship years. Under the leadership of Luiz Inácio Lula da Silva, compensation for families of victims was extended and the possibility of establishing a Truth Commission was debated for the first time (Goes, 2013). Dilma Rousseff's presidency presented an opportune moment for the creation of a Truth Commission with a president who was herself a victim of human rights violations under the military regime (Engstrom, 2012). Alongside the institutional steps taken by the PT a number of Brazil's cultural industries have also started to claw back the past, replicating a fixation on traumatic historical events experienced elsewhere on the continent (Bilbija and Payne, 2011; Atencio, 2014). Curiously however, Brazil's street artists and their chroniclers have so far failed to take up 'memory' as a leitmotif. Resistant to 'looking backwards', they leave a whole generation of anti-regime art-activism unrecognised and underexplored. This sets Brazil apart from other countries on the continent where both street artists and art historians have worked to unpack and draw on anti-system antecedents from the authoritarian era.[6]

---

[6] In Argentina for example, the 2002 *Argentina Arde* initiative recalled the *Tucuman*

Most people would claim to have a good idea of what street art is, yet a precise definition can be hard to devise since the characteristics that are commonly used to describe it are inescapably broad. Street art has become a descriptive label for more or less any creative work visible on the street, where 'the street' refers rather broadly to any determinable public space. There are good reasons for this inclusiveness, particularly in Brazil, where street art is a medium constantly evolving as new techniques and surfaces are brought together. As any travel guide will attest, in Brazil today street art is ubiquitous and dramatic, existing in all corners and stretches of the country's urban zones. Today's street art - or *graphite*, as it is often called - is bold in both scale and style. It is highly decorative and striking to behold. Often highly abstract and brightly coloured, Brazilian graphite has become commonly associated with themes such as celebration, happiness and progress. In contrast to street art from neighbouring Latin American states, the content of the interventions rarely, if ever, recalls the past.

Increasingly too, graphite production in Brazil is sponsored by corporations and city councils. The city of São Paulo now integrates street art into its policies for regenerating and improving levels of social capital in impoverished neighbourhoods. It has also become common for residential and commercial landlords to invite artists to decorate their walls in order to increase the economic and aesthetic value of the premises. Since 2009, street art has been de-criminalised in Brazil, a clear recognition of the medium's growing commercial and touristic appeal (Young, 2012). In this way, much of today's street art is decidedly pro-system, feeding into private commercial and even national economic imperatives.

The international popularity and appeal of Brazilian street art has led to a surge in the publication of books, art-zines and even street art tours, many of which offer a cursory examination of street art's history and evolution in Brazil. Notably though, many of these sources inaccurately link the birth of Brazilian street art to the import of hip-hop codes and culture in the late 1980's. Notably, anti-system street artists took to the streets at least a decade earlier than is popularly assumed. In contrast to much of today's highly decorative graphite, the work done by Brazil's early street artists did not seek to uphold the status quo. Instead, it provided an important counter-discourse and way of expressing oppositional views in a context marred by the circumscription of rights and threat of violence under the dictatorship.

There are good reasons for considering the functions of this early anti-system street art as a part and source of social history in Brazil. Firstly, in work-

---

Arde art-action of 1968. Graffiti which appeared during the 2001 crisis also recalled the years of the *Guerra Sucia* as an indictment of the political class. Anti-regime art in Argentina has been extensively documented by a number of scholars Longoni (2006; 2007; 2008) Longoni and Bruzzone (2008) and Kozak (2004).

ing to undo a hegemonic memory that pushed the brutality of the regime, the plight of its victims and its contenders out of view, social historians like Bickford (1999; 2000) and Serbin (2006) urge us to scope out new forms of 'evidence'. These scholars have led the call for relevant actions and initiatives to unlock and amplify buried histories. Whilst Bickford (1999; 2000) for example speaks of an 'archival imperative', Serbin (2006) implores fellow scholars to uncover the marginalised, overlooked, unpopular and even distasteful stories in order to build a fuller picture of the authoritarian experience in Brazil. Street art, as an ephemeral medium with a 'built-in impermanency' can in fact provide an expedient, if unconventional, form of 'evidence' similar to that which Tschabrun (2003:305) attributes to posters:

> The built-in obsolescence of political posters endows them with a quality not always shared by more permanent forms of primary source material, namely that the creators of posters rarely, if ever, thought they were creating historical evidence…political posters may sometimes attest to underreported or even illegal activities that may be documented in no other way.

Carrying this argument forward, we might also think about the ways that forms of ephemera might provide a more candid insight into the strength of circulating ideologies as well as the existence and force of anti-system views at a particular historical moment. In his study of street art as a tool for democratization in Hispanic countries, Chaffee (1993) draws attention to the utility of posters, murals and tagging in political struggle. He suggests that in the absence of an open and pluralistic political system, street art can provide an underground or alternative media system that gives voice to a sidelined or censored opposition and serves an important role in breaking the complicity of silence under authoritarianism. The presence of oppositional slogans or even unsanctioned decorative interventions indicates that a noncompliant fringe endures, signaling to the public the possibility of resistance. As a result, regimes are often quick to cover up oppositional street art and to retaliate against street artists, if or when they are found. In fact, hardline reactions may be conceived as a testament to street art's very power.

A second reason for focusing on oppositional street art is that it may prompt us to identify and explore alternative ways of 'doing' politics. On the one hand as indicated above, street art may be seen as a type of anti-politics; a recourse for those who have been excluded from or choose to turn away from institutional channels. On the other hand though, an exploration of anti-system art-activism may prompt us to think more creatively about how we might engage in politics and in particular, what art has to offer that other instruments of protest cannot. Art produces experience of a form and type that differs from other political encounters. It allows for an extra-discursive form of expression which is free from the confines of established linguistic categories. As such, it can offer crucial spaces through which to imagine, experiment with and build new worlds. Thomas More's original sixteenth-century conceptualization of 'Utopia' has recently been revisited by interdisciplinary scholars (Duncombe, 2012; Demos, 2011) interested in exploring the intersections between art and politics. 'Utopia', as a beautiful no-place, itself implies the rejection of the present and initiates a process of active reflection on the possibility of alternative futures. Street art can thus be seen to mediate in the development of an individual sense of self and political community, having great relevance for how the authoritarian experience is felt, processed and resisted.

Political scientists are often hesitant to engage with creative and cultural material, worried in part about the problem of intentionality, or what Shaw (2010: 275) describes the 'question of aboutness'. In media and reception studies a similar question relates to the presumed gap between the coding and decoding of a source (Hodkinson, 2010). But this gap may be precisely the location of politics. And in determining the political effects of street art, we should look not only to the content of the intervention but to the experiences and reflections of the producers.

Within the Brazilian context, *Grupo Tupinãodá* were one of the first street art collectives to use the street as a medium for documenting and projecting their experiences and reflections of the dictatorship's repressive nature. Thus, detailed examination of their work adds a previously unexplored dimension to the body of research and study of Brazil's transition to democracy. In this way, examination of *Grupo Tupinãodá's* work presents an opportunity to build on the work of social historians such as Serbin (2006), Chaffee (1993) and Bickford (1999) and to document the collective's work as a living and vibrant historical tapestry of São Paulo's social history during the dictatorship and later during the political opening of the transition to democracy. Moreover, examination of the collective's work exposes the political roots of street art in Brazil and helps contextualise the post-transition nature of contemporary pro-system Brazilian street art.

IV. Grupo Tupinãodá

During the late 1970's, the artist-activists Milton Sogabe, Eduardo Duar and Zé Carratu began re-appropriating public spaces in São Paulo. They were later joined by César Teixeira, Jaime Prades, Rui Amaral and Carlos Delfino to form São Paulo's first street art collective *Grupo Tupinãodá*. *Tupinãodá* were a strong visual force of resistance in São Paulo during the dictatorship era. They intervened in a range of public spaces including areas of São Paulo that are now designated as world-renowned street art hubs.[7] As well as producing some of

---

[7] The Paulista/ Rebouças tunnel, running beneath São Paulo's financial centre is now one of the most famous graffiti spots in the city. It is passed daily by thousands of commuters.

the Brazil's earliest examples of political stencilling and chalked graffiti, they also produced large-scale outdoor installations and striking 'mega-graffiti' that pre-empted the abstract and bold styles of today's *graphite*.

Through combining the limited existing documentation of the group's activities together with information from a series of unstructured interviews conducted with Jaime Prades and Rui Amaral in 2011 and 2012, it has been possible to build a clearer timeline and picture of *Tupinãodá's* anti-system interventions. The group's story is recounted below, offering insights into what factors influenced the artists to take to the streets; the political aims and effects of their art, as well as their experiences as part of a movement for political change.

i. Surfacing

Tupinãodá's members had divergent backgrounds and political beliefs. Rui Amaral, for example, began his street art interventions as a part of the PT's youth mobilisation, whilst Ze Carratu described himself as the son of Italian anarchists and a student of the 'French May' (Carratu, 1989). By contrast, Jaime Prades became absorbed into the organised Brazilian opposition in his late adolescent years and began producing political cartoons and pamphlets for left-wing activists at the publishing house *Editora Abril* (Prades, 2011a). Having all grown up during the dictatorship era however, the youths shared a grievance. Their opportunities had been formed and in many ways impeded following the imposition of the Institutional Acts. They looked on as swathes of the city's cultural and historical buildings were demolished as real estate speculation went unregulated (Carratu, 1989). Moreover, as adolescents, tales of violence and harassment directed at students and workers in the São Paulo area compounded their animosity towards the military police and government. Prades notes that, 'It was the time of the military regime, and in our generation you could not remain neutral. Our generation was militant, we took that to heart… And this manifested in the mobilisation of *Tupinãodá*' (Prades, 2011a).

The artists who came together to form *Grupo Tupinãodá* were heavily influenced by the work of modernist poet Oswaldo de Andrade. In particular, his *Manifesto Antropófago* [Cannibal Manifesto], which sought to play with the old colonial notion that Brazil was a land inhabited by cannibals. In the 1920's, de Andrade encouraged his fellow Brazilians to think about the possibilities of a cultural rather than a physical cannibalism, suggesting that Brazilians embrace (or ingest), and transform the received morsels of European culture in ways that would engender and elaborate a uniquely Brazilian way of life. Identity thus became a strong organizing theme for the artists, with their works challenging dominant narratives about Brazil's past, its present and its future.

The group's critical stance was reflected in their choice of name, taken from a playful reference to de Andrade's work in a poem by the geographer Antonio

Robert de Moraes: '*Você é tupi daqui ou tupi de lá, e tupiniquim ou tupinão-da?*' [Are you Tupi from here? Or Tupi from there? Are you *Tupiniquim*, or *Tupinãodá*?] (Prades, 2011a). '*Tupiniquim*' was the language and name of the indigenous inhabitants of Brazil who made up the majority of the population when European colonisers arrived on the continent. In modern-day Brazil, the term is often used as a perjorative term for 'Brazilian national'. *Tupinãodá*, is a word play based around the refusal to comply.

ii. The art of stealth

Initially all of the artists worked alone on the streets. Writing on the origins and practice of the *Tupinãodá* collective, curator Fabio Magalhães (2009) explains that, in order to stay ahead of the police, the street artists had to develop quick production techniques, giving their art distinctive stylistic features that often drew its ephemerality into sharp focus.

In 1983, Milton Sogabe produced an array of simple figurative stencils in and around the neighbourhood of Pinheiros, São Paulo. Sogabe's crude stencils often depicted Brazil's tribal peoples and hunter-gatherer communities, armed with spears and arrows. Meanwhile, Carratu took to producing hasty chalk drawings, including abstract emblems and coloured patterns sketched over previously blacked out squares. Prior to meeting Carratu and the other members of *Tupinãodá*, Rui Amaral set about plastering the streets of Vila Madelena with hundreds of tiny hand-drawn stick figures that danced energetically and gesticulated wildly.

Working alone, the artists would often exploit the cover of darkness, or choose desolate areas such as abandoned recreation centres and demolition zones. As Carratu (1989) states, one of the reasons for this was to rescue cultural spaces. Since years of repression directed at students organisations and learning groups had led to a decline in creative local and community projects. However, another more strategic imperative for painting in abandoned areas was the need to skirt the gaze and censorship of the authorities. Amaral, who was arrested and imprisoned for his work on the streets, described the need for caution and vigilance among street artists. He explained that prior to the political opening, to self-attribute or work publicly would have been to invite brutality from the *Departamento de Ordem Política e Social* [Department of Social and Political Order or DOPS] (Amaral, 2011).

Anthropologist James C. Scott (1992) describes these deliberate attempts to veil acts of insubordination as 'infrapolitics'. He underlines the often overlooked power of the *art of stealth*, which can protect activists from retaliation and allow opposition movements to grow outside of the view and reach of the repressive state apparatus. The decision to organise formally as a collective can be seen as an extension of this strategic drive: 'We wanted to go bigger, bolder and reach more people' (Prades, 2011b). The need for constant vigilance posed limits to the size and detail of the street art interventions that could be produced on an individual basis. Artists thus began to look out for each other. Familiar artists collectivised their efforts; one or more would keep a look out while the rest worked. They began to paint (and chalk) alongside one another, mixing styles and expanding their coverage in order to heighten visibility and impact.

iii. Identity and insubordination

The re-appropriation of identity was a recurrent theme in the group's works. Sogabe's tribal stencils, supplanted those traditional groups afflicted by the regime's developmental projects in the Amazon Basin to the centre of São Paulo, giving them an urban presence. Meanwhile, Jaime Prades' stencil of Tarsila do Amaral's 'Uma Negra', sought to give the famed Brazilian painting a greater visibility by bringing it back to the poor and 'excommunicated' (Mattelart, 2008) of Brazil:

> ... the goal of my own work was to bring to the streets this highly regarded painting; to dislocate it from the institutions of high art and make it truly accessible to the mass audience by bringing it to the street. I suppose that in a way it was like a type of Brazilian 'pop art'...(Prades, 2012).

As the political opening presented new opportunities for political expression and heightened tolerance, the group became bolder in their collective projects to invoke critical engagement around the concept of Brazilian identity. In 1984, *Tupinãodá* created a provocative installation of 'found objects' in the gardens around the University of São Paulo. Over the course of several months, the group collected a vast number of full rubbish bags coloured black, yellow and blue. They fashioned these bags on an expansive rectangular green lawn in a geometrical composition that recalled the *Bandeira do Brasil* [the Brazilian flag]. Conscious of the *continuismo*, the artists seem to have offered little commentary on this inflammatory juxtaposition at the time. However, many years later, Jaime Prades explained that the intervention was conceived collectively as an affront to the regime's monopoly on Brazilian identity and its appropriation of the national colours to justify the abuse of Brazil's indigenous people and the poor (Prades, 2011b).

iv. The power and virtue of aesthetic expression

Reflecting on his early chalk graffiti, Carratu (1989) inferred that society at the time was headed for a radical break and that role of the artist was to help bring this about, by signalling 'chãos' through art. Meanwhile, Amaral has described his stick figures as 'part of an invented utopia', a non-real, ideal place where people might express themselves freely without harassment from the police. (Amaral, 2011). These ephemeral expressions, offering visions of chaos and utopia respectively, worked on different levels to offer cues for political change. First, each offered a suggestion that the world might be different and provided a means for the street artists to reach beyond the present and re-envision day-to-day life. Even if onlookers did not fully understand these gestures to other worlds, the presence of unsanctioned urban inscriptions in itself signalled a breach in the regime's machinery and capacity for total control. It is perhaps no surprise then that as Amaral (2011) reflects: '[the government] made every effort to cover up our graffiti'.

Amaral also made a point of explaining that whilst his dancing figures and later collective works with *Tupinãodá* had an instrumental function, they were also important to him at a more personal level. He suggests that:

> ...producing the figures gave to me some kind of release, they were freedom, presence... Art is determined by something more than what goes on in your head. It is also your heart (Amaral, 2011).

Amaral's message here reminds us that any understanding of how street art gains its power must take stock of the complex, sticky and sometimes indeterminable entanglements of emotions that human beings feel and the ways that these too can impel political action.

During the mid 1980's, as Brazil emerged from over two decades of military government, *Grupo Tupinãodá* produced an array of large-scale wall-paintings around the city of São Paulo, increasingly working in the light of day and tackling expansive public spots with less regard for the authorities. Perhaps most notably, *Tupinãodá* were the first to paint in the now famous *beco do Batman* [Batman alleyway] as well as the large concrete tunnel running beneath the Avenida Paulista in São Paulo's financial centre. As Magalhães (2009) describes, these new works were playful in terms of the imaginary, invoking bold patterns and innovative, sometimes abstract themes. In terms of both style and scale, these works pre-empted contemporary *graphite*.

When asked about this shift in the group's style and fervour, Prades provides two responses. Firstly, he suggests that the re-instatement of rights and freedoms accompanying the political opening gave them the confidence to paint in the open. But he also states, 'What I think is that when the pressure cooker started to open, paint gushed out!' (Prades, 2011a). He compares the painting experience to an eruption or wave of feeling that was unleashed with the transition. Brian Massumi's introduction to *Parables for the Virtual: Movement, Affect, Sensation* (2002), is insightful here. Massumi states,

> When I think of my body, and ask what it does to earn that name, two things stand out. It moves. It feels. In fact, it does both at the same time. It moves as it

feels, and it feels itself moving. Can we think of a body without this: an intrinsic connection between movement and sensation, whereby each immediately summons the other?

Sometimes, bodies move as they feel and they feel themselves moving. An engulfing mood or state of feeling can - as much as any instrumental objective - spur street art production. As Halsey and Young (2006) put it, street art production does things to the artists' bodies as much as it does things to the surfaces on which they write. It may provide an outlet for feeling and an opportunity for renewal.

The change in scale and intensity seen in the group's later works reflects the shifting opportunity structure and political conditions as the country moved through the *distensão*. It also reflects the force of their sentiments as the country emerged from the long 'years of lead'. Through *Tupinãodá's* works it is possible to trace the stylistic evolution of Brazilian street art, including important pre-cursors to today's globally popular but largely decorative *graphite* form. The group's story and indeed their art thus forms an important bridge to the present, illuminating the manifestly political origins of street art in Brazil.

V. Colouring the streets: Reflections on Brazil's street art against authoritarianism

As this chapter has argued, the authoritarian experience in Brazil was characterised by a confluence of factors that made the country something of a regional outlier in terms of its memory politics. Unlike neighbouring Argentina and Chile, Brazil's political and cultural institutions have been slow to emerge from a pervasive and collective 'amnesia' around the dictatorship years. Whilst aspects of this amnesia are increasingly contested today, Brazil's street artists and street art chroniclers have remained resistant to cues for 'looking backwards'. Memory has not been taken up as a theme or as a motif by these actors and Brazil's very first generation of street artists has been under documented as a result.

The chapter discussed São Paulo's first known street art collective, *Grupo Tupinãodá*, whose story of opposition and resistance has fallen far outside of the scope of hegemonic collective memory. Through exploring *Tupinãodá's* street art interventions, this chapter offers one way of answering Serbin (2006) and Bickford's (1999) calls for more innovative approaches to historiography in Brazil. Of course, the act of 'recovering' their story also offers a new cue for 'remembering' in itself. As such this chapter self-consciously feeds into a broader cycle of cultural memory, as described by Atencio (2014).

Tupinãodá's resort to an 'art of stealth' during the most repressive period of military rule is suggestive of the strong obstacles and disincentives for oppositional political expression. Meanwhile, the collective's persistent insubordination and recurrent endeavours to contest and re-present the idea of 'Brazilianness' directs us to places, groups and political beliefs that remained outside the control of the state's machinery. Linked to this, *Tupinãodá's* street art reveals alternative ways and options for engaging politically under authoritarianism. Firstly, through their imagined utopias and pre-emptions of chaos, the group served an important political function by proposing and maintaining that the world could be otherwise. Indeed, the power of utopian imagery lies not in the specificity of future visions themselves but in the very fact that such imagination is possible.

Additionally, the artists' comments suggest at the affective interplay that occurs around street art, illuminating the way that street art production, by offering a channel for expression, can in fact enable a process of personal renewal to take place. The possibility of healing, renewal and regeneration through art production and reception is a timeworn area of focus for scholars of aesthetics, with heralds dating back to the classical works of Aristotle. *Tupinãodá's* experience draws attention to the past 'healing' work that has been done through street art production, underlining its historic, intrinsic and community value.

Yet, rather than 'looking backwards', young and aspiring *graffiteiros* in today's Brazil have become more fixated on prosperous futures and street art's extrinsic and commercial value. They increasingly pursue corporate and even state sponsorship for a medium that was once considered subversive and intolerable by the very same patrons. Few are aware of the battle to re-appropriate the public space which took place from the 1970s and even fewer are perhaps aware of *Tupinãodá's* daring initiatives which played a determinable role in the spaces and distinctive graphite style that brought Brazilian art into international focus during the 1990s. Recuperating *Tupinãodá's* story prompts us to question street art's political purpose in today's Brazil. In particular, the tolerance for and de-criminalisation of street art may suggest that the state and other institutions of power no longer deem the medium to pose a commercial or ideological threat. One might thus wonder whether Brazilian street art has lost something of its critical edge and power, with consequences for available modes of resistance.

References

Amaral, R. 2011. Interview with H.E. Ryan. 28 September. São Paulo, Brazil.

Arturi, C. S. 2001. 'O debate teórico sobre mudança de regime político: o caso brasileiro'. *Revista de Sociologia e Política* 17. 11-31.

Atencio, R. 2014. *Memory's Turn. Reckoning with Dictatorship in Brazil*. Madison, WI: University of Wisconsin Press.

Bickford, L. 1999. 'The Archival Imperative: Human Rights and Historical Memory in Latin America's Southern Cone'. *Human Rights Quarterly* 21:4. 1097-1122.

_____ . 2000. 'Human Rights Archives and Research on Historical Memory: Argentina, Chile and Uruguay'. *Latin American Research Review* 35.2. 160-82.

Bilbija, K. and Payne, L. 2011. *Accounting for Violence: Marketing Memory in Latin America*. Durham, NC: Duke University Press.

Bocchini, B. Lourenço, I. and Virgilio, P. 2014. 'Brazil's economic miracle, social exclusion and state violence'. *Agência Brasil*. Available: http://agenciabrasil. ebc.com.br/en/politica/noticia/2014-03/brazilian-economic-miracle-social -exclusion-and-state-violence. Last accessed 01/08/2014.

Carratu, Z. 1989. Interview with C. Carlsson and Manning for the documentary *Brazilian Dreams*. São Paulo, Brazil.

Chaffee, L. 1993. *Political Protest and Street Art: Popular Tools for Democratization in Hispanic Countries*. Westport, CT: Greenwood Press.

Coehlo, J. 2013. 'Globo media organisation apologises for supporting Brazil's dictatorship'. *The Independent Online*. Available: http://www.independent. co.uk/news/world/americas/globo-media-organisation-apologises-for-supporting-brazils-dictatorship-8795277.html. Last accessed 01/08/2014.

Demos, T. 2011. 'Is Another World Possible? The Politics of Utopia and the Surpassing of Capitalism in Recent Exhibition Practice' in Hlavajova, M and Sheikh, S (eds) *On Horizons: A Critical Reader in Contemporary Art*. Utrecht and Rotterdam: BAK. 52-82.

Duncombe, S. 2012. .Imagining No-place'. *Transformative Works and Cultures* 10.

Engstrom, P. 2014. 'Brazilian Foreign Policy and Human Rights: Change and Continuity under Dilma'. *Critical Sociology* 38. 835- 49.

Flynn, P. 1973. 'The Brazilian development model: the political dimension'. *World Today* 29:11. 481-94.

Goes, I. 2013. 'Between Truth and Amnesia: State Terrorism, Human Rights Violations and Transitional Justice in Brazil'. *European Review of Latin American and Caribbean Studies* 94. 83-96.

Gugliano, A. and Gallo, C. 2013. 'On the Ruins of the Democratic Transition: Human Rights as an Agenda Item in the Abeyance for the Brazilian Democracy'. *Bulletin of Latin American Research* 32:3. 325-38.

Halsey, M. and Young, A. 2006. 'Our desires are ungovernable: Writing graffiti in urban space'. *Theoretical criminology* 10:3. 275-306.

Hawlbachs, M. 1992. *On Collective Memory*. Chicago, IL: University of Chicago Press.

Hodkinson, P. 2010. *Media, Culture and Society: An Introduction*. London: Sage.

Jorge, F. 1987. *cale e boca, jornalista!* São Paulo: New Century Press.

Kozak, C. 2004. *Contra la pared: sobre graffitis, pintadas y otras intervenciones urbanes*. Buenos Aires: Libros del Rojas, Universidad de Buenos Aires.

Latinobarometro. 2014. *Análisis Online*. Available: http://www.latinobarometro. org/latOnline.jsp Last accessed 01/08/2013.

Levine, R. 1980. 'The Burden of Success: "Futebol" and Brazilia Society through the 1970s'. *Journal of Popular Culture* 14:3. 453-64.

Linz, J. and Stepan, A. 1996. *Problems of Democratic Transition and Consolidation. Southern Europe, South America, and Post-Communist Europe*. Baltimore.MD: Johns Hopkins University Press.

Longoni, A. 2006 'Is Tucumán Still Burning', Translated by Marta Ines Merajver. Sociedad (Buenos Aires). Vol.1, Selected edition. Available: http://socialsciences .scielo.org/scielo.php?pid=S0327-77122006000100003&script=sci_arttext. Last accessed 06/04/12.

_____. 2007. 'El Siluetazo: On the Border between Art and Politics'. *Frontiers*. Available: http://www.sarai.net/publications/readers/07-frontiers /176-186_longoni.pdf. Last accessed 01/08/2011.

_____. 2008. 'Crossroads for Activist Art in Argentina'. *Third Text* 22:5. 575-87.

Longoni, A. and Bruzzone, G. 2008. *El Siluetazo*. Buenos Aires: Adriana Hidalgo Editora.

Magalhães, F. 2009. 'Jaime Prades: Art in Context' in Prades, J. (ed.) *A Arte de Jaime Prades*. São Paulo: Olhares.

Mainwaring, S. 1986. 'The Transition to Democracy in Brazil'. *Journal of Interamerican Studies and World Affairs* 28:1. 149-79.

Massumi, B. 2002. *Parables for the Virtual: Movement, Affect, Sensation*. Durham, NC: Duke University Press.

Mattelart, A. 2008. 'Communications/excommunications: an interview with Armand Mattelart'. Conducted by Costas M. Constantinou. Available: http:// www.fifth-estate-online.co.uk/comment/Mattelart-   intervie%5B1%5D. pdf. Last accessed 10/08/2012.

Picq, M. 2013. 'Rescuing the Memory of Latin America'. *Al Jazeera Opinion*. Available: http://www.aljazeera.com/indepth/opinion/2013/06/ 20136611144173414.html. Last accessed 01/08/2014.

Prades, J. 2009. *A Arte de Jaime Prades*. São Paulo: Olhares.

_____. 2011a. Interview with H.E. Ryan. 29 September. São Paulo, Brazil.

_____. 2011b. Interview with H.E. Ryan. 30 November. São Paulo, Brazil.

Scott, J. 1992. *Domination and the Arts of Resistance: Hidden Transcripts*. New Haven, CT: Yale University Press.

Schneider, N. 2010. 'Breaking the "Silence" of the Military Regime: New Politics of Memory in Brazil'. *Bulletin of Latin American Research* 30:2. 198-212.

_____. 2011. 'Impunity in Post-authoritarian Brazil: The Supreme Court's Recent Verdict on the Amnesty Law'. *European Review of Latin American and Caribbean Studies* 90. 39-54.

Serbin, K. 2006. 'Review Article: Memory and Method in the Emerging Historiography of Latin America's Authoritarian Era'. *Latin American Politics & Society* 48:3. 185-98.

Shaw, R. 2001. 'Processes, Acts, and Experiences: Three Stances on the Problem of Intentionality'. *Ecological Psychology* 13:1. 275-314.

Skidmore, T. 1988. *The Politics of Military Rule in Brazil 1964-1985*. Oxford: Oxford University Press.

Snider, C. 2013. 'Get to Know a Brazilian – Emílio Garrastazu Médici'. *Americas North and South*. Available: http://americasouthandnorth.wordpress.com /2013/02/03/get-to-know-a-brazilian-emilio-garrastazu-medici/. Last accessed 10/07/14.

Tschabrun, S. 2003. 'Off the Wall and into a Drawer: Managing a Research Collection of Political Posters'. *The American Archivist* 66. 303–24.

Young, M. 2012. 'The Legalisation of Street Art in Rio de Janeiro, Brazil'. *The Huffington Post*. Available: http://www.huffingtonpost.com/michelle-young/ post_3047_b_1307119.html. Last accessed 01/08/2014.

Zaverucha, J. 1994. *Rumor de sabres: tutela militar ou controle civil?* São Paulo: Atica.

IV. Uneasy Presence

11

WHOSE STREETS? OUR STREETS! THE PLACE OF THE STREETS IN THE OCCUPY MOVEMENT

Ashley Lavelle

The streets were the home of the Occupy movement that erupted spectacularly following the anti-Wall Street protests of 17 September 2011. Influenced by the Arab Spring and European resisters such as the Spanish *Indignados*, Occupy represents a deepening of radicalism and a heightening of the stakes since the path-breaking 'anti-globalisation' protests that commenced with the late-1999 siege of the World Trade Organization (WTO) meeting in Seattle. But whereas the latter harassed international organisations whenever and wherever they met, Occupy was less reactive and episodic (Klein, 2011). Indeed, the audacity of a movement that strove to 'occupy' Wall Street – a global behemoth whose financial power is rivalled only by the City of London's – is hard to overstate. The diversity, colour, and militancy of the combatants injected a shot of adrenaline into the bloodstream of the western left. The capture of world attention by this new force was indicated not just in the reverberations of solidarity Occupying in some 1500 cities across the globe, but also in 2011's hottest word: 'Occupy' (Gallman, 2012).

Yet the Occupy movement's relationship to the streets and public space – as central points of resistance to global capital – is worthy of critical examination. There are lessons to be drawn from the events of 15 November 2011 when the New York Police Department (NYPD) swooped on Occupy Wall Street headquarters at Zuccotti Park and cleared it with chilling and brutal precision (Writers for the 99%, 2012: 180; 181). Occupy is about more than taking to the streets. But, as indicated by its name and one of its favourite chants – 'Whose Streets? Our Streets!' – demonstrations and the occupation of public space are the movement's trademark features; since the America-wide evictions in November 2011 it has been significantly – probably fatally – wounded.

It is suggested below that, while mass protests in urban districts are instrumental to any radical movement, the streets have limitations as sites from which to launch campaigns for fundamental social change. Power in capitalist society is located in institutions of the state, the education system, the media, the Church, the family, and, most importantly, in economic centres of capital accumulation. Drawing on the experience of some 1960s radicals, it is argued that any movement too focused on the streets risks neglecting the power structures and relations that perpetuate the social horrors that brought it into existence. Capitalism is a global *system* of profit-making whose oxygen is the countless hours of daily toil by the world's labourers, a system that can only partially be confronted through street demonstrations and public encampments. It follows that extending links with organised labour should be a high priority: the protest and the occupation should complement the economic muscle of the strike.

As well as outlining an argument for a movement more broadly concentrated on capitalism's sites of power, this paper suggests that the modern state is increasingly equipped to manage discontent in the streets. While new technology and social media assist activists in unique ways, at the same time the arsenal of weaponry in the hands of police forces and authorities has expanded ominously. Finally, the dominance of the streets in recent movements should be seen in the context of recent political trends, particularly since the 1990s, when the marginalisation of Marxism and class politics pushed the labour movement well down the pecking order as an agent of change in the minds of many radicals.

Power and Capitalism

In late-2011 the Occupy chorus, 'Whose Streets? Our Streets!', rang out through cities across the United States, where festivals of conviviality were interspersed with running battles against riot police.[1] Here it is important to recognise, however, that Occupy's nemesis, global capitalism, is a *system* of class relations defined by the constitutive antagonism between capitalists and workers (Callinicos, 2010: 18).[2] Needless to say, 'Occupy' meant different things to its many different participants: to some it was primarily about being there, revelling in the carnival-like atmosphere of the campouts in the spirit of a 1960s style 'be-in'. But clearly inequality was a leading motivator, with many Occupiers identifying as part of the '99%' majority, pitted against the '1%' minority (Writers for the 99%, 2012). Capitalism's elite and its hangers-on may constitute more than 1%

---

[1] It is difficult to generalise about a movement that involved hundreds of thousands of people and spanned hundreds of cities across the US and approximately 1500 worldwide (van Gelder, 2011: 2), so this paper is focused on the US movement, and partly based on the author's experience in Oakland in October-November 2011.

[2] As opposed to approaches emphasising 'blue' and 'white' collars and subjective assessments, the 'working class' is defined here in objective terms as encompassing those with little or no control over their labour, which they are compelled to sell to an employer (see Ste. Croix 1981, 43-4). In other words, in most industrialised countries a majority of people, when we include pensioners, the unemployed, and those dependants of wage labourers, are working class.

of the population, but the social fractures that gave rise to Occupy are undeniably deep.

These, however, cannot be confronted merely on the streets or by occupying public space. Capitalism is perpetuated by 'fraud' and 'force'. The 'fraud' used to ensure capitalism's reproduction includes subtle means such as the maintenance of conformity through a mass media that reifies capitalist social relations, as well as through the more general intellectual and cultural hegemony enjoyed by the ruling class (Herman and Chomsky, 1994; Gramsci 1989, esp. 12-13). But pro-capitalist ideas are hegemonic in specific circumstances, which the likes of Gramsci tended to ignore: many people accept authority and hierarchy because of the effects of capitalist alienation, which means that any individual person has little or no control over one's labour or the broader events that shape a person's life, making it more natural to submit to a king, a president, or a general (Rees, 1998: 243). When workers get uppity after awakening to the fraud of capitalist society's fairness – the wage paid for labour that masks the exploitation inherent in the relationship between boss and worker – as a result of economic and political crises, or through their own activity, they potentially confront 'force' in the form of mass state repression by the police, armed forces, and intelligence services. The responses and strategies employed by activists in coping with this violence go a long way towards explaining their success or failure, as we shall see later.

Yet, on a more day-to-day basis, capitalism endures essentially because of the human labour that keeps the profits flowing for capital. Wall Street, in this sense, is an order built on sand without the wage labour that generates the corporate 'earnings' on which the speculators and desk-jockeys hedge their bets. The location of power in the hands of the capitalists who own the bulk of productive resources on which the world's workers expend their energies explains why those reformist politicians who have sought to change society through existing political structures have so often failed: by focusing on parliament or other bourgeois assemblies, they have left intact the wealth-making – and therefore politically powerful – institutions that transcend any government, party, or president, and whose decisions determine the fate of economies and nations. As Occupy's New York City General Assembly (2011: 36) put it, corporations 'run our governments'. Reformist politicians have often been rudely awakened to where power lies in capitalist society, as in the case of the military coup in Chile on September 11, 1973, when General Augusto Pinochet's forces crushed the democratically elected Socialist government of Salvador Allende (Prieto, 1974).

The latter was an extreme example of a long history of left governments hopelessly compromised by attempts to legislate for socialism via the capitalist state (Herman, 1999). Occupy's birth is partly explained by the dismal failure of the rhetorical President, Barack Obama, to go anywhere near rewarding the hopes many Americans invested in his candidature. While part of this failure owes to Obama's market-friendly politics and his conciliatory *modus operandi* (Klinenberg and Manza, 2012), underlying it all is the mistaken belief that the political system can challenge the domination of Wall Street and America, Inc. In contrast, as St. Clair and Frank (2012: 303) point out, the object of Occupy 'isn't reform…but radical systemic change'.

Capitalism is a system that must be assailed by targeting its life-blood, the human labour undergirding its profit-making. This requires an orientation to the working class whose daily, hourly efforts keep the wheels of capital grinding over people and planet. The power of organised labour is symbolised by the strike, which has effected important social change in the industrial capitalist era. As Cameron observed, the 'strike is the only weapon for which the opponents of labour have real respect' (Cameron, 1970: 1). From a more radical perspective, the German Marxist Rosa Luxemburg stressed the revolutionary potential of the mass strike, which offered the most effective way to galvanise workers into action collectively as well as 'a means of undermining and overthrowing the old state power and of stemming capitalist exploitation'. She added that, with the growth of industry and the development of the working class, the antagonism between classes sharpens, and consequently the 'more effective and decisive must mass strikes become'. Thus the lynchpin of resistance in bourgeois revolutions, 'the fight at the barricades [on the streets], the open conflict with the armed power of the state, is in the revolution of today only the culminating point, only a moment in the process of the proletarian mass struggle' (Luxemburg, 1986: 72; 73).

The steadily growing power of the proletariat and its unique capacity to wield this strike weapon explains why the labour movement has been critical to many great social upheavals since the beginning of the twentieth century – from the Russian revolution of 1917 to the present Arab Spring. While none of these has thus far succeeded in demolishing global capitalism as Marx had hoped, they nevertheless reveal the potential economic potency of working class strike action.[3] And it is true that in the industrialised core of the system struggle by workers and unions remains at a low level, partly the residual effects of the defeats of Thatcherism and Reaganism in the 1980s: in the US, in which we are most interested for the purposes of this paper, the total number of work stoppages involving more than 1000 workers was just 19 in 2012, compared to 470 in 1952 and 412 in 1969 (BLS, 2013: 3-4). Even allowing for changes in sizes of workforces, this says something about the presence strength of labour. But this can change – and quickly – as it did in the late-1960s after a period of ebb (Bentley, 1980: 31). Unions and workers have been in worse situations before

---

[3] Some of these great upheavals are discussed in Barker (1987); the Russian (1917) experience is dealt with at greater length in Rees (1991).

– whether it be the late-nineteenth century or in the period after the Great Depression – only to reassert their power triumphantly at a later stage.

Needless to say, there has been extensive discussion among commentators and activists about the revolutionary potential of different agents. Like some of these discussants, the more recent proponents of the 'multitude' over the working class as the agent of radical change often ignore the latter's unique economic power at the point of production (e.g. Hardt and Negri, 2004: xiv; xv). Indeed, they often mistakenly assume the diminution of the global working class, all the while capitalism continues to transform more of the world's population into wage labourers who might one day begin digging the system's grave (Harman, 2010: 331). This is also a salient point for union activists excited by Occupy's *élan*. One union official in New York predicted: 'You'll see more unions on the street, wanting to tap into the energy of Occupy' (Appelbaum, cited in Greenhouse, 2011). It's worth remembering, however, that what makes organised labour *sui generis* is not its ability to mobilise on the streets but rather the economic bargaining clout it can deploy at short-notice. Thus unionists ought to be wary if any of their wily leaders try to dragoon them into a street march as a substitute for wielding the graver – but ultimately more effective – strike weapon. For this reason, we must take issue with David Harvey's assessment of Occupy. While he does argue for Occupy to build links with 'students, immigrants, the underemployed' and others negatively impacted by the policies of the 1%, the central lesson that he draws from the movement is that it 'shows us that the collective power of bodies in public space is still the most effective instrument of opposition when all other means of access are blocked' (Harvey, 2012: 161-2).

Such a conclusion ignores the relative ease with which the NYPD shut down Occupy (see below). The proletariat does need to be out in force in the streets and neighbourhoods with its allies, but because of its power at the point of production it must seek a leading role among the 99%. Strikes have the effects of not only hitting the bosses where it hurts in lost production, but they also can produce mass pickets, themselves sites of collective resistance that can draw in wider members of the public and throw up a range of questions about the role of the state, in particular the police, who seek to repress the pickets and allow non-union labour a safe passage to nullify the strike.

The synergies between the labour movement and Occupy should already be clear. Occupiers stood shoulder-to-shoulder with workers at union pickets (Greenhouse, 2011). Meanwhile, unions provided material support to hard-up Occupiers in the form of financial donations, food, toilet facilities, and salaries for organisers (Gitlin, 2012: 206). But more often than not organised labour was represented in the movement by individual protestors rather than by strikers: in the case of Oakland Occupy, for example, the 'general strike' of 2 November 2011, in which the author was a participant, was declared by Occupy rather than by unions. The port closed on the day not as a result of workers walking off the job but of protestors marching to shut it down – no mean feat, but not quite the same as a labour forced closure. The individuals who struck on 2 November did so with the blessing of their union, but without formal action being taken to bring out workforces *en masse* (Gee, 2011).

This was likely to be true of Occupy at large. One reason for this is the constitutive conservatism of the labour hierarchy, which usually desires to harmonise the labour-management relationship rather than dismantle the economic system undergirding it (Bramble, 1996). Union leaderships, and often their memberships, are frequently prone to a narrow-minded 'economism' that focuses on the 'bread-and-butter' issues of pay and conditions in the workplaces they inhabit, in contrast to the more global outlook characteristic of much of Occupy. Also, union membership rates have been in long-term decline in the US, weakening labour's confidence (Gitlin, 2012: 209; 210). Nevertheless, as noted above, organised labour remains an extremely powerful force, which makes it a political imperative for Occupy to maximise the support and activity of workers, whose importance owes not to any moral superiority over the rest of the oppressed but simply to their industrial might. This point was missed by elements of Occupy Los Angeles who opposed formally allying with local retrenched hotel workers in October 2011 on the grounds that their union had ties to the Democratic Party (Wilson, 2011). Occupiers should ally with striking workers. This should not be construed as a one-way process, but rather as a dialectic of mutual education: unions and workers have been inspired by the imagination, courage, and militancy of the Occupy activists (Greenhouse, 2011). It has been suggested that student protestors in the 1960s played a part in the upsurge in strikes at the time by alerting workers to the merits of direct action, beckoning them to walk off the job through their heroic example (Bentley, 1980: 31). It is to be hoped that Occupy may have a similar catalysing effect today. Every strike and resistance to layoffs should be infused with Occupy's global vistas of alternative worlds, while Occupiers should adopt the day-to-day struggles of the working class over labour rights, public housing, education, and welfare (Farnham, 2012: 25).

Hitting the Streets – in the 1960s

Whose streets? For the early Walter Benjamin, the streets were the natural habitat of the 'eternally restless, eternally moving' masses, the arena in which the teeming voiceless could find their voice and become architects of their own emancipation (cited in Suleiman, 1994: 61; 62). Yet, past radicals who resisted capitalism almost exclusively in the streets were denied the long-term radical social change they sought. One reason for this is the modern state's relative ability to parlay such forms of resistance, for it was a co-ordinated police assault in New York that evicted the activists from Zuccotti Park, effectively closing down the historic Occupy Wall Street movement (Writers for the 99%, 2012: 180-1).[4] In the words of Adbusters, who issued the call for the original occupation on 17 September 2011, 'they smashed our encampments with midnight paramilitary raids' (Adbusters, 2012).

The state is more comfortable at responding to set-piece battles in the streets: anyone who has attended a demonstration will know that a relatively small group of police can control a significantly larger number of protestors, in part because of the steadily expanding weaponry at their disposal, but also because of their discipline, chain of command, and organisation in the context of police forces' increasingly militaristic operations and training (e.g. McCulloch, 2001). The Russian revolutionary Vladimir Lenin's description in 1917 of states as 'bodies of armed men which have prisons, etc., at their command' (Lenin, 1970: 10) will resonate with any contemporary rebel confronted in the streets by columns of muscle-bound Robocops bedecked in grotesque armoury.

Authorities have a decisive advantage on urban terrain, not just in terms of the use of force to arrest and drive protesters off the streets, but also through their ability to control and co-ordinate cities' traffic and public transport, and through their access to increasingly sophisticated monitoring equipment, which has ushered in the 'surveillance society' (Lyon, 2001). More generally the state is better at managing protest action isolated to a specific locale. While unlimited in its political imagination, as Dyer-Witheford argues Occupy has been limited by the 'boundaries of the squares, plazas and parks it has seized. These are sites of assembly, but not sites of production. To the extent Occupy stays within them, it remains a symbolic protest, stopping nothing' (Dyer-Witheford, 2012: 4).

The politics of public space has been an area of great productive scholarship, including the work of, among others, Marxists Mike Davis (e.g. 1992) and David Harvey (2012). Yet, in the latter's case we also saw earlier the potential limits of such analysis when the state's ability to marshal its forces against protestors on the streets – especially if they are not backed up by mass industrial action in the workplace – is ignored. If the anti-globalisation protests were more reactive than was Occupy, the former had the advantage of directly assailing powerful political decision-makers and sometimes capital itself (e.g. at the World Economic Forum in Davos), even if the confrontations were more physical than economic in nature. Some have stressed the 'decentralized' nature of Occupy (van Gelder, 2011: 10). But to city police forces such as the NYPD, the occupation appears as a protest firmly lodged in one space – in this case Zuccotti Park, lower Manhattan – thereby rendering it more manageable and, ultimately, dissolvable. The short-term answer to police atrocities is to build bigger and wider demonstrations that are more difficult for the state to disperse. Protestors can

---

[4] When I visited Zuccotti Park in July 2013 all that was left of this great movement was a thinly stocked book stall. Seemingly, it had sunk without a trace.

toy with any number of different tactics with all the resources at their disposal – including cyber tools of hacking and more elementary internet campaigns – to thwart the cops and authorities, some of which will have greater impact than will others. But the longer-term answer is building a mass, democratic anti-capitalist movement that strikes simultaneously at capitalism's profits in workplaces across jurisdictions.

While it may be true that after the police crackdowns and the onset of the American Winter some sections of Occupy executed a *tactical* shift away from presences in public space towards moving into foreclosed homes and vacated buildings (Adams, 2012), in a *strategic* sense it was more of the same. This is not an argument for the staid and predictable methods of organising from times gone past. Battling with police in the streets is par for the course in any radical social movement. Moreover, it is important to distinguish between the different types of dissent in open spaces, which can vary between the picnic-style gathering in the park and the full-scale riot in the streets. Some forms of outdoor protest undoubtedly are more effective than are others. But any movement focused largely on the streets and in public spaces is restricted in what it can achieve long-term in the sense of unravelling capitalist social relations. Thus, the typical Reclaim the Streets (RTS) protest can be exhilarating,[5] disruptive of 'business-as-usual', creative, and thought-provoking, but seriously challenging corporate and state monopolisation of public space would require a movement that targets the profit-driven economic system underpinning decisions, for example, that prioritise road-building and car usage over public transport and preservation of parks.

There are numerous examples of the limits of action in the streets from the last great anti-capitalist movement of the 1960s and early 1970s – a movement with which Occupy can be seen as the most recent chapter in a continuing narrative (Hayden, 2012). A case in point is Joschka Fischer, whose youthful brushes with authority eventually gave way to a stint as a German Green foreign minister (1998-2005). In its January 2001 edition, Germany's *Stern* magazine published dramatic photos of the so-called 'stick man' – Fischer was known in his past life as a protestor who distributed sticks to break windows at demonstrations – engaged in fisticuffs with a police officer on the streets of Frankfurt in 1973 (Berman, 2001; Harman, 2001). Fischer had been an advocate of violent resistance, urging the overthrow of the capitalist system and the institution of a socialist republic (Hockenos, 2008: 4). But in the late-1970s Fischer and fellow future Green politician Daniel Cohn-Bendit (see below) abandoned revolutionary politics to pursue careers in reformist politics (Berman, 2005: 272). Fischer compromised his radicalism to the point where nothing was left but memories. Formerly an opponent of state violence, Fischer was now proposing state

---

[5] Something for which the author can personally vouch.

violence of the most lethal kind: he provided unstinting support in 1999 for NATO's bombing rampage in Yugoslavia and in the early 2000s for what were then the most punishing austerity measures enacted in Germany since WWII (Theil, 2003).

Following a similar trajectory was Fischer's colleague and possibly the best-known European student radical of the 1960s, Daniel Cohn-Bendit (Berman, 2005: 14). As a radical, Cohn-Bendit mistakenly believed that capitalism could be overturned by 'insurrectional cells' and 'nuclei of confrontation' (cited in Roszak, 1972: 5). Over 40 years later, Cohn-Bendit sits as a German Green politician in the European Parliament, completely unmoved by revolutionary 'confrontation' – an ironic twist in a political career that began with him *a priori* rejecting leaders and political parties (Singer, 2002: 16-7; 134). In other words, his quasi-Guevarist approach was superseded by a parliamentarist strategy even less likely to deliver tangible results for radicals.

How did it all go so wrong? These European militants' adoption of more consensual forms of political activity was partly the consequence of strategic setbacks in the streets. Key actors among this 1960s generation had pursued a political strategy involving small-scale individualist tactics that isolated militants from the working masses. Some German radicals who realised that capitalism would not be defeated by skirmishes with police in the streets turned to ultra-militancy (e.g. the Baader-Meinhof Red Army Faction), while others, including Fischer and Cohn-Bendit, opted for elite party politics (Harman, 2001). In explaining similar developments in France, Alain Badiou focused on the strategic flaws of some 1960s radicals who imagined that ideas and disruptive incidents alone could trigger a social revolution. The failure of this strategy saw some of their careers take a trajectory that included, in the case of André Glucksmann, plumping for Nicolas Sarkozy in the 2007 presidential elections. Badiou portrays the fickleness of their actions as akin to: 'That wasn't the right card, so I'll play a different one' (Badiou, 2008: 126-7; 130).

The 1960s movements were complex phenomena whose 'success' or 'failure' cannot be pithily summarised (see Harman, 1988). Any discussion of the period ought to account for the role of diverse political cultures and their impacts on organisation and strategising (Johnston, 2009). But an emphasis on urban warfare at the expense of a strategy seeking to fuse street protests with the economic potential of the proletariat was not something exclusive to sections of Europe's far left. One of Tariq Ali's books on the 1960s is aptly titled *Street Fighting Years* (Ali, 2005). Among American 1960s radicals it was widely believed that 'democracy is in the streets' (Miller, 1987). The preference of Jerry Rubin, the anti-Wall Street radical and co-founder of the Yippies (Youth International Party), was for acts of political theatre aimed at attracting the media spotlight. According to Rubin's confidante, the protest singer Phil Ochs, the Yippies sought 'to act out fantasies in the street to communicate their feelings to the public' (Ochs, 1969-

70). As a hallmark of 1960s carnival-style politics, the widest range of political expression, including street theatre, should be encouraged (Stam, 1988: 136). But theatre and action in the streets have obvious limits in terms of their capacity to upset the daily violence of capitalism and the state. While it is possible to argue that the urban terrain in contemporary major cities has been shaped by neo-liberal policies in ways that are increasingly attuned to the needs of corporations and the wealthy (Davis and Monk, 2007), what was true even in the 1960s is that the streets can be dead end for radicals if militant and symbolic actions are not accompanied by economically – and therefore strategically – powerful strikes.

Alas, the likes of Rubin had shied away from the ideological and organisational ramifications of such an analysis (see Lavelle, 2013: 142-3). Thus, when the 1960s movements ended, a disoriented Rubin underwent years of experimentation, soul-searching, and lifestyle changes before ending up as a Wall Street stock analyst in 1980 (Rubin, 1980). This was richly ironic in light of Rubin's participation in a famous anti-Wall Street protest in 1967, when he and other protestors dropped dollar bills onto the floor of the New York Stock Exchange (Ledbetter, 2007). The irony of Rubin's tryst with the streets does not stop there: in 1994 he was killed in the street, not in the midst of dangerous political protest, but while jaywalking across Wilshire Boulevard in Los Angeles near his $5000/month apartment. As Berger (1994) sardonically commented, jaywalking was then about the extent of Rubin's rebelliousness. But it is possible to draw a connection between Rubin's emphasis on street theatrics and his later evacuation of the streets when the political tide turned in the 1970s and his antics were no longer of interest to the mass media.

Along with Rubin, Tom Hayden was tried for conspiracy to riot at the August 1968 demonstration against the Democratic Party's convention in Chicago. Hayden declared at the time: 'When they bring the troops against us we have to show a fighting spirit in the streets' (Hayden, 1969: 172). But within a decade Hayden was a candidate for the Democratic Party in the Senate (California) – the same party against which he was indicted for inciting a riot. Undoubtedly there were important distinctions between Hayden, Rubin and other 1960s militants: a confluence of personal and political factors explains their drifting away from radicalism (see Lavelle, 2013). But what united many of these was a predilection for the streets, which was not without effect: according to Myers, that unforgettable decade was the first 'period in American history in which people took their protests to the streets and actually forced changes in the way the country went about its business'. On the other hand, not since the civil war had the streets been so drenched in blood (Myers, 1993: ix; x). Despite important outcomes from the 1960s movements, including recognition of the legal rights of Blacks, women, and lesbians and gays, the goal for many of revolutionary change went unfulfilled, and capitalism stabilised in the 1970s (Ali, 2005: Ch.11).

It was not just an over-emphasis on the streets that was part of the problem, but also the state's ability to acquit itself against a street-based movement, for when not simply murdering activists (see Berger, 2006: 63), it endeavoured to beat them off the streets. At the aforementioned Chicago Democratic convention in 1968, demonstrators infamously were on the receiving end of a 'police riot' when they were charged and clubbed relentlessly in a frenzied rage (Katsiaficas, 1987: 80). Similarly, at an action initiated by the Yippies earlier the same year at Grand Central Station, New York on 22 March 1968, police viciously attacked the protest without provocation. One member of the press attending the event blamed the Yippies for failing to take a lead (cited in Gitlin, 1993: 238). This absolves the police of responsibility for the violence. But the example did illustrate the lackadaisical nature of the Yippies 'organisation', as well as the limits of street protests, which authorities could cope with provided that militants were in relatively small numbers and unable to draw upon the solidarity of the working class, whom American radicals were accused – perhaps overly so (Levy, 1994) – of either neglecting or affronting with their behaviour.

As was the case across the Atlantic, in the US it was partly the defeat of street based movements that led some former radicals into handshake politics, as in the case of Tom Hayden and others whose preferred arena of struggle became the graveyard of the Democratic Party (Davis, 1986: 256). Others resorted to ultra-militancy: the Weather Underground, like their German counterparts in the Red Army Faction, turned disastrously to armed struggle against military, corporate, and political targets in a futile effort to bring the system to its knees (Varon, 2004).

Any attempt to draw lessons from the radical 1960s movements raises the question as to what has happened between then and now. The backlash against the 1960s and the defeats of the late-1970s and 1980s were symbolised in 'Thatcherism' and 'Reaganism'. Overlapping with this shift to the right was the 'end of history', which coincided with the decline of visible conflict in the workplace and the marginalisation of Marxist critiques of the capitalist system, now heralded after the collapse of the Soviet Bloc as a peerless economic model for the satisfaction of human needs (Callinicos, 2003: 2). Even on the left, Marx and his agent, the proletariat, had dropped out of fashion. It has been argued along these lines that the impact of post-modernism was to take female students 'off the streets and into the salons' (Salleh, cited in Burgmann, 2003: 137).

Conversely, part of the explanation for why the streets have predominated as places of resistance in recent years is that working class politics still for many on the radical left represent part of a bygone age. The larger than ever global proletariat has only started to stir – as measured either empirically through rising rates of strikes, or ideologically through an emphasis by actors on the power of organised labour – to reassert its place in resistance movements (Moody, 2004). The amorphous 'multitude' is more at home on the streets than is the less trendy proletariat. Yet, in the wake of the global financial crisis, Marxist analyses of capitalism and its awesome destructive nature have proven more relevant than ever (Harman, 2010). Success in challenging the dictates of politicians, 'the market', and the forces of the state warrants a reengagement with the classical Marxist tradition, which has much to offer both in terms of comprehending the present juncture as well as offering strategies for winning radical social change.

Conclusion

The Occupy movement represents an audacious extension of the radical anti-globalisation movement – politics as the 'art of the impossible' in the age of austerity and imperialism. The movement boldly took to the streets and occupied public land, demanding another world. This paper has argued, however, that the searing injustices of our epoch are part and parcel of global capitalism, which relies on the continued exertions of workers to generate corporate profits at the expense of people and planet. Any radical movement for change needs to tackle that system and its power sources, including institutions of the state as well as centres of economic accumulation. The deepening of roots in organised labour, coupled with efforts to build a vibrant countercultural movement in the streets, should be a priority.

In this sense, it is important to absorb the lessons of the past, including the strategic weaknesses of the last great radical movements for change in the 1960s and early 1970s. Sections of the radical left were fixated on street battles with police, and when that failed to achieve the dissolution of capitalism and the state, some resorted to ultra-militancy or to the deal-making of elite party politics. Yet, constructing the widest possible radical movement – one cognisant of the strategic importance of labour – will not be easy, especially in light of attempts to divide the working class with racism, as in recent crackdowns on Mexican immigrants in the US and the wider Islamophobia plaguing fortress Europe. Nor will such a movement be sufficient. Debate needs to be had about such matters as: what we are against – capitalism in general or merely its neo-liberal variety, how to defeat state violence, and whether the oppressed in turn should use force; what forms of organising and decision-making to adopt; and whether the radical left should contest power. But the Occupy movement has been a shining example of twenty-first century resistance in the United States, the belly of the capitalist beast. The task in the coming years is to fulfil the promise of that resistance.

References

Adam, J. 2012. 'Occupy Time.' *Radical Philosophy* 171, January/February.

Adbusters. 2012. 'The Battle for the Soul of Occupy', *Adbusters*, April 12, Available: http://www.adbusters.org/blogs/adbusters-blog/jump.html. Last accessed 17/07/2014.

Ali, T. 2005. *Street Fighting Years: An Autobiography of the Sixties.* London: Verso.

Badiou, A. 2008. *The Meaning of Sarkozy.* London: Verso.

Barker, C. (ed.) 1987. *Revolutionary Rehearsals.* London: Bookmarks.

Bentley, P. 1980. 'Recent Strike Behaviour in Australia: Causes and Responses', in Ford, G.W., Hearn, J.M. & Lansbury, R.D. (eds) *Australian Labour Relations: Readings.* 3rd Ed. South Melbourne: Macmillan.

Berger, D. 2006. *Outlaws of America: the Weather Underground and the Politics of Solidarity.* Oakland, CA: AK Press.

Berger, J. 1994. 'Born to Be Wild. Scratch That. Born to Be Mild.' *The New York Times.* December 4. Available: http://www.nytimes.com/1994/12/04/weekinreview/born-to-be-wild-scratch-that-born-to-be-mild.html. Last accessed 17/07/2014.

Berman, P. 2001. 'The Passion of Joschka Fischer: from the Radicalism of the '60s to the Interventionism of the '90s.' *The New Republic.* August 27. Available: http://www.tnr.com/article/78957/the-passion-joschka-fischer. Last accessed 17/07/2014.

_____. 2005. *Power and the Idealists: Or, the Passion of Joschka Fischer and its Aftermath.* Brooklyn, NY: Soft Skull Press.

BLS. 2013. 'Major Work Stoppages in 2012', *Bureau of Labor Statistics U.S. Department of Labor.* Media Release. February 8. Available: http://www.bls.gov/news.release/archives/wkstp_02082013.pdf. Last accessed 17/07/2014.

Bramble, T. 1996. 'Managers of Discontent: Problems With Labour Leadership', in Kuhn, R. & O'Lincoln, T. (eds) *Class and Class Conflict in Australia.* Melbourne: Longman.

Burgmann, V. 2003. *Power, Profit and Protest: Australian Social Movements and Globalisation.* Crows Nest: Allen & Unwin.

Callinicos, A. 2003. *An Anti-Capitalist Manifesto.* Cambridge: Polity Press.

_____. 2010. *Bonfire of Illusions: The Twin Crises of the Liberal World.* Cambridge: Polity Press.

Cameron, C. 1970. 'Industrial Protest: The Right to Strike.' Paper delivered by Shadow Industrial Relations Minister Clyde Cameron to the University of Adelaide Seminar on 'Social Order and the Right to Dissent.' November 27/28. Adelaide, South Australia.

Churchill, W. 2001. ' "To Disrupt, Discredit and Destroy": the FBI's Secret War Against the Black Panther Party,' in Cleaver, K. & Katsiaficas, G. (eds.) *Liberation, Imagination, and the Black Panther Party*. New York, NY: Routledge.

Davis, M. 1986. *Prisoners of the American Dream: Politics and Economy in the History of the US Working Class*. London: Verso.

_____. 1992. *City of Quartz: Excavating the Future in Los Angeles*. London: Vintage.

Davis, M. and Monk, D.B. (eds) 2007. *Evil Paradises: Dreamworlds of Neoliberalism*. New York, NY: The New Press.

Dyer-Witheford, N. 2012. 'Net, Square, Everywhere?' *Radical Philosophy* 171, January/February.

Farnham, D. 2012. 'Chomsky's Occupy Fails to Address Movement's Impasse.' *Solidarity* 51, November-December.

Gallman, S. 2012. 'Linguists Name "Occupy" as 2011's Word of the Year.' *CNN*. January 8. Available: http://edition.cnn.com/2012/01/07/us/2011-word-of-year/index.html. Last accessed 17/07/2014.

Gee, R. 2011. 'Teachers, Service Workers Support Oakland's Strike Without Striking.' *Huffington Post*. Blog. November 2. Available: http://www.huffingtonpost.com/turnstyle/teachers-service-workers_b_1071604.html. Last accessed 17/07/2014.

Gitlin, T. 1993. *The Sixties: Years of Hope, Days of Rage*. New York, NY: Bantam Books.

_____. 2012. *Occupy Nation: The Roots, the Spirit, and the Promise of Occupy Wall Street*. New York, NY: HarperCollins.

Gramsci, A. 1989. *Selections from the Prison Notebooks of Antonio Gramsci*. New York, NY: International Publishers.

Greenhouse, T. 2011. 'Occupy Movement Inspires Unions to Embrace Bold Tactics.' *New York Times*. November 8. Available: http://www.nytimes.com/2011/11/09/business/occupy-movement-inspires-unions-to-embrace-bold-tactics.html. Last accessed 17/07/2014.

Hardt, M. and Negri, A. 2004. *Multitude: War and Democracy in the Age of Empire*. New York, NY: Penguin.

Harman, C. 2001. 'Street Fighter Turned Salesman.' *Socialist Review*, Issue 249.

_____. 2010. *Zombie Capitalism: Global Crisis and the Relevance of Marx*. Chicago, IL: Haymarket.

Harvey, D. 2012. *Rebel Cities: From the Right to the City to the Urban Revolution*. London: Verso.

Hayden, T. 1969. 'The Battle for Survival', in Babcox, P., Babcox, D. and Abel, B. (eds) *The Conspiracy*. New York, NY: Dell.

_____. (2012) 'Participatory Democracy: From Port Huron to Occupy Wall Street.' *The Nation*. April 16.

Herman, E. 1999. 'The Third Way: the Politics of Betrayal.' *Z Magazine*. November. Available: http://www.thirdworldtraveler.com/Political/Third_ Way.html. Last accessed 17/07/2014.

Herman, E.S. & Chomsky, N. 1994. *Manufacturing Consent: the Political Economy of the Mass Media*. London: Vintage.

Hockenos, P. 2008. *Joschka Fischer and the Making of the Berlin Republic*. Oxford: Oxford University Press.

Johnston, H. (ed.) 2009. *Culture, Social Movements, and Protest*. Surrey: Ashgate.

Katsiaficas, G. 1987. *The Imagination of the New Left: A Global Analysis of 1968*. Boston, MA: South End Press.

Klein, N. 2011. 'Occupy Wall Street: the Most Important Thing in the World Now.' *The Nation*. October 6. Available: http://www.thenation.com/article/163844/occupy-wall-street-most-important-thing-world-now. Last accessed 17/07/2014.

Klinenberg, E. and Manza, J. 2012. 'Obama Misses His Historic Moment', in Kristianasen, W. (ed.) *The Best of Le Monde Diplomatique 2012*. London: Pluto Press.

Lavelle, A. 2013. *The Politics of Betrayal: Renegades and Ex-Radicals from Mussolini to Christopher Hitchens*. Manchester: Manchester University Press.

Ledbetter, C. 2007. 'The Day the NYSE Went Yippie'. *CNN Money.com*. Available: http://money.cnn.com/2007/07/17/news/funny/abbie_hoffman/index.htm. Last accessed 17/07/2014.

Lenin, V. 1970. *The State and Revolution: the Marxist Teaching on the State and the Tasks of the Proletariat in the Revolution*. Peking: Foreign Language Press.

Levy, P.B. 1994. *The New Left and Labor in the 1960s*. Urbana, IL: University of Illinois Press.

Lyon, D. 2001. *Surveillance Society: Monitoring Everyday Life*. Philadelphia, PA: Open University.

Luxemburg, R. 1986. *The Mass Strike*. London: Bookmarks.

McCulloch, J. 2001. *Blue Army: Paramilitary Policing in Australia*. Carlton: Melbourne University Press.

Miller, J. 1987. '*Democracy is in the Streets*': *From Port Huron to the Siege of Chicago*. New York, NY: Simon and Schuster.

Moody, K. (2004) 'Workers of the World.' *New Left Review* 27, May-June. Available: http://http://newleftreview.org/II/27/kim-moody-workers-of-the-world. Last accessed 17/07/2014.

Myers, D.W. 1993. *Malcolm X: By Any Means Necessary*. New York, NY: Scholastic.

New York City General Assembly. 2011. 'Declaration of the Occupation of New York City', in van Gelder, S. (ed.) *This Changes Everything: Occupy Wall Street and the 99% Movement*. San Francisco, CA: Berrett-Koehler.

Ochs, P. 1969-70. 'Testimony of Phillip David Ochs in the Chicago Seven Trial', exact date unknown. Available: http://law2.umkc.edu/faculty/projects/FTrials/Chicago7/ochs.html. Last accessed 17/07/2014.

Prieto, H. 1974. *Chile: the Gorillas are Amongst Us*. London: Pluto Press.

Rees, J. 1991. 'In Defence of October.' *International Socialism* 52, Summer.

_____. (1998) *The Algebra of Revolution: The Dialectic and the Classical Marxist Tradition*. London: Routledge.

Roszak, T. 1972. *The Making of a Counter Culture: Reflections on the Technocratic Society and its Youthful Opposition*. London: Faber and Faber.

Rubin, J. 1980. 'Guess Who's Coming to Wall Street.' *The New York Times*. 30 July.

Singer, D. 2002. *Prelude to Revolution: France in May 1968*. Cambridge: South End Press.

Stam, R. 1988. 'Mikhail Bakhtin and Left Cultural Critique,' in Kaplan, E. A. (ed.) *Postmodernism and Its Discontents: Theories, Practices*. London: Verso.

St. Clair, J. and Frank, J. 2012. 'Occupy the System', in St. Clair, J. and Frank, J. (eds) *Hopeless: Barack Obama and the Politics of Illusion*. Oakland, CA: AK Press.

Ste. Croix, G., de.1981. *The Class Struggle in the Ancient Greek World: From the Archaic Age to the Arab Conquests*. Ithaca, NY: Cornell University Press.

Suleiman, S.R. 1994. 'Bataille in the Street: the Search for Virility in the 1930s.' *Critical Inquiry* 21:1, Autumn.

Theil, S. 2003. 'Reform Now, or I'll Quit.' *Newsweek International*. 12 May.

Van Gelder, S. 2011. 'Introduction: How Occupy Wall Street Changes Everything', in van Gelder, S. (ed.) *This Changes Everything: Occupy Wall Street and the 99% Movement*. San Francisco, CA: Berrett-Koehler.

Varon, J. 2004. *Bringing the War Home: the Weather Underground, the Red Army Faction, and Revolutionary Violence in the Sixties and Seventies*. Berkeley, CA: University of California Press.

Wilson, S. 2011. 'City Council Unanimously Passes Occupy L.A. Resolution – Protesters Struggle to Distance Themselves from Democrats, Unions.' *LA Weekly*. October 12. Available: http://blogs.laweekly.com/informer/2011/10/city_council_passes_occupy_la_resolution_democrats_unions.php. Last accessed 17/07/2014.

Writers for the 99%. 2012. *Occupying Wall Street: the Inside Story of an Action that Changed America*. Melbourne: Scribe.

12

WALKING IN THE STREET: SLUTWALK AND THE STREET

Linda Stupart

Introduction

The SlutWalk movement began in January 2011 with a refusal of 'advice' from a Toronto policeman who suggested to a personal security class at York University that 'women should avoid dressing like sluts in order not to be victimised' (*BBC Online*, 2011).

SlutWalk is a movement formed against victim blaming – that double negation where the raped woman is both victim (powerless, without speech) and to blame (aggressor, inciter, whore) as well as a specific reclamation of the word 'slut' as an indicator of sexual freedom - an appropriation of dirtiness, which is also the dirtiness of the surface of the street.[1]

SlutWalks occur throughout the world, including in Morocco, South Africa, Delhi and Mexico as well as in Western centres - not just the 'Global North' as is often assumed by European and American commentators. Each local protest is specific to time and place, however every SlutWalk has an element of site in common: they all take place in city centres, and on the (well-lit) street: proposing a complex and potentially disruptive intersection of looking, pleasure, inscription and embodiment.

Slut

The use of the word 'slut' in the SlutWalk movement has split Feminist and other commentators on fairly predictable lines. I think that dissent that speaks of the problem of privileging promiscuity, or sexual excess, over all other kinds of sexual choices is an important one, which should also be considered along racial and cultural lines of inclusion and exclusion and I am also sympathetic to the argument that the use of the word 'slut' as sight of reclamation contributes

---

[1] The word was used as early as 1402 to describe a 'dirty, untidy, or slovenly woman' and has retained its current usage since 1450.

to a misleading focus on libidinal as opposed to traumatic sites; that is that sex, as opposed to sexual violence, may become the focus of the protest-event.

However, more often the critique of using the word slut follows a very straightforward and self-replicating logic: that the word *slut* is misogynistic, thus women using it to describe themselves and other women is merely perpetuating misogyny. Many commentators following this logic also seem steeped in a deep sense of both disbelief and discomfort as to why women would want to embark on the apparently self-hating gesture of referring to themselves as sluts, when this is clearly such a demeaning word (linked both to dirt and excessive sexuality). This position is summed up in anti-porn, anti-sex worker 'activist' Gail Dines who ends her 2011 *Guardian Comment is Free* piece, 'SlutWalk is not Sexual Liberation', with the categorical statement that 'Women need to take to the streets – but not for the right to be called "slut"' (Dines and Murphy, 2011).

It is difficult to engage in these kinds of arguments without regressing to the so-called 'pro' versus 'anti' sex arguments that have divided Feminists for decades, a divide linked to the second vs. third wave debates, which continue to produce a familiar range of generational, racial and class-based antagonisms that I would very much like to avoid. So, while treading carefully, I would argue that this comment, which supposes that the SlutWalk participants are fighting for a right *to-be-called* slut, misses the point not only of the protest, even as it is defined by its spokespeople, but also of the idea of claiming a word as one's own – that is that one is never fighting for the right *to-be-called* x by an injurious other, but rather the capacity to take up the name that we have been called and to inhabit it without the shame that the hateful speech act produces – it is an act that attempts to leech a word of its power to wound, and in this way to take power away from those who would wield this word to hurt.

To be *self-defining* sluts is to enable the woman subjected to sexual violence, victimized by her sexual or social habits, or, even class, to speak from and against the position of victim-subject. The argument of whether a word itself has immanence, or particular power inferred to it through history, use etc., or whether words and naming are always contingent on an addressor and addressee is one too long for this text, however I would argue, at least, that the act of reclamation is not a simple nor merely reactive one.

Particularly, given that many of the women who participate in the SlutWalks and especially those who are given the role of speakers at these events have been subjected to sexual violence, it seems unfair and reductive to align the use of the word slut (as many have) with an uncritical, liberal, cheerful and necessarily 'pro sex', postfeminist attitude that demands sexual-pleasure-as-emancipation, encourages the purchase of expensive sex toys, wearing playboy t-shirts etc. Though here we should also be wary of an outright denigration of any kind of sexual and identificatory choices – though the choice to go to expensive pole dancing lessons is by no means liberatory in itself, we should also not degrade those women who are able to choose these modes of sexual expression as part of their sexual identities.

Rather, we might consider, as Judith Butler proposes in *Excitable Speech*, that:

> one is not simply fixed by the name that one is called. In being called an injurious name, one is derogated and demeaned. But the name holds out another possibility as well: by being called a name, one is also, paradoxically, given a certain possibility for social existence, initiated into a temporal life of language that exceeds the prior purposes that animate that call. Thus the injurious address may appear to paralyze the one it hails, but may also produce an unexpected and enabling response... (Butler, 1997:23).

This particular claim for reclamation is one that seeks to shift the power of patriarchal language generally (that calls us sluts, or 'unclean' when we behave as they do or, worse, as we want) and to call into being a self-defining feminine sexuality: A sex that means wearing short skirts, without being told we are 'asking for it' by men and other woman on the street or wearing pink dresses and not being told we are infantilizing ourselves by academic feminists. A sexuality that means wearing burkas without attempts made to rescue us by white feminists and Richard Dawkins.[2] A sex that is written in a new script, a sex that is ours, to do with as we want, to fuck who we want, a sex that does not end when you are 'finished'. A sex that is trans* inclusive, shifting, grounded on each of *our own utterances*.

While it may be accurate that we do not need to march for the right to be called sluts, surely it is important to position ourselves as able to fuck who we want, if we want and how we want, without being called unclean, immoral; without being subjected to shame, abuse and violence? And surely the space of the street, the public, the erotic encounter with the beautiful stranger and the fearful encounter with the violent one, is the appropriate site for this resistance, this assertion, this claim?

---

[2] Richard Dawkins consistently instrumentalises violence against women as a way to perpetuate racism, particularly islamaphopia, as well as casual misogyny. Dawkins claims include that no Muslim woman is *able* to make the decision freely to wear a burka, and thus require white western saviours, as well as consistently pushing the 'we should hate Islam because we want to protect women' mantra popularised in the Bush and Obama administrations in the United States. At the same time, Dawkins reproduces neo-Darwinian claims for 'natural' and 'genetic' differences in the sexes as well as dismissing everyday sexism in the west as not 'real' or 'violent. See Rebecca Watson's piece including Dawkin's shocking comments here: http://skepchick.org/2011/07/the-privilege-delusion/.

Bodies

The SlutWalk is defined through its own internal nomenclature as a protest produced by an embodied participant/protestor who walks, moves.

This highlighting of the protester's body fits into a slew of public protests since 2010 and also follows a very long tradition of Feminist and Women's protest, particularly the Take Back the Night protests, which began in the early 1970s in American colleges as a response to particular incidents of violence against women walking home at night.

'Our bodies, our lives, our right to decide!'

An embodied protest about women's rights to sexual freedom right now, though, has a particular point, an edge. Post-political-correctness, cultures of the virtual (which include the much documented misogyny of blog comments on women's writing, online Men's Rights Activists and violently sexist groups and specific attacks permitted on Social Networking site *Facebook*), contemporary art's insistence on indeterminacy, the hangover of postmodernity's ideal of elective affinities, the instrumentalisation of Feminism and neoliberal fence-sitting and non-positioning are all indicative of a culture where a performance of a specifically embodied subjectivity is itself a rupturing act. The embodied nature of the SlutWalk speaks the urgency of a recorporealisation of identity and a repoliticisation of desire, here situated on the surface of protesters' bodies.

In South Africa lesbian women in townships are regularly raped to 'cure' them of their desire in what is known as 'corrective rape'. Turkey banned elective caesareans in July 2012. In June the same year the fight for reproductive rights in the West is typified by House Republicans barring Democratic Representative Lisa Brown from speaking on the floor of the Michigan state legislature because she said the word 'vagina' during a heated debate over abortions. Huge billboards all over Dublin, where abortion is illegal, claim 'Abortion tears her life apart' and 'There's always a better answer'. Todd Akin, the Republican nominee for Senate in Missouri in August 2012 justified his opposition to abortion rights even in cases of rape with a claim that victims of 'legitimate rape' have unnamed magical biological defenses that prevent pregnancy. More recently and most notably, the persistence of violence against women both and the street was embodied in the Elliot Rodger killing spree in which Rodger produced a video describing how he would seek retribution against women who have sexually rejected him, before murdering six people. That the visibility and safety of women, our bodies and our voices must be protected is evident everywhere in the world. However, this remains to be noted in a neoliberal culture which so often claims that the work of feminism has already been done. Feminism, protest and the fight for our safety is still as necessary as ever, no matter how many wealthy white women claim the meritocratic successes of equality in the boardroom, for example.

That the SlutWalks always happen during the day (unlike the *Take Back the Night* protests) also highlights the movement's imperative that bodies, both desiring and desirable, be both visible and safe in the world, especially on the street. In considering the function of SlutWalker's bodies in the street, this particular visibility is important in thinking about how the SlutWalk does *not* just reproduce the kinds of objectifications we are familiar with from conventions of cinema, the peep show, and other images of moving women's bodies. This darkness, Mulvey tells us, functions as a distancing mechanism in the cinema that is instrumental in producing the subject/object separation that scopophilia proper requires, where: 'the extreme darkness in the auditorium [...] and the brilliance of the shifting patterns of light and shade on the screen helps to promote the illusion of voyeuristic separation' so that the position of the spectators (and, by extension, the male controlling gaze) is 'blatantly one of repression of their exhibitionism and projection of the repressed desire onto the performer (Mulvey, 1989:17).[3]

'Self-Objectification'

Mulvey's project in *Visual Pleasure and Narrative Cinema* is foundational for Feminist resistance to modes of objectification and speaks at length about the manner in which women become a particular type of object - an image - produced by and for a masculine economy where:

> In a world ordered by sexual imbalance, pleasure in looking has been split between active/male and passive/female. The determining male gaze projects its fantasy onto the female figure, which is styled accordingly. In their traditional exhibitionist role women are simultaneously looked at and displayed, with their appearance coded for strong visual and erotic impact so that they can be said to connote to-be-looked-at-ness (ibid).

The mechanisms of objectification thus seem to require an autonomous subject exterior to, and acting on, the subject-becoming-object. The external (masculine) Other produces a subject → object transfiguration (which is also analo-

---

[3] My return to Mulvey and her remarkably influential *Visual Pleasure and Narrative Cinema* is political in the same way that Mulvey claims her use of psychoanalysis uses the oppressive tools of the discipline to analyse and ultimately disrupt its mechanisms. Though Mulvey's conception of the male gaze is vital for understanding how objectification and fetishization functions, and for understanding how to look at popular culture, I feel it is also appropriate at this juncture to use this essay (one of the foundations of any theory of objectification) to undo some of the accusations of more contemporary Feminist projects that also speak to Feminine sexual objectification and the male gaze. That is, while I feel critiques of Mulvey's thesis are vital, I think it is useful to reconsider this text in light of more positive, queer conceptions of objectification.

gous to the human → corpse abjection of death) so as to manufacture a passive object-commodity-corpse to be inserted into circulations of their (masculine, heterosexual) desire and pleasure.

However, the neoliberal terrain of late capitalism has produced a new set of mechanisms for objectification, many of which appear to shift the abjecting agency on to the bodies of women themselves.: The 'pornification' of Western popular culture produces drunken hen parties, stripper parties, pop burlesque – LET'S ALL TAKE POLE DANCING LESSONS TOGETHER IT WILL BE SO MUCH FUN - constituting an apparent 'mainstreaming' of sex,[4] and an escalating commodification of feminine desire visible in shows like *Sex and the City* as well as an exponentially increasing market for feminine sex toys (*you must have this vibrator shaped like an adorable animal to be a real woman*). On what may feel like the other side of the spectrum of woman-as-object or determining subject is the apparent rise in self-harming and stress-related behaviour (anorexia, depression, cutting and anxiety disorders) in women; cutting, which like much of the mechanisms of sexual 'empowerment' detailed above, both asserts and negates its own being.

The SlutWalk movement is often and easily associated with the aesthetics of extreme beauty practices; labiaplasty, complete hair removal, 'vajazzling'[5] as well as participation in projects such as the *Girls Gone Wild* franchise,[6] posing for porny photoshoots on social media, all under the rubric of self-objectification, a term used colloquially and in postfeminist texts to describe the process whereby the emancipated feminine subject (who is surely also subjected to various modes of expectation, projections of desire, social requirements etc.) willfully becomes object (and apparently loses their freedom and ability to act and speak), often under the auspices of empowerment, liberation and individualism; the very same discourses that drive the progress of the Post-Fordist free market, which welcomes women into the workforce only so long as they both continue to be paid less as workers, and spend more as consumers, than their male counterparts.

Nina Power insightfully notes: 'That the height of supposed female emancipation coincides so perfectly with consumerism is a miserable index of a politically desolate time.' Power is also correct in noting the 'death of the object/

---

[4] According to Feona Attwood, in the introduction to *The Mainstreaming of Sex* (2010), this phrase is used simply to denote the ways that 'sex is becoming more visible in contemporary Western cultures' (xiii), though the book focuses specifically on pornography and other 'sexually explicit media representations' (ibid).

[5] 'Vajazzling' is a beautification practice whereby Swarovski crystals are applied, temporarily, to a women's pubic area.

[6] *Girls Gone Wild* is an adult entertainment enterprise made famous for its amateur, 'real life' strategy of convincing drunk college-aged girls to strip, kiss each other, masturbate and so on, on camera, usually in exchange for some kind of merchandise, and also usually while in a crowded social situation.

subject divide' (Power, 2009:25) via the logic of person-as-CV, an assertion that hints at the possibility of an autonomous pre-object feminine position from which woman may objectify herself.

In Angela McRobbie's *Aftermath of Feminism*, the author defines the landscape of 'post-feminism' as the simultaneous incorporation of elements of feminist struggle (emancipation, empowerment, sexual freedom) by aspirational, consumerist models of capitalism and the subsequent revulsion of rigorous critiques of culture; the belief, in the West, that the work of Feminism is already done. In McRobbie's acidic damning of the 'phallic' girl, the imagined object of Post-feminism, she writes of the 'girl' who apparently aspires to be like the soft porn glamour model and who is 'prone to drinking to excess, getting into fights, throwing up in public places, swearing and being abusive, wearing very short skirts, high heels, and skimpy tops, having casual sex, often passing out on the street and having to be taken home by friends or by the police' (McRobbie, 2009:85). This remarkable list, which can probably be summarised as slut-who-is-definitely-asking-for-it (and by 'it' I mean to be raped and/or brutalized) is a clear indication of the problematics of some Post-Feminist critiques of self-objectification, which posit a knee-jerk response to new feminine subjectivities and objecthoods, allowing no space for propositions of rupture, strength or revenge, which might be possible from these new feminine subject/object positions.

McRobbie's description of the phallic girl is slut-shaming – a phrase that has largely, though not entirely, entered the popular lexicon *because* of the SlutWalk movement – suggesting an equivalence between 'excessive' drinking, casual sex, 'skimpy' clothing and the disgusting abjection of a corporeal public expulsion; vomiting on the street. Worse, McRobbie suggests that this set of behaviours inevitably leads, rightfully, to girls 'having to be taken home [by friends or] by the police' – that brutal figure of The Law and hegemonic authority 'having' to take her back home; returning her to the domestic realm, because her phallic behaviour necessitates it. Because she is asking for it.

McRobbie, Power and other writers such as Ariel Levy (who authored *Female Chauvinist Pigs: Women and the Rise of Raunch Culture* in 2005) are by no means wrong to raise concern about the links between consumer culture, late capitalism and the framing of the emancipation of women through distinctly Western, privileged operations, which often seem to work in the service of a white male hegemony instead of disrupting it. They are also correct in alerting us to the danger of a culture that mistakes participation for consent, and that is derisive of celibacy, asexuality and other sexual choices, as well as alert us to the possibilities of feminine misogyny. However, the postfeminist critique of certain kinds of 'raunchy' behaviour and much kneejerk derision of the Slut-Walk falls short in that it fails to consider the complexity of contemporary feminine socio-sexual positions, refusing a possibility for resistance and rupture with arguments that often sound very similar to those used in masculine heterosexual economies, where it is already impossible to *take a woman seriously*, to acknowledge her voice, her resistance, her autonomy. So, when a woman does appear to conform to a heterosexual binary presentation of the 'slut', if she tries to reconfigure this position on her own terms; dares to participate in the heterosexual matrix, she is doubly bound, and doubly dismissed by both patriarchal and feminist institutions.

Moving

The SlutWalk is different to, for example, the Occupy Movement, where the imperative is to remain stationary, to block passage, to not be moved. Instead, the SlutWalks claim a physical, literal movement through the street as primary signifier of protest. In considering how the body functions as a site for the transmission of affect, Brian Massumi defines the body thus:

> when I think of my body, and ask what it does to earn that name, two things stand out. It moves. It feels. In fact, it does both at the same time. It moves as it feels, and it feels itself moving. Can we think a body without this: an intrinsic connection between movement and sensation, whereby each immediately summons the other? (Massumi, 2002:5).

The SlutWalks posit subjects who reside in a corporeal body and a body that states its presence through a visible movement through lived spaces. However, this body is the potential of more than just a meat envelope. Rather, SlutWalk participants might imagine their moving, feeling bodies as conduits for affect, sites of translation, moments of discourse.

Not curtailed by skins, the walkers' movement creates more feeling, feeling more movement, with bodies, discourses, desires and demands spiraling outward...

The SlutWalk movement has considerable drive and currency in that other city grid of Cyberspace; going viral - *as a sickness through a body or bodies* – using authority's tools of information dissemination as catalyst for affect, but each time finding host in real, physical (predominately women's) bodies, on actual streets.

The Street

In referring to 'the street' there is a slippage between the urban planner's, the theoretical street, the *Grid* and the lived–in street produced by the encounters therein. The street is an ideological space, both as it is experienced daily and as it is mapped, planned, written. To be 'out on the streets late at night' is still considered as unquestionably unsafe for women globally, and street harassment is taken for granted as a regular feature of daily life for women in public. Fear of assault, rape, robbery and violence dictate our behaviour in public city space even as what is still a deeply misogynistic culture of advertising perpetuates the violence of representation, billboards, shop windows and images assault us too on the street.

The street of the urban planner or the authorities is a crucial element of the Modernist and postmodern teleological grid and constitutes an integral set of codes in the language of patriarchy. The image of the male body is pervasive in the body of the city, from phallic skyscrapers to muscular civic architecture, masculine power is reified and legitimized through the city and its architecture. Buildings; erect.

To return to the grid; we imagine the straight intersecting lines simultaneously written by logos and writing logos on the map. This grid contradicts the actual bustling, living, heaving, breathing city street down below. And while this street still very much belongs to men, perhaps it is this real street, which slithers between its framing phallic buildings, which escapes the urban planner's eye, this street of the walker, even as she moves with and through the circulatory mechanisms of capital, that becomes the most productive site for speaking feminine desire whilst simultaneously protesting our own unsafeness on it. To walk a different path, to inhabit; to play.

Performance, Pleasure

> Woman has sex organs just about everywhere. She experiences pleasure almost everywhere.... The geography of her pleasure is much more diversified, more multiple in its differences, more complex, more subtle, than is imagined-in an imaginary [system] centered a bit too much on one and the same. 'She' is infinitely other in herself. That is undoubtedly the reason she is called temperamental, incomprehensible, perturbed, capricious-not to mention her language in which 'she' goes off in all directions and in which 'he' is unable to discern the coherence of any meaning. Contradictory words seem a little crazy to the logic of reason, and inaudible for him who listens with ready-made grids, a code prepared in advance. In her statements-at least when she dares to speak out-woman retouches herself constantly (Irigaray, 1985: 23).

As women we are still seeking geographies of pleasure that resists the grid, the plan, the single lines. Might we find these in the street, not as it is marked as straight, linear lines on the urban planners map, but as it is walked; a crevice, void, crater *in between* the unmoving architecture? A site of affect and of shifts, multiplicities, desires. The street, which enters, passes through, surpasses, joins, *penetrates* the architecture of the city is a dangerous, desirable and complete site for feminist protest, particularly regarding sex and language.

The seemingly incongruous nature of the SlutWalk; the celebration, the weirdness, the joy amongst derision suggests cartographies of pleasure that are complex, unsure, that protest the very stage on which they perform: An embodied event that speaks louder than the phallogocentric plan on which it treads, even if only for a moment.

Walking in the City[7]

> The act of walking is to the urban system what the speech act is to language or to the statements uttered. At the most elementary level it has a triple enunciative function: it is a process of appropriation of the topographical system on the part of the pedestrian (just as the speaker appropriates and takes the language); it is a spatial acting-out of the place (just as the speech act is an acoustic acting-out of language) and it implies relations among differentiated positions, that is amongst pragmatic contracts in the form of movements (just as verbal enunciation is an 'allocution', 'posits another opposite' the speaker and puts contracts between interlocutors into action) It thus seems possible to give a preliminary definition of walking as a space of enunciation.
>
> ... the pedestrian speech act has three characteristics which distinguish it at the outset from the spatial system: the present, the discrete, the phatic (Certeau, 1985: 98).

The SlutWalk states it is about the reclamation of the term 'slut', about a challenge to the normalized/androcentric definition of what is 'acceptable sexual behaviour', what female desire should look like, what complicity means and what sex *is*. Each discrete performance of the event, each lived protest, each conversation, each greeting, performs a challenge to the language of desire, and to language itself, as well as grabbing at, to hold, women's rights to be a pedestrian, a *flâneur* (/*flâneuse*); safe.

Indeed the wandering feminine pedestrian marks a challenge to the institution of the *flâneur*; the privileged Parisian man who can enjoy the city (and her women, as objects) through an abundance of leisure time, which allows them the particularly sensitized single-eyed vision of the Man on the Street. Instead, the woman pedestrian who marches with the SlutWalk in a claim for the right to freely inhabit the street without particular productive end interrupts the *flâneur*'s gaze whilst also exceeding the supposition that equality may somehow be found within the work place, since the *flâneuse* is necessarily outside of work.

Fear

Women feel unsafe on the street, in the city. We warn our daughters and our friends not to stay out too late, we walk in groups, we are told by the authorities to hide our bodies lest we provoke (and I have always wondered what it means to dress *provocatively*), lest we incite or cause violence against us.

---

[7] 'Walking in the City' is the title of Chapter VII in Michel de Certeau's *The Practice of Everyday Life* (1985).

It is not that the street is unsafe for women because it is filled with evil men, nor that we are unprotected there, on the street, *outside*, but rather that on the street, walking its surfaces, we are transgressing our proper place *inside* in the private/public; reproduction/production; active/passive dichotomies that define Woman.

To quote from Margaret Atwood's increasingly prophetic *Handmaid's Tale*, 'There is more than one kind of freedom [...]. Freedom to and freedom from' (Atwood, 1985:103). SlutWalks are about both kinds of freedom. They say that women need to be free to have as much sex as we want *if* we want to and to dress however we please, to be empowered sexual beings, to claim agency. And most importantly, that women need to be free from sexual abuse, rape and violence.

Sluwalks perform a simultaneous assertion of subjectivity and choice; to wear, to walk, to fuck what we want and when we want so that the SlutWalk also performs the possibility for feminine power *outside of* and without 'the work-place' (for why would we want to be equal to men, when men are slaves?) and of the right to be safe from sexual violence. Both of these demands, for subjectivity and choice, are centred around consent and it is integral that these arguments become relocated and made visible on our bodies, in 'public' and in the street. If, on the street, women are on parade, surely we should get to choose that parade?

Representation

The sexual politics of looking function around a regime which divides into binary positions: activity/ passivity, looking/being seen, voyeur/exhibitionist, subject/object. Thus, it is very difficult to image the SlutWalks without the structural violence of representation - in one article I found an author completely puzzled and totally derisive of one SlutWalker's request not to be photographed, as if participating in the protest and wearing a minimal amount of clothing totally negated her right to chose how she is represented.[8]

The imaging of the SlutWalk movement, particularly within the non-real grids of cyberspace, necessarily negates its rigour – allowing the spectator to position himself as voyeur and potentially reducing the protestors to symbol/ object as well as only presenting a still, as opposed to a walking, moving, speaking body. If the SlutWalk participant becomes scopophilic spectacle, floating signifier in the chains of production, it is very easy to lose its immediacy, its physicality, its fluidity; its ground. There is much about the SlutWalk that is uncomfortable, difficult, hard to swallow: its immediate, perhaps simultaneous, recuperation via social networking and online branding, often through the imaging of normatively 'hot' women and men who look 'good' naked and a non-inclusion of racial and ethnic minorities are real issues with the overarching structure of the movement.

---

[8] See http://www.edrants.com/occupy-wall-street-SlutWalk-nyc/.

This problematic is typified in a comment by South African Public Enterprises Minister, Malusi Gigaba, who tweeted at another government official, 'Let's talk about the slut walk [sic]. Now, I wanna attend as an observer. Might get lucky.'

Conclusion

The SlutWalk as movement is not without major problems, which perhaps reassert criticisms of the SlutWalk within a neoliberal 'happy feminist' framework. In September 2012, SlutWalk London joined rape apologists in issuing statements on Twitter in support of Julian Assange, who has never faced up to his charges, immediately believing in his innocence, and disbelieving the women accusing him, although Anastasia Richardson later claimed responsibility for the statements and issued an apology. SlutWalk DC held a fundraiser in a 'Gentleman's Club' in 2011 and the Johannesburg SlutWalk somehow ended up with an anti-Feminist (male) spokesperson. The biggest problem with the movement structurally is its failure to address and include the work of trans* and black women, groups and organisations who have been working against rape, against victim blaming and against the police for decades (and who are sexualized in violent ways that far exceed the bodies of white women. However, the solidarity engendered in the simple act of walking on the street with other women, and knowing that women around the world are engaging in this activity feels like a moment of punctuation, of rupture, of movement, where there feels like a real possibility for mass mobilisations of women claiming a position within sexual economies that does not leave us always as the victims of violence; a space without hurt.

References

Atwood, M. 1985. *The Handmaid's Tale*. Toronto: McClelland and Stewart.

BBC News. 2011. '"SlutWalk" marches sparked by Toronto officer's remarks'. 8 May. Available: http://www.bbc.co.uk/news/world-us-canada-13320785. Last accessed 25/07/2014.

Butler, J. 1997. *Excitable Speech: A Politics of the Performative*. New York, NY: Routledge.

Dines, G & Murphy, W. 2011. 'SlutWalk is not Sexual Liberation'. *The Guardian*. 8 May. Available: http://www.theguardian.com/commentisfree/2011/may/08/slutwalk-not-sexual-liberation. Last accessed 25/07/2014.

Luce Irigaray. 1985. *The Sex Which is Not One*. Ithaca, NY: Cornell University Press.

Massumi, B. 2002. *Parables for the Virtual: Movement, Affect, Sensation*. Durham, NC: Duke University Press.

McRobbie, A. 2009. *The Aftermath of Feminism*. London: SAGE Publications.

Mulvey, L. 1975. *Visual Pleasure and Narrative Cinema* in Mulvey, L. 1989 [2009]. *Visual and Other Pleasures*. London: Palgrave MacMillan.

Pollock, G. 1987. *Vision and Difference: Femininity, Feminism and the Histories of Art*. London: Routledge.

Power, N. 2009. *The One Dimensional Woman*. London: Zero Books.

13

IMBIBING NEOLIBERALISM

Tom Henri

While intoxication in the city has often been celebrated by scholars as both creative content and creative inspiration for novels such as Emile Zola's *L'Assomoir* (1877) and, more recently, artistic mapping projects like Francis Alÿs' *Narco-turismo* (1996), the relationship between alcohol consumption and the modern city remains largely unproblematised (Jayne, Holloway & Valentine, 2006). Moreover, the absence of focus within the social sciences and more specifically urban geographers can also be extended to public drinking. Given urbanists' contemporary concerns with how groups compete for space within the built environment (Keith, 2005), this oversight seems strange and worthy of further enquiry. This chapter is an attempt to pop the cap on how we might begin to consider popular notions of street drinkers and what these representations potentially inform us about social control in the public thoroughfares of the contemporary city. I focus on the London neighbourhood of Deptford, not as an idealised type, but as one example of how the processes of urban regeneration can be analysed through the presence of street drinkers. This analysis serves as a compass for understanding contemporary anxieties about urban redevelopment. The conclusion is that urban renewal in the neoliberal form of gentrification, cyclic decay and renewal, is a process which places controls on both who is and who is not permitted to drink in public spaces and relies on competing notions of street drinking subjectivities in order to enact its cyclic processes.

> Liquor licencing and control systems, whatever their particularities, all share the difficult position of having the regulation of personal consumption as their objective – an object out of keeping with the logic of liberalism (Valverde, 1988: 145).

The current hegemonic political ideology has little in common with liberalism as John Stuart Mill would construct it in which the government has little role in the regulation of personal behaviour (Mill, 1859) but rather neo-liberalism which while appearing to preach a lack of government intervention in the lives of the citizenry actually endorses and increases regulation, as long as government regulation mimics the market. In this mode of political ideology, regulation and government intervention are permitted, despite their illiberalism, as long as they are marketised (Mirowski, 2013), under the neoliberal mode of social organisation governments take on the form of markets (Foucault, 1994). Here, it is useful to cite Nick Couldry's definition of neoliberalism as:

> ... broadly a range of policies that evolved internationally from the early 1980s to make market functioning the overwhelming priority for social organisation (Couldry, 2010: 4).

Yet the regulation of alcohol consumption which exists under neoliberalism remains without significant examination or challenge from academic discourses.

At the same time public discourses of alcohol controls usually relate to the form and severity of regulation rather than its ideological legitimacy. Take, for example, the recent if ultimately doomed intention to introduce minimum alcohol pricing in the UK. Research on this area of public policy tends to focus on the potential impact on health behaviours (Brennan et al., 2014), sidestepping or ignoring how the politics of exclusion are reinforced through the bolstering of social class divisions (Brockley, 2012) or the discrimination of immigrants (Henri, 2012). The health economists can tell us how many lives could be saved from modelling the policy, but they can't tell us at whose expense this will occur. Thus it seems that wherever the political consensus resides a consensual academy will follow. Beyond the potential impact on people's health, academics have little to say on how alcohol regulation in neoliberal contexts enables both regulation and exclusion of certain imbibing subjects.

This is not to say that the merits and reality of neoliberalism have not been contested and debated. However the rise of neoliberalism over the last forty years has coincided with a concomitant shift of productive forces in the United Kingdom. This shift has seen a move from an industrial to post-industrial mode of production. With this the regulation of public spaces and leisure activities of the working classes has shifted from containment in the interests of defending capital (Thompson, 1963) to marketised consumption as the dominant form of social control (Bauman, 2005). Within the framework of neoliberalism we can also observe the increasing control, regulation and surveillance of public spaces (Klein, 2008), subsumed to the market-form of post-Fordism social control, particularly in relation to producing the night time economy (Haywood & Hobbs, 2007). The liberalisation of liquor licencing hours in the United Kingdom is a clear example of this shift from containment to marketization. Pubs no longer cease their service at 10:30pm on a Sunday evening in order to regulate industrial workers, instead the constant lure of consumption offered by extended opening hours conditions the neoliberal worker to 'work hard, play hard' (Deal & Kennedy, 1988).

This shift from traditional-industrial modes of regulation to neoliberal modes of marketised social control has occurred in relation to the consumption of alcohol. During the New Labour years (1997-2010), the UK experienced a significant liberalisation of the existing regulatory regime regarding the sale and consumption of alcohol.[1] Most famously the 2003 Licencing Act introduced flexible opening hours for licenced premises with the potential for the 24-hour sale of alcohol. The previous regime of fixed licencing hours had been in force in some variant since the Defence of the Realm Act of 1914. However, further liberalisation of alcohol sales defenestrated the requirement that a licensee had to demonstrate 'need' for a further drinking establishment in the locality.[2] The proponents of this change heralded it as a benefit to the night time economy and the reinvigoration of many post-industrial city centres (particularly in the North of England – the once industrial heartland). Detractors of the scheme blame the introduction of the legislation on creating 'binge drinking' zones (Haywood & Hobbs, 2007).

As there has been a recasting of the regulation of personal consumption there has also been a shift in the regulation of public spaces. One of the most prominent tools for the regulation of individuals within public space is the Anti-social behaviour order. Anti-social behaviour orders (ABSO) are a civil court order and therefore require much less of a burden of proof than a criminal conviction. A recipient of an ASBO is perceived to be causing 'or likely to cause alarm, harassment or distress' (Crime and Disorder Act 1998) in a particular locality. An ASBO may have many conditions including non-association, a curfew, banning from certain streets or localities, being electronically tagged or prohibited from participating in certain behaviours. It is worth noting that although an ASBO is not a criminal order; a breach of an ASBO will potentially result in a criminal conviction. So one does not have to be committing criminal acts to become the recipient of an ASBO, yet the breach of an ASBO will make you a criminal. With regards to the particular topic of this chapter, public drinking and public space, the Greater London Authority further defines anti-social behaviour as;

> ... - threatening or physically obstructive behaviours stopping people using public or semi-public places e.g. intimidating behaviour by groups of youths, aggressive begging, street drinking or drug misuse and kerb crawling (Millie et al., 2005: 9).

In this specific example, 'alarm, harassment and distress' are spatialized. Behaviours and acts which are perceived to obstruct the flow of peoples participating in legitimate activities, or to put this in the language of neoliberalism – behaviour which obstructs consumers from consuming – require regulation, censure and control.

---

[1] This is an over simplification of the process of alcohol liberalisation for the sake of brevity. For a full account see Chapter 15 of *The Politics of Alcohol: A History of the Drink Question in England* (Nicholls, 2009).

[2] Again see Nicholls 2009 for a useful and clear explanation of how the alcohol industry and the central UK government were in league to deregulate alcohol consumption.

It is necessary to consider the enduring subject of the street drinker within the context of these shifts in regulatory cultures and practices. One might expect the liberalisation of alcohol consumption and the increased regulation of public space to have a deterrent effect on those considered to be 'derelict' street drinkers.[3] With pubs open longer, competition reducing the price of alcoholic beverages and an increased chance of being judicially reprimanded for public drinking, incidences of street drinking should have decreased. However, until 2013 the street drinkers of Deptford were a regular and consistent feature of life at the Southern end of Deptford High Street.

Street Drinkers

The enduring historical imaginary of street drinking in London emerges from the 1750s during the period referred to as the 'Gin craze' (Nicholls, 2012). Hogarth's famous print 'Gin Lane' rendered in detail a depiction of morally deficient behaviour brought on by the overconsumption of Gin. However, there is another subtext to the image. The setting is a public place, the street. The dress and demeanour of the characters are intended to represent working class mass drinking. Thus Hogarth was making apparent the connection between public drunkenness and poverty (Nicholls, 2009: 46). It is not public drunkenness itself which is of concern to Hogarth, rather the artist is alerting his audience to the potential caused by public drunkenness by the poor in newly urbanised London. Gin Lane is not just a morality tableau about the evils of public drinking, it also highlights Eighteenth Century anxieties about the threat to public order of the new urban working class.

More recent concerns with street drinking in London emerge in the 1950s and 1960s. The UK's first Alcoholics Anonymous group started in Croydon, South East London in 1952. Imported from the United States, Alcoholics Anonymous with their 'twelve step' treatment programme introduced the idea of alcoholism as a disease for which the cure is abstinence. This is not to say that abstinence movements had not existed previously in the UK (There were many Victorian temperance movements) but Alcoholics Anonymous brought with it a new way of problematizing drinking and drunkenness, and with it the modern notion of the habitual drunk. By the early 1960s a group of psychiatrists at the Maudsley hospital in Camberwell, South East London started to develop ideas

---

[3] I find the term 'derelict street drinker' problematic as it defines the street drinker as either jobless or homeless and this might not necessarily be the case. As Mills et al. (2007) demonstrate many homeless people drink in public yet Ross et al. (2005) confirms that not all street drinkers are homeless. However in this chapter I use the term 'derelict street drinker' taken directly from Archard (1979) to identify a mode of street drinking which is deemed to be a marker of urban blight whereas the 'respectable street drinker' is a marker of urban renaissance.

about how to 'treat' 'skid row' drinkers, homeless drunks unable to help themselves (Nicholls, 2009: 203-4). This laid the groundwork for the treatment, both medical and cultural, of the street drinker.

It is from this popular imaginary that we have the image of the derelict drunk. At this point I wish to add a word of caution to the typology of street drinkers. The work of the Camberwell Council on Alcoholism (Nicholls, 2009: 204) as well as that of Peter Archard (discussed further below) make clear reference to homeless drunks and derelicts. I want to suggest a decoupling of homelessness from street drinking. This is not to contest extensive evidence that some street homeless people habitually drink (Mills et al., 2007) or the basic fact the homeless have little choice as to where they drink. However there are many street drinkers who may in fact be securely domiciled (Ross et al. 2005).

Surprisingly there is little social research into street drinking. The primary text we can refer to dates from the 1970s, when Peter Archard befriended a drinking school on Camberwell Green in South East London. Archard (1979) demonstrated through his ethnographic work that there were four modes of social control of street drinking – moral, penal, social and medical. Each of these four modes of social control, according to Archard, seeks to recuperate street drinkers through salvation, correction, rehabilitation or treatment and each mode of social control is linked to a particular institution – the church, the courts, social services and the medical profession. This chapter will consider the idea that since Archard published his seminal work, a fifth mode of social control of street drinking has emerged, a mode that comprehensively rewrites our understanding of the public drunk, which redefines who is permitted to be inebriated in the street and by logical extension who is not allowed to drink alcohol in public. This mode of social control is the mode of rational-legal urban planning we know as regeneration which seeks to eliminate the derelict street drinker from an idealised public view.

Deptford, South East London

Deptford is a district of South East London within the London Borough of Lewisham. Deptford is currently undergoing a period of regeneration (Prynn, 2013). An illustrative example of this regeneration occurred during 2014 when the old job centre, effectively a labour exchange for the destitute, reopened as a bar called 'The Job Centre' featuring 'quirky design features inspired by its function as a place that once served the unemployed' (Elliott, 2014). As we will see this redevelopment of the area has impacted on those now referred to in the sociological literature as 'Street-life people' (Manders, 2009: 146), particularly street drinkers.

Until very recently one of the most prominent signs of entry into Deptford was a large anchor (Chandler, 2013). installed on a low brick plinth at the junction of Deptford High Street and New Cross Road.[4] The importance of this road to shipping and trade cannot be understated. Deptford was an important sea trading port in its time, with a strong maritime tradition, including some unfortunate links to transatlantic slavery (Back, 2007). The anchor sat at the Southern end of Deptford High Street, fully visible from the A2, a reminder to continental haulage and global trade of the role Deptford played in the development and maintenance of Empire. It was probably due to the location of the anchor at the point where Deptford High Street adjoins the A2, providing a vista onto the comings and goings of continental trade, along with the low brick plinth which made it a perfect height for sitting down, that the anchor became a popular place for a group of street drinkers (Crosswhatfields, 2013). Most days one could observe a number of regular street drinkers who would congregate and socialise at the anchor. As of June 2013, the anchor has gone from public view, removed by London Borough of Lewisham Council along with the plinth – and so has the group of drinkers. The anchor was removed as part of the council's regeneration plan for Deptford High Street. Although the plan does not mention the existence or the removal from public view of the Deptford anchor drinkers, there are subtle clues that removing a particular street drinking aesthetic and replacing it with another street drinking aesthetic, is an intentional element of the regeneration plan which will eventually have inflationary effects on both commercial and residential property prices in the area, effectively enabling 'developers' to extract greater value from an area which had been left to decay for at least 20 years.

The Paradox of Street Drinking

The neoliberal mode of social organisation is based on Chicago school neo-classical economic theory. Within neoliberal doctrine the mythical market is the greatest information processor in existence. According to this doctrine, the market when left to its own devices, in a neoliberal utopia, will find the correct price for all goods and services based on the laws of supply and demand. As long as the market is free from unnecessary regulation, it *can* and *will* meet all human needs (Klein, 2008; Mirowski, 2013). The paradox of street drinking in neoliberal contexts is that street drinkers have access to the best 'prices' for alcohol in terms of cost per unit, surely the goal of the Friedmanian self-correcting system. Yet street drinkers constitute abject figures within the neoliberal economy subject to many and various forms of social control. There are several ways in which derelict street drinkers are cast as abject, one of which is due to their consumption of low price per unit alcoholic beverages. The source of this para-

---

[4] New Cross Road is a section of the A2, a major arterial road that links London to the Port of Dover. The A2 therefore provides a direct, physical link from one of the world's pre-eminent financial centres to the World's busiest passenger port.

dox can be reduced to taste – and here I mean taste in both the sensory meaning and the sociological understanding (see Rhys-Taylor, 2013 for an indepth discussion on connections between taste and distinction). It is the abject street drinkers' 'taste' for cheap yet strong alcoholic beverages which often marks him or her out from the 'respectable' drinker. The derelict street drinker plays by the neo-liberal rules, he or she finds the best price for the product he or she wishes to imbibe, yet by doing this the derelict street drinker is marked out as unruly. His or her lack of appreciation of 'craft beers', 'real ales' and vintage wines is both evidence that they are playing the drinkers' ultimate game of political economy yet he or she is simultaneously cast as degenerate and certainly lacking in moral and economic worth by doing so.

According to Millie, disgust and distaste relates to people's behavioural expectations. It is behaviour which is '… beyond conventional norms of acceptability and […] beyond people's behavioural expectations for that particular environment' (Millie, 2008: 380). Thus it is not street drinking per se which is condemned as distasteful or disgusting but rather the context of this drinking and the subjugation of the drinker. In order to illustrate this point I consider briefly at another neighbourhood in South East London, namely Camberwell. Camberwell is an important locale in the development of both the personification of the street drinker and the social control mechanisms which have been developed over the last fifty years to reform his or her public libations (Nicholls, 2009: 203-4). If you were to walk around Camberwell and look at the lamp posts you would notice a small sign on them indicating an 'Alcohol Control Area'. Smaller print reads, 'A police officer or authorised person can ask you to stop drinking in this area.' On a number of occasions I have witnessed police offices taking cans of drink off derelict drinkers in the area and pouring the beverage away. Yet at the same time there are a number of pubs in Camberwell with tables and seating on the street outside their establishments enabling their customers to drink in the street. This category of street drinker I refer to as the respectable street drinker.[5]

On the one hand there is a form of street drinking which can be censored while on the other hand similar behaviour can be tolerated or even promoted. Street drinking in the context of the derelict drinker can be subject to a myriad of social control measures including antisocial behaviour orders (Millie et al., 2005), and Alcohol Control Zones yet street drinking as a form of 'café society' leisure activity has been accepted, if not promoted, as a respectable form of street drinking (Hobbs et al., 2005). During the 1990s there were two alternative and contradictory public discourses of public drinking. We have both local and

---

[5] Again this term is problematic but I use the term 'respectable' to denote someone who within the current regulatory regime of public space is allowed to imbibe in public without experiencing the social control methods and mechanisms described by Archard (1979) and therefore does not require recuperating.

central government authorities, with the encouragement of the alcohol industry, promoting policies towards the acceptability of drinking in public places as
a consumption-based driver for post-industrial urban renewal. Yet at the same
time we have the development of mechanisms for controlling those who drink
in the street in the form of antisocial behaviour orders and alcohol control zones
(Liberty Central, 2009). A rudimentary discourse analysis of these two diverging policy orientations enables us to identify who is allowed to drink in public
without censure and conversely, whose public drinking will potentially be constructed as problematic, anti-social or even criminal. The message is clear even
if the policies are conflicted, there is respectable street drinking and there is
distasteful street drinking. What appears to separate the two is aesthetics.

This aesthetic contradiction of ways of being in the street appears in other
forms. Graffiti is a street art form which is both admired and simultaneously
categorised as evidence of urban blight. Banksy, a Bristol-based graffiti artist is
often deemed to create works of artistic merit worthy of preservation by local
authorities, the same local authorities that spend millions of pounds each year
cleansing streets of graffiti. Indeed in January 2007 *The Brighton Argus* newspaper reported that 'Two men have been convicted of criminal damage after
painting over one of Brighton's most photographed pieces of graffiti' and a year
earlier the same newspaper reported:

> A graffiti vandal has been jailed for 90 days in what the police believe is a new
> 'get tough' approach to the crime by courts. One senior policemen said: 'It is very
> unusual to see a tag "artist" put behind bars but we are delighted – graffiti blights
> our city' (qtd in Millie, 2008: 385-6).

This contradictory approach to graffiti exposes the paradox of urban aesthetics.
Both Banksy and those who damage his 'works' are essentially committing acts
of vandalism yet one form is celebrated as a symbol of post-industrial urban
renaissance and the other as evidence of decline and urban decay. The same
paradox applies to street drinking. The promotion of 'continental style' night
time economy destinations aims to rejuvenate urban centres, yet street drinking
outside of these terms is deemed to be potentially anti-social behaviour (Millie
et al., 2005).

Regenerating Deptford

So where does this leave us in terms of aesthetics, urban space, public
drinking and Deptford? Deptford is currently undergoing a number of urban regeneration projects, the most ambitious and contentious of which is

the Convoys Wharf development.[6] These developments will undoubtedly bring money into an area of London which has so far seen little post-industrial revival; however these regeneration projects will shift the character and the social milieu of the district. One effect of the overheated housing market in London is that property developers are constantly on the lookout for the next area they can turn to profit. The formula is familiar to anyone who has lived in any of the following areas of London in the last 20 years – Notting Hill, Shoreditch, Dalston, Stoke Newington, Hackney, Peckham – areas are left to decay until property prices are such that artists and other creative types move in, open small boheminan-type businesses creating a sense of an area 'happening.' This is seen as urban renaissance. Then the property developers move in, with the blessing of the local authority, citing urban renewal, buy the cheap property and sell it at fantastic profit. As people of a wealthier strata move into the area the existing population gets squeezed out and the process of gentrification is complete.

> The cycle of urban regeneration relies upon a longer-term pattern of running down of city areas until the timely intervention of developer capital and Government 'reconstruction' (Henri & Hutnyk, 2013: 207).

Deptford is an area currently being transformed from urban blight to urban regeneration through gentrification. Part of this process of improving property values involves changing the spatial aesthetic of the neighbourhood. Returning to the paradox of street drinking, the drinkers who used to frequent the Deptford anchor represent and even embody a Deptford of relatively low rents and urban decay, a prerequisite for urban renaissance. Yet the forthcoming 'continental style' street drinkers of Deptford represent and embody both urban renaissance and legitimate taste. By designing out the existing street drinkers, urban planners and the architects of urban gentrification can create spaces of public imbibing reserved for 'respectable' drinkers. Again the paradox persists, the street drinkers at the anchor in Deptford signified that this was an area of urban blight 'ready' for investor capital to swoop in and extract huge profits, yet to increase the value of the properties in the area requires the absence of derelict street drinkers from public view. Thus the question of who drinks in the street informs us whether the bourgeois gentrification project has been successful in 'civilising' the area.

The presence of both the derelict street drinker and the respectable street drinker reveals at what point in this process an area currently finds itself. The acceptance of the public derelict drinker in a neighbourhood marks out the area as experiencing urban blight. If this is the case, the presence of persistent derelict street drinking also serves as a precondition to urban renaissance. During

---

[6] For a comprehensive account of the gerrymandering associated with the Convoys Wharf development see the Transpontine blog at http://transpont.blogspot.co.uk/2013/10/johnson-caves-in-to-convoys-wharf.html.

this period of urban renaissance, it might be possible for derelict street drinkers and respectable street drinkers to coexist. However as the developer capitalists move into the area, the derelict street drinker needs to be cleansed from public view in order to increase the potential profits. It is at this point that that legal measures may start to be deployed against the derelict street drinkers. As the money comes into the area, the disreputable street drinkers get pushed out.

What marks out the derelict street drinker from the respectable street drinker is aesthetics not behaviour. This is not to deny that other frameworks for regulation and exclusion might yet apply – race, nationality, gender, immigration status and so on. Yet in order to censure the unwanted street drinker his or her behaviour is pathologised and criminalised. In essence there is little to separate the behaviour between the street drinker representing urban regeneration and the street drinker representing urban decay. Both are engaged in similar activities but the aesthetics or rather the representations of drinking aesthetics, transform the individual from a mere public drinker to either a human manifestation of either 'Broken windows' (Kelling & Wilson, 1982), signifying urban blight or gentrification, which can be viewed as either a purifying force or a marker of greater social inequality (Jayne et al., 2006).

In this way, the conflicting demands by drinkers on public space in urban centres echoes the themes which tend to dominate the academic literature on alcohol consumption; either as pathology (particularly in the medical sciences but also in much of the social sciences) or as everyday life. The derelict street drinker is a pathogen in need of cleansing from public view whereas the respectable street drinker representing regeneration and post-industrial vigour is participating in everyday social relations and cultural practices of sociability and pleasure (Jayne et al., 2006). Of course the street drinking group that existed at the Deptford anchor also involved sociability and pleasure but symbolised urban decay rather than urban renewal.

As I draw towards the close of this chapter I want to return to a historical theme mentioned earlier, in order to consider its relevance in the light of this discussion. Hogarth's famous print 'Gin Lane' represented anxieties of the time about urbanisation. I wish to posit that, in a way, representations of street drinking persist in reflecting our anxieties about the urban environment. However in the contemporary city, the concerns are not about urbanisation but urban regeneration with its dual scourges of urban blight and gentrification.

References

Archard, P. 1979. *Vagrancy, Alcoholism and Social Control*. London: Macmillan.
Back, L. 2007. 'Written in Stone: Black Writing and Goldsmiths College.' *Sociology Working Papers*. London: Goldsmiths, University of London.

Bauman, Z. 2005. Work, Consumerism and the New Poor. Maidenhead: Open University Press.

Brennan, A., Meng, Y., Holmes, j., Hill-McManus, D., & Meier, P. S. 2014. 'Potential benefits of minimum unit pricing for alcohol versus a ban on below cost selling in England 2014: modelling study.' British Medical Journal 349. doi: http://dx.doi.org/10.1136/bmj.g5452.

Brockley, B. 2012. 'Drunkennes is a Right not a Privilege.' 17 February. Available: http://brockley.blogspot.co.uk/2012/02/drunkenness-is-right-not-privilege.html. Last accessed 18/11/2014.

Chandler, M. 2013. 'Deptford High Street Anchor Removed by Lewisham Council.' News Shopper. 15 April. Available: http://www.newsshopper.co.uk/news/10356100.Deptford_High_Street_anchor_removed_by_Lewisham_Council/?ref=mr. Last accessed 18/11/2014.

Couldry, N. 2010. Why Voice Matters: Culture and Politics After Neoliberalism. London: Sage.

Crosswhatfields?. 2013. 'Goodbye to the Anchor!' 12 April. Available: http://crossfields.blogspot.co.uk/2013/04/goodbye-to-anchor.html. Last accessed 18/11/2014.

Deal, T.E. & Kennedy, A.A. 1988. Corporate Cultures: The Rites and Rituals of Corporate Life. Harmondsworth: Penguin.

Elliott, J. 2014. 'The Job Centre Bar's Attempt to do Gentrification Ironically is an Insult.' The Guardian. 9 July. Available: http://www.theguardian.com/commentisfree/2014/jul/09/job-centre-bar-gentrification-ironically-deptford. Last accessed: 18/11/2-14.

Foucault, M. 1994. 'Governmentality.' In L. Wrigley & D. McKevitt (eds.), Public Sector Management: Theory, Critique and Practice. London: Sage. 11-24.

Haywood, K., & Hobbs, D. 2007. 'Beyond the Binge in "Booze Britain": Market-led Liminalization and the Spectacle of Binge Drinking. The British Journal of Sociology 58:3. 437-456.

Henri, T. 2012. 'The Borders of Booze Britain: Alcohol Controls and Nationality'. Contemporary Social Science 8:1. 36-45.

Henri, T., & Hutnyk, J. 2013. 'Contexts for Distraction'. Journal for Cultural Research 17:2. 198-215.

Hobbs, R. F., Winlow, S., Hadfield, P., & Lister, S. 2005. 'Violent Hypocrisy: Governance and the Night-time Economy. European Journal of Criminology 2:2. 161-183.

Jayne, M., Holloway, S., & Valentine, G. 2006. 'Drunk and Disorderly: Alcohol, Urban Life and Public Space'. Progress in Human Geography 30:4. 451-468.

Keith, M. 2005. After the Cosmopolitan? Multicultural Cities and the Future of Racism. Abingdon: Routledge.

Kelling, G., & Wilson, K. 1982. 'Broken Windows: The Police and Neighbourhood Safety'. March. The Atlantic.

Klein, N. 2008. *The Shock Doctrine*. London: Penguin Books.

Liberty Central. 2009. *Criminal Justice and Police Act 2001*. Available: http://www.theguardian.com/commentisfree/libertycentral/2009/jan/14/criminal-justice-police-act. Last accessed 18/11/2014.

Manders, G. 2009. 'The Use of Anti-Social Behaviour Powers with Vulnerable Groups: Some Recent Research'. *Social Policy and Society* 9:1. 145-153.

Mill, J. S. 1859. *On Liberty*. London: Longman, Roberts and Green.

Millie, A. 2008. 'Anti-social Behaviour, Behavioural Expectations and an Urban Aesthetic'. *British Journal of Criminology* 48:1. 379-394.

Millie, A., Jacobson, J., Hough, M., & Paraskevopoulou, A. 2005. *Anti-social Behaviour in London: Setting the Context for the London Anti-Social Behaviour Strategy 2005*. London: King's College London.

Mills, K., Knight, T., & Green, R. 2007. *Beyond Boundaries: Offering Substance Misuse Services to New Migrants in London*. London: Centre for Community Research, University of Hertfordshire.

Mirowski, P. 2013. *Never Let a Serious Crisis go to Waste: How Neoliberalism Survived the Financial Meltdown*. London: Verso.

Nicholls, J. 2009. *The Politics of Alcohol: A History of the Drink Question in England*. Manchester: Manchester University Press.

_____ . 2012. 'Drink: The British Disease.' In History Today. *Last Orders: A Social History of Drinking*. [ebook]. Available: www.historytoday.com. Last accessed 18/11/2014.

Prynn, J. 2013. '£1bn plan to turn Deptford into the "Shoreditch of South London."' *London Evening Standard*. 2 May. Available: http://www.standard.co.uk/news/london/1bn-plan-to-turn-deptford-into-the-shoreditch-of-south-london-8600714.html. Last accessed 18/11/2014.

Rhys-Taylor, A. 2013. 'Disgust and Distinction: The Case of the Jellied Eel'. *The Sociological Review* 61:2., 227-246.

Ross, A., Heim, D., Flatley, K., Davies, J., & Sudbery, M. 2005. 'An exploration of street drinking in Drumchapel, Scotland'. *Health Education Research* 20:3. 314-322.

Thompson, E. P. 1963. *The Making of the English Working Class*. London: Penguin.

Valverde, M. 1998. *Diseases of the Will: Alcohol and the Dilemmas of Freedom*. Cambridge: Cambridge University Press.

Index

99%, The, 190, 193

access,1, 6-7, 17-20, 26, 28, 67, 89, 92-3, 97, 100, 102, 107, 150, 193, 195, 224

activism, 3, 4, 7, 8n, 16, 34, 91, 109, 149-50, 154-5, 172, 174, 176-9, 190-1, 193-4, 199, 206, 208

Adbusters,195

advertising, 3, 14, 19, 35-40, 45, 50, 53, 59, 156, 161, 164-5, 213

alcohol, 28, 82, 98, 155, 161-2, 219-228

Alcoholics Anonymous, 222

Alcohol Control Zones, 225-6

licensing laws, 221

see also drinking

alienation, 5, 23, 64, 71, 75, 85, 98, 101-5, 107, 135, 191

Anonymous, 37

anti-globalisation, 189, 195, 200

anti-social behaviour, 22-6, 28-9, 104-5, 114, 120, 125, 226

anti-social behaviour order (ASBO), 221

Arab Spring, The, 81-2, 108, 189, 192

architecture, 4, 5, 13, 18, 19-20, 28-9, 34, 42, 58-9, 63, 71, 74, 213, 227

Arendt, Hannah, 17, 24

Argentina, 169, 170, 172, 174n, 175n, 182

augmented reality, 47-8, 58-60

Baader-Meinhof Red Army Faction, 197

Badiou, Alain, 81, 101, 197

Balzac, Honoré de, 75

Banksy, 33-4, 44, 226

barricade, 35, 192,

Benjamin, Walter, 34, 71, 98, 146-7, 194

blackness, 101-2, 113-127

Blek le Rat, 33

bodies, 2-3, 6-7, 28, 57, 143, 182, 193, 208-10, 212, 214-16

Bogotá, 131-5, 137-9

Brazil, 3, 4, 81, 109, 144, 148-50, 169-83, dictatorship, 170, 172-5, 177-8, 182

Breton, Andre, 71, 76

built environment, 47, 48, 53, 57, 60-1, 164, 219

Butler, Judith, 3, 6, 207

capitalism, 122, 145, 190-4, 196-8, 200, 210-11

cartography, 41-3, 45, 144, 213

see also mapping

Certeau, Michel de, 5, 34, 45, 60, 135, 140, 214

child abuse, 147, 162

Church, The, 147, 161, 189, 223

Catholic, 131

citizenship, 83-5, 88, 144

city centre, 15, 40-1, 105, 144, 147, 148, 177n, 180, 181, 205, 221, 226, 228

class, 4, 26, 84, 90, 92, 98, 102, 106, 107, 109, 120, 146, 190-2, 206, 220

middle, 24, 25, 40, 86, 100-3, 105, 107, 109, 149

working. 40, 86, 97, 98, 100-9, 190n, 192-4, 199, 200, 220, 222

Cohn-Bendit, Daniel, 196-7

collective, 6, 9, 34, 41, 63, 74, 90-1, 100, 102-3, 123, 126, 133, 169, 177, 179-82, 192-3
  amnesia, 170, 172, 174, 182
  memory, 169-70, 173, 174, 182
  Wooster Collective, 43

consumerism, 4, 6, 14, 21, 24, 37, 38, 99, 144, 156, 166, 210-11, 221

crime, 24-5, 28, 39n, 99-100, 104, 118, 124, 170, 172-3, 221

cyborg, 56-8, 60-1

Dean, James, 85-6

Debord, Guy, 41, 64-6, 68, 70-2, 75, 135

demonstration, 81, 84, 140, 149, 171, 189-90, 195-6, 198
  see also protest

dérive, 65, 67, 71
  drift, 65, 66-7, 74

Derrida, Jacques, 65, 70
  Derridean, 76, 148

design, 7, 13, 18, 19, 22, 24, 28, 33n, 34, 52, 67, 170, 223, 227

disability, 6-7, 17-18, 147

drinking,
  binge, 211, 221
  street, 219, 221-8
  see also alcohol

Engels, Friedrich, 69

enlightenment, 4, 144-7, 156, 158, 161, 164, 166

Europe, 7, 83, 85, 92-3, 144, 145, 178-9, 197, 205
  European Parliament, 197
  fortress Europe, 200

Facebook, 7, 38, 43, 56, 105, 156, 208

Fanon, Frantz, 124-5, 146

fashion, 102-4,

fear, 7, 25, 29, 40, 85-6, 89, 100, 122-3, 207, 213, 214

feminism, 57, 208, 211
  post-, 211

flâneur; flâneuse, 61, 98, 144, 148, 214

football, 100, 102, 105, 107, 149-50, 156, 172n
  hooligans; hooliganism, 98, 104, 106-7
  Hillsborough, 104

Foucault, Michel, 7, 109, 135, 140, 220

Free Fare Movement, 81

freedom, 5, 16, 21, 24, 101, 120, 171-2, 181, 205, 208, 210, 211, 215

gentrification, 4, 8n, 33, 40, 219, 227-8

Gezi Park, 16, 81-2

graffiti, 14-16, 33, 35n, 36, 39, 144, 148-50, 160, 175n, 177n, 178, 180-1, 226
  see also street art

grid, 212-13, 215

grime, 3, 97, 115-27

Habermas, Jürgen, 138, 145

Harvey, David, 6, 88, 193, 195

hate speech, 206

Haussmann, Georges-Eugène, 34-5

homeless, 21, 25-6, 29, 222n, 223
  anti-homeless spikes, 25, 29

hoodie, 102-3, 105, 107

human rights, 146, 156, 174
  violation of, 154-5

immigration, 82-4, 86, 92, 106, 108, 193, 200, 220, 228

Iran, 89-90

Islamaphobia, 207n

Jones, Owen, 104, 106, 113

journalism, 103, 118-20, 171

Klein, Naomi, 35-6, 189, 220, 224

labour, 190-4, 199-200, 223

law, 1, 64, 85, 93-4, 97-8, 115, 118, 123-5, 127, 134, 138, 149, 170n, 172-3, 211

Lefebvre, Henri, 5, 13-14, 23, 135, 143

Lenin, Vladimir, 195

Letterist, 4, 64-66, 72-3

lighting, 22-3, 25, 27-8,

logo, 35-8, 45, 49, 213

London, 3, 7, 8, 33, 40, 47-8, 54, 60, 71, 99-100, 102-3, 108, 116-21, 123, 216, 221-2,

227
  2011 riots, 4, 35, 40, 81-4, 86, 99, 115
  Camberwell, 222-3, 225
  City of, 24, 48, 189
  Convoys Wharf, 227
  Deptford, 219, 223-4
  Tottenham, 99
maps, 41-3, 73, 144, 213
  mapping, 3, 24, 41, 69, 212, 219
      see also cartography
Marx, Karl, 192, 199
Marxism, 66, 68, 70, 190, 192, 195, 199-200
Mauritius, 3, 144, 154-65
media, 39, 44, 50, 67, 154-5, 171-2, 176, 189, 191, 197, 198
  analysis, 67, 102, 177
  representation, 16, 35, 40, 82, 85, 102, 106, 118, 135, 136-7, 148, 154, 210n
  social, 7-8, 43, 74, 99, 105, 156, 190, 210
Mill, John Stuart, 219
misogyny, 206, 207n, 208, 211, 213
neoliberalism, 1, 74, 93, 102, 208, 210, 216, 219-21, 224
New Labour, 220
New York, 8, 33, 189, 191, 193-4, 199
  NYPD, 189
  Wall Street, 189, 198
  Zuccotti Park, 189, 194
Newsnight, 113-14, 116, 123
Nuremberg, 147, 162
Obama, Barack, 9, 191-2, 207n
Occupy, 6, 37, 81-2, 108-9, 189-96, 200, 212
outside, 14, 215, 225-6
Paris, 33-5, 39-42, 44-5, 63, 71-2, 75, 81-2, 100, 214
patriarchy, 207, 212-13
pedagogy, 132, 134, 137, 143-4, 146, 166
pedestrian, 14, 16-18, 22, 29, 135, 139, 144, 145, 147-8, 151, 165, 214
photography, 9, 36, 40-1, 44, 52, 56, 59, 71-3, 103, 145-7, 215, 226
pirate radio, 118, 122-3, 126-7

police, 8, 16, 24, 28, 34, 35n, 40n, 82, 86, 93, 97, 99, 101-2, 104, 107-9, 123-4, 131n, 134, 143, 150, 151, 154, 155, 171, 178, 179, 181, 190, 191, 193, 194-7, 199, 200, 205, 211, 216, 225, 226
  London Metropolitan, 99, 113, 117-18
  see also NYPD; violence
poverty, 83, 84, 100, 102, 118, 149, 151, 156, 172, 222
privatisation, 4, 34, 56, 98, 105
profiling,
  ethnic, racial, 84, 86, 117-18
proletariat, 192-3, 197, 199-200,
property, 2, 21, 24, 87, 109
  development, 33, 227
  prices, 224, 227
protest, 1, 8n, 13, 16-17, 35, 63, 81-2, 90, 92, 97, 99-101, 108-9, 113, 132, 149-50, 172, 176, 189-90, 193-9, 205-6, 208-9, 212-15
  see also demonstration
public space, 1-9, 13-14, 16, 17-18, 19, 21, 22, 23-5, 28-9, 45, 47, 50, 54, 56-9, 86, 89, 98, 105, 118, 132, 139, 144, 159, 175, 177, 183, 189, 191, 193, 195-6, 219-22, 225n, 228
  see also privatisation
racism, 86, 104, 149, 200, 207n
rap, 114-15, 121
rape, 28, 205, 208, 211, 213, 215-16
resistance, 3-4, 16, 34-5, 73, 86, 98, 176, 177, 182-3, 189, 192-4, 196, 199-200, 207, 209, 211-12
São Paulo, 149-50, 169, 171, 175, 177-82
Sarkozy, Nicolas, 35, 82, 197
security, 14, 21, 24-5, 28, 101, 133, 135, 165, 172, 205
sex, 155, 163, 205-7, 208, 210-11, 213-16
Situationist International, 64
skateboarding, 21, 23-4, 26, 34
skinhead, 98, 102-7

spectacle, 7-8, 54, 61, 74-5, 135, 137, 139-40, 215

stairway, 13-29

street art, 33-45, 47, 144, 146, 169-70, 174-83, 226

   3D, 47-50, 52-61

   stencils, 36, 179-80

      see also graffiti

street theatre, 138-40, 197-8

strikes, 41, 84, 103, 192-4, 196-7, 199

students, 8n, 14-15, 35, 63, 100, 133, 134n, 172, 178-9, 193-4, 197, 199

subculture, 98, 102-4, 106-7

surveillance, 8, 21, 24-5, 28-9, 101, 104, 195, 220

Sydney, 13-15, 19-24, 26-8

tactics, 5, 34-6, 123, 135, 140, 196-7

tourism, 16, 18, 19, 35, 41-3, 47, 59, 151, 169, 175

urban renewal, 34, 219, 226-8

vandalism, 2, 36, 150, 226

video games, 58, 105-6

violence, 1, 2, 5, 17, 82, 83, 87, 97-9, 102-4, 106-7, 108-9, 114-15, 117-18, 120-1 122-3, 125, 137-8, 141, 143-51, 154-6, 159, 161, 164-6, 173-4, 191, 198

   domestic, 144, 146, 148, 163

   gender-based, 155-6, 162, 206-8, 213-16

   police, 16, 93, 171, 178, 199

   state, 169-70, 174-5, 196-7, 200

youth, 41, 81-6, 92, 97, 98, 100, 102-7, 109, 144, 147, 178, 197, 221

Žižek, Slavoj, 8, 84

www.ingramcontent.com/pod-product-compliance
Lightning Source LLC
Chambersburg PA
CBHW050808270326
41926CB00026B/4632